EXPLORING THE POWER WITHIN

A Resource Book For
Transcending The Ordinary

EXPLORING THE POWER WITHIN

A Resource Book For
Transcending The Ordinary

by Brad Steiger

Insights from over 30 present day spiritual leaders
who have demonstrated remarkable
powers of mind-body-spirit

Whitford Press

1469 Morstein Road
West Chester, Pennsylvania 19380 USA

Exploring the Power Within:
A Resource Book for Transcending the Ordinary
by Brad Steiger

Copyright © 1989 by Brad Steiger

Cover design by Bob Boeberitz

Library of Congress Card Number: 89-50769
International Standard Book Number: 0-914918-97-4

Manufactured in the United States of America

Published by Whitford Press,
A division of
Schiffer Publishing, Ltd.
1469 Morstein Road
West Chester, Pennsylvania 19380
Please write for a free catalog.
This book may be purchased from the publisher.
Please include $2.00 postage.
Try your bookstore first.

CONTENTS

PART FOUR: TRANSCENDING THE ORDINARY

Introduction

The span of interviews and discussions in this book encompasses almost my entire thirty-five year career as an investigator of the paranormal. But rather than focusing on peculiar happenings and unexplained phenomena that somehow blend together to comprise this fascinating universe (as does my book *Mysteries of Time and Space*) this present volume places its emphasis on the psychic sensitives, the spiritual guides, who have provided us with inspiration and with evidence of a much greater reality and an even more fascinating universe in which we co-exist with higher intelligences – both seen and unseen.

It was in the autumn of 1988 that I suggested to Peter Schiffer, the wonderfully cooperative president of Whitford Press, that a compilation of the many conversations that I have enjoyed with the leading psychic-sensitives, mystics, clairvoyants, and seers of the past nearly four decades would provide a marvelous resource book for serious students of metaphysics. After all, in those 35 years of prowling around the paranormal, I have discussed everything with psychically gifted people from their favorite breakfast food to their most traumatic childhood experience.

But most often, I have asked them about how one might go about developing those abilities of the psychic that we most often term "extrasensory." Are there special techniques that can more readily enable one to become psychic? Are there certain diets to follow? Certain mantras to chant? And if it is possible to develop psychic abilities, what precautions should be followed to prevent one from being seduced by the Dark Side of the Force?

As you meet these individuals possessed of talents as yet unexplained by the orthodox sciences, you will find them one and all to be very practical, down-to-Earth men and women. Regardless of their personal philosophies, regardless of their belief structures, they are all people who came to terms with their society's ethics, values, and norms. Although certain of their concepts if vocally expressed might raise an eyebrow or two at the local Rotary Club, each of these psychic geniuses would pass unnoticed in any crowd – if judged by physical appearance, that is. Depending upon your own psychic sensitivity, you might receive a jolt of recognition if you passed too close to them in that aforementioned hypothetical crowd, for they all have decidedly powerful, if not electric, personalities.

Each of them is by nature a sharer – even those who are somewhat reclusive or reserved. Each of them has a strong sense of mission and a clear idea of why they put on the fleshly clothes of Earth in the first place. Each of them is secure in his or her role as a teacher of important metaphysical truths. Each of them knows that the material plane is a schoolhouse in which even the lessons that are harsh present opportunities for growth.

In the final analysis, that is what this book is all about – spiritual growth. How to get right with yourself so that you are able at last to recognize the Divine Spark of the Creator within the temple of your own body. How to become your own guru.

And once you have learned how best to balance your own entity, you will find, as these wonderfully talented men and women have discovered, that you now have the ability to link with an Eternally Powerful Energy Source that is external to your own being but which is central to the Universe. Then you will be on the way to becoming One with the god within and with the God without – and that is what it has always been all about.

Brad Steiger
Scottsdale, Arizona

CHAPTER ONE

Seeress of
the Golden Path

From her serene office of the Golden Path, Irene Hughes commands a mighty position in the metaphysical world. Seeress, clairvoyant, teacher, speaker – this lady is very nearly a walking public relations department for the entire psychic field. Irene Hughes first became known widely for her many accurate predictions, and she was catapulted into national attention in 1966 with her prognostication of a great Chicago blizzard. She has since come to be respected also for her psychic development classes which she has taught since 1959. She has also assisted the police repeatedly with her clairvoyant abilities in criminal investigations, and her lectures have brought her before women's clubs, businesses, prison inmates, and religious orders.

Irene's list of correct predictions has been validated by notarized statements, personal letters of affirmation, and newspaper records.

Among her many predictions:

Twice in 1966 the seeress predicted the Middle Eastern War of June, 1967.

In January, 1968, she predicted that President Johnson would not seek another term, which he announced in April of that year.

The summer of Ted Kennedy's crisis at Chappaquidick she predicted a "tragedy for Senator Kennedy, in or around water."

In November, 1967, she foresaw the assassination of Robert Kennedy, which occurred in June, 1968.

She has since foretold deaths, assassinations, marriages, divorces, winning teams in sports, major weather disasters, and the outcome of elections. She has also maintained for years a high score of "hits" for her personal clients, who have written her letters of confirmation which she keeps carefully filed in her office.

In her capacity of clairvoyant Irene Hughes has located missing bodies, missing persons, and stolen goods. She has given case-breaking leads to harried policemen who have exhausted all possible clues. She has sat across the room from people and given them detailed descriptions of their lives, from the mundane to the spectacular. She has investigated haunted houses and unearthed information about the houses' previous events and occupants that no one present could verify – but exhaustive research could.

FROM A SMALL TENNESSEE CABIN

Irene Hughes has come a long way from a poverty-stricken childhood in Tennessee. The many people whom she has taught, spoken to, or counseled would scarcely suspect that the gracious Irene was the former "Rene" Finger, who had lived with her ten brothers and sisters in the small Tennessee cabin and had worked alongside them in the fields.

As soon as Irene could talk, it was apparent that she had inherited the "special feelings" of her half-Cherokee mother. As a four-year-old, Irene helped schedule her father's farming with her uncanny premonitions of the weather. On evenings when the family would swap tall tales, Irene had the knack of telling "tales" that later came true.

THE FAIRY QUEEN IN THE ATTIC

One day the small child had an experience that crystallized her latent clairvoyant gifts. In symbology very assuring to a four-year-old, Irene encountered a fairy queen.

The queen was up in the attic, and she lifted Irene miraculously up to her. There the entity told the child that she had the ability to "feel many strange and wonderful things." Before leaving the amazed girl, the queen promised gifts of a doll and a string of beads, items far beyond the reach of the Finger household budget. The next thing Irene knew she was standing back down in the kitchen.

Irene described her strange experience to a very perceptive mother. "She made me understand I was a normal child with a special God-given gift of being able to see what was hidden to others," Irene recalled in later years. "She never laughed at me or made me feel foolish. She never scolded me or tried to whip the 'devil' out of me."

Irene's mother did not want her child to expect the doll and beads, and then be disappointed if they did not materialize, nor did she want summarily to dismiss her child's experience.

That night Irene and her sister visited a dying elderly woman who had often helped the Fingers with house and field work. The old woman explained she was going to die, so she wanted Irene to have something. She reached for an old shoebox and pulled out two strands of beads, then draped them around Irene's neck. The first promised gift had been realized.

Irene went running home to her mother to show her the beads. As she entered the cabin she saw two older girls with an object. They insisted they had outgrown it, and wanted Irene to have it. The object was a beautiful doll.

THE VALUE OF HEEDING SPIRIT VOICES

Irene's opportunity to realize the fairy queen's other promise of feeling "strange and wonderful" things very nearly failed to happen, for a year later the girl contracted a terrible case of dysentery. The disease struck twenty-one other children in that rural area of Tennessee, all of whom died painfully from bleeding through the bowels.

The doctor had given up all hope of saving the girl, and in despair Irene's mother had gone for a solitary walk in the woods. Then, from nowhere, a disembodied voice commanded: "Give Rene peach leaf tea!"

Irene's mother hastened to follow the strange instruction and administer it to her child. In days the terrible diarrhea had stopped, and the doctor pronounced Irene a miraculous cure. From that time on both Irene and her mother learned the value of heeding spirit voices.

By the time Irene was fifteen years old, her life was replete with psychic impressions, clairvoyant visions, and precognitive glimpses into the future. She had already formulated many of the essential guidelines that were to comprise her lifelong spiritual creed. This written creed begins with a fundamental premise:

"We must create our own lives. If one intensely desires anything in life, he shall have it. 'Image' what your heart desires, and it shall be yours."

"IMAGE WHAT YOUR HEART DESIRES"

In her late teen years Irene went to New Orleans to live with an older sister. There she embarked on another aspect of what would be a lifelong concern. She went to work for the Baptist Hospital of New Orleans, where her compassion for the patients led one doctor to remark that Irene did more for the patients with her smiles than he did with his pills.

Irene came to the attention of a staff doctor, who offered to help the girl through school. Irene gratefully attended business school, going half days so she could retain her hospital job and be self-supporting. She still finished the two year program in nine months, scoring high on the government civil service test.

On December 23, 1945, Irene Finger married Bill Hughes, and the two moved to Chicago. From there Irene eventually launched her office of the Golden Path. The clients began to come in, and Irene became a firmly established Midwestern psychic.

Irene has ventured in many directions from her base at the Golden Path. An area in which she has devoted particular attention in the last two decades has been that of offering psychic assistance to criminal investigators. As psychic investigator she has worked with the Cook County Sheriff's office, in Chicago, the Kankakee, Illinois Sheriff's office, and other law enforcement agencies. In all these cases Irene's aid is solicited by the police. She does not enter a case unless she is specifically asked to do so.

Irene Hughes, Chicago's Seeress of the Golden Path

PSYCHIC CRIME INVESTIGATIONS

One of Irene Hughes' most spectacular experiences in psychic crime investigation came during a crisis of national proportions. On October 5, 1970, British diplomat James Richard (Jasper) Cross was abducted from his Montreal, Canada, home, by French [Quebec] terrorists. This group, known as the FLQ, was an organization dedicated to bringing equality to the French-speaking, yet English-dominated, province of Quebec. Their avowed means was violence.

The FLQ made contact with the Canadian government, asking for Cross' ransom. The abductors were refused and another terrorist faction of the FLQ retaliated by abducting Pierre LaPorte, senior Cabinet member of the Quebec government.

Canadian Premier Pierre Trudeau responded by invoking an obscure emergency war powers act, which effectively placed the entire Dominion in a state of declared war.

A SUMMONS TO HELP

Into this emotional and political turmoil entered the Chicago seeress, summoned by a radio broadcaster in the far western province of British Columbia. Bob Cummings, a broadcaster for Prince George station CJCI, decided to interview the psychic over the air for her spontaneous impressions regarding the Canadian crisis.

Almost immediately Irene began stating her predictions: "With the first gentleman that was kidnapped by the radical group, I feel that no physical harm will come to him [Cross]. However, I feel that there will be physical harm that will come to the second [LaPorte]."

Irene also predicted that the case would not break for another "two to three months," and she felt that the kidnap victims had not been taken far from the original area of Montreal.

Over the next several weeks Irene Hughes continue to check in regularly with Bob Cummings, to offer further psychic impressions. The material, which had originally been aired live, was thought to be so significant that Cummings sent the tapes to the Royal Canadian Mounted Police, and other government branches. He was requested to refrain from air play, and to send all further impressions from Irene to their offices.

ACCURATE PREDICTIONS OF LIFE AND DEATH

Although Irene did not work officially with the Canadian government, the accuracy of her predictions indicates that they might have been advised to work more closely with her! For, as Irene predicted, no harm did come to Jasper Cross, and the harassed diplomat was finally released on Decem-

ber 14, 1970, within the two to three-month period that Irene had designated.

Unfortunately, her impression regarding the "physical harm" that
would come to the second abductee, Pierre LaPorte, also proved tragically
correct. Within days of her initial prediction, the Cabinet Minister's brutally
murdered body was found in the trunk of a car. The police had been led to
the corpse by a tipoff from the kidnappers.

Neither Cross nor LaPorte were taken far from the original area, either,
as Irene had also predicted. LaPorte was discovered in the St. Hubert area
of Montreal, and Cross was released from a residential district in the
northern section of the city.

In addition to these predictions, Irene imparted many other details of
the terrorists and their circumstances, the method in which LaPorte was
killed, the abductors' car, and the physical condition of Jasper Cross. And,
as if all this were not enough, the seeress proved that her psychic juices were
flowing by giving many additional predictions regarding general news in
the Canadian Dominion. An astonishing number of these were also proved
correct.

POLICE SHOULD HAVE TRAINING IN ESP

Irene's close professional work with law officers in the Chicago-Kankakee
area has given her insights into the way the police solve cases. She also has
an interesting suggestion which could further aid in the prevention of crime
and the apprehension of criminals:

"I think police should have training in ESP because some of them use it
anyway – whether they mention it to their bosses or not. It seems they have
no reluctance to talk to each other about it, though. Often in my work with
them I hear them saying, 'I have a hunch this is where we should go,' or `I
have a hunch this is what happened.' These comments do not go down in
the police report, but the results of the hunch usually pay off."

WORKING BEHIND THE SCENES IN LEGAL MATTERS

Because of Irene's years of experience with the law and her own
research into all phases of psychic phenomena, she has had ample time to
give serious thought to the matter of psychics and possible legal conflicts.

"It should be absolutely stressed that the information a psychic gives to
police officers should be for their use alone to check out and turn into factual
evidence," believes Mrs. Hughes. "No psychic information should ever be
used in court without the police having first checked it out and proved it to
be accurate."

Irene Hughes firmly believes that in legal matters such as these, the
psychic should work behind the scenes. The very nature of the psychic

work leaves room for misinterpretations and possible error. Conviction is too serious for there to be any doubts whatsoever as to a particular person's guilt.

Mrs. Hughes has also considered the liability of psychics who offer impressions regarding a case on trial. She believes that it would be ". . . extremely unethical for any psychic to give a name to the press on any case that was in the courts at the particular time." If comments such as these influenced the outcome of the trial, then that psychic could definitely be sued.

Over and over again psychics emphasize that the work they do is not admissible evidence, that it is never intended to get as far as the courts where it could influence the proceedings. Psychic impressions are given as an informer gives tips. They are meant to be investigated by police officers. If the impressions can be supported by solid evidence, then the evidence is the only testimony given in court.

THE ETHICS OF PSYCHIC CRIME DETECTION

Also included in Irene Hughes' ethical code is a strict injunction against predicting the outcome of a particular trial. Her one firm rule is "no public disclosures," and she guards herself well in this area.

"If I confided to a columnist the outcome of a trial and that columnist betrayed my confidence, I would take legal action against him," she has stated. "I would feel that was a breach of faith and a breach of ethics."

In Irene's code a psychic should use discrimination, work only with the particular authorities who originally contacted the psychic, and never release anything of his or her own accord. "Let it be up to the authorities to determine when certain information should be released," she believes.

A DIALOGUE WITH IRENE HUGHES ON ESP AND CRIME

Brad Steiger: Could there be cases wherein a psychic impression could help apprehend a suspect?

Irene Hughes: I think that is possible only in certain cases. For example, if the psychic is in the courtroom listening to the case and the person lies about where he was at a given date. The psychic can immediately perceive this and perhaps determine where the suspect really was. This information could be given to someone in authority, then during a recess it could be quickly checked to see if the psychic is right. Then that evidence can be presented in court.

Would there be a role for a psychic in jury selection?

I do not feel that psychics could, or ever should, be involved in jury selection. As a matter of fact, I was called upon to be on a jury. I told them my ability, and they did not ask me to be a juror.

What would be your attitude if you were retained by a defense attorney to come into the court for a particular case? Could you or would you?

I would if I were retained by the defense attorney, but only on a quiet basis. I would not want it known what I was really there for. I would get psychic impressions on the case, and then I would give these to the attorney outside the courtroom. The attorney could then have these checked for evidence.

I am totally sold on the fact that no psychic should ever be allowed to be a witness, no psychic should be allowed to be on a jury. The psychic should work behind the scenes, giving impressions, and letting the actual evidence be brought forth by the authorities, based on these impressions.

Would your opinion change if there were a better acceptance of ESP?

I don't feel my opinion would change, because I think there is an ethic involved here. The psychic deals with things unseen; therefore, the psychic cannot prove what he is seeing unless someone else checks it out. I just don't see how a psychic could ever be a really useful witness or a juror, because a good psychic would always have to go above and beyond the facts and employ his psychic abilities. His abilities might unearth something he could not prove, and this would create too much confusion and frustration.

IRENE HUGHES ON PSYCHIC SAFARI

In the summer of 1970, Other Dimensions, a research group that I had established, used the talents of Irene Hughes to cut a swatch through Iowa, Illinois, and Nebraska on a haunted house psychic safari. In her wake she left numerous dumbfounded skeptics-turned-true-believers. Among these were police officers, journalists, caretakers, local historians, and the hosts and hostesses of the haunted homes.

The tour was organized by my associate Glenn McWane who had investigated all the homes prior to our visit to ascertain the validity of the hauntings.

One of the stops of the tour was a very old house in Clinton, Iowa. In a darkened, sub-basement Irene got an impression of "... a stream ... a river. There was a passage here, somewhere over there, that went to a river."

The sub-basement was so dark that not even the light of my flashlight could pick out a possible passageway. I was aware of the house's history, but I had told Irene none of it. All information she received would have to be on the basis of psychic acuity alone.

"Why would there be a stream of people moving through here? I almost feel like these people are prisoners or something. Slaves I see slaves, black slaves streaming through this place," Irene announced.

The psychic could not have been more accurate. The house in Clinton had been a station of the Underground Railway during the Civil War era. The slaves had slipped out of the house through a tunnel leading from the sub-basement to another depot further north, and further on the way to

Irene is also an author, newspaper columnist, and
editor of her own psychic astrology magazine.

freedom. Records indicated that there had been a small stream running
through the tunnel, which Irene also correctly sensed.

The amazing part of the psychic's success is that there was no reason for
her to go out on a limb and speak of an underground railroad station so far
north of the Mason-Dixon line. Anyone familiar with the "road to freedom"
would naturally assume that Iowa, which was definitely pro-Union, would
be a safe place for a former slave to surface. It is little known, however, that
the town of Clinton was strenuously pro-Confederacy, because the town's
lumber barons had a prosperous trade in the South and had invested in
many Southern plantations. The fate of a runaway slave caught in Clinton
would have been cruel, and more than one Abolitionist was tarred and
feathered for speaking out against slavery. Hence, it was essential that the
railway depot be a well-kept secret.

A GLOWING ORB OF MISTY LIGHT

One of the strangest nights of the psychic safari occurred in front of the
Sumpter mansion in Iowa City, Iowa. We had made arrangements to visit
the house on a particular night, but had decided to drive out unofficially the
evening before to check the place.

Suddenly a large, glowing orb of misty light appeared before us, some
fifty yards from our parked car. Irene grew quiet and seemed unwilling to

follow the others' excited conversation until I suggested that they go forward to investigate the eerie light. Immediately Irene found her voice.

"No, not tonight," she told the group. "I have a very bad feeling that it would not be good for us to walk down that lane right now."

The psychic's voice was so adamant that we agreed to her wishes immediately. Whatever the thing was, Irene's psychism had definitely told her that the time was wrong. We left and returned the next evening with the house's caretaker and a police officer from the Iowa City force.

A wispy vapor huddled in one specific spot on the next night, but the glowing orb did not reappear. The light had been seen for years, though, by the two spinster sisters who had lived in the house; and after the place was deserted, passing patrol cars frequently had reported the presence of a strange light.   No one knows where the light came from or what it represented, but three years after witnessing the ghostly orb, Irene finally opened up regarding her impressions of the preternatural thing. Her comments appear in the interview section of this chapter.

Brad Steiger on "Psychic Safari," 1970

Irene Hughes has repeatedly proved her psychic prowess in front of skeptical newsmen, policemen, and other observers. On the haunted house safari she often encountered caretakers and homeowners who were willing to open their homes to her, but doubtful of any information she might produce. In each case she startled these disbelievers, telling them things about themselves and their homes that they never dreamed another person could know. She also challenged them to investigate her psychic impressions regarding events of which they were not aware, but had been connected with the houses. Wherever sufficient records could be found, Irene's information was proved amazingly accurate.

THROUGH THE DOOR OF THE GOLDEN PATH

Irene can have this same effect on those who come to her through the door of the Golden Path offices. They may be students, housewives, doctors, lawyers, businessmen, ministers, and shop girls, but they all get the full attention and compassionate concern of this lovely lady. They may come to her only half-believing that she can help them, or curious only to "check her out," but they all invariably leave her office feeling encouraged and strengthened by her inspirational manner.

In the development classes which I have observed, Irene tries to teach her students an awareness of their spiritual selves through the medium of evolving psychic abilities. She opens each class with a Bible reading, and encourages her students to discuss their problems and successes with the many psychic exercises she gives them. Each night the students engage in some aspect of psychic training, with guidance and encouragement from Irene.

Irene has devised a series of meditations for her students, as well as a very practical series of techniques to increase their psychic awareness. On various nights the students will experiment with telepathy, with clairvoyance, and with precognition. The classes engage in practice through such methods as trying to impress a thought upon undeveloped film, teaming up for home telepathic experiments, and prediction-making during meditation.

It is for predictions that Irene is best known on the national scale. The seeress maintains that she has 80% accuracy, and the claim is backed up by an invitation to study her files, which contain her "hits" as well as "misses."

A criticism frequently made against psychics is that their predictions are worded so generally that "anyone" could predict such-and-such an event. These critics do not realize that a psychic often deliberately generalizes a very specific prediction, especially if the prediction is a negative one. An ethically based psychic is aware that the faith she inspires in her devotees may actually cause these people subconsciously to create the negative event. Or, worse, an explicitly worded prophecy may incite an individual to take fate into his own hands and make the prediction come true.

THE "DOOMSDAY BOOK"

For this reason, Irene Hughes will not always publicly announce the name of an individual whom she feels may die, but she will privately record the specific information in what she calls her "Doomsday" book. This book is shown to a small number of persons, who sign affidavits affirming that the predictions were made well in advance of the date.

Once Irene was present on a radio show in Chicago with this book in her hands. The radio commentator asked for a few predictions that he could pass on to his listeners, and Irene complied by opening the book. At the top of the page was a prediction stating: "Martin Luther King will be killed in April, 1968."

The startled broadcaster began to blurt out the information, but Irene hastily covered the prediction with her hand. The man immediately caught himself and told his listeners that "a man who is a national leader will die in April, 1968." Irene later informed the man that it would have been highly unethical for the full information to be given out over the air.

Of the future in general, Irene foresees major crises – but nothing that a balanced humanity cannot survive:

"Within each of us is a deep desire for the type of peace for ourselves and the rest of the world, but each of us goes about it in a different way...Man will have to face, according to the revelations of mystics and astrologers, major crises within the next few years that are devastating to behold, but the right light of knowing in advance, being able to prepare, and gaining a greater knowledge of man will see us through to a greater and more peaceful world! Cheer up! We are here to stay for a very long time yet!"

Such optimism is typical of a woman who has devoted her life to helping others. She has guided too many people through personal crises and seen them survive as stronger, more spiritual people, to fear for humankind, as we battle our way through the twentieth century.

With spiritual guides of the caliber of Irene Hughes, we are bound to make it.

ESPECIALLY, IRENE

Brad Steiger: Irene, if you were in a position of great authority and someone bequeathed you a million dollars for the investigation of psychism, how would you spend that million dollars?

Irene Hughes: I would spend it, first of all, on getting a proper place and bringing in doctors and scientists who are interested in this type of research – particularly criminology and medicine. Those are my two greatest areas, and I have always been interested in them. Then I would certainly allow these people all the time they needed, with sufficient pay, to carry out their research. I would urge open-mindedness so that a person with just the slightest psychic abilities could be brought in and checked out, too.

Would you do this in more natural conditions for the psychic or would you have strict laboratory conditions?

I think it would be like a farm, in a very relaxed atmosphere, but still strictly controlled. I feel that is the best way to do it. Also not to let the psychic know how he is doing, even though I like that. It frustrates me not to know how I am doing, but in the final analysis I think it works out. Also, there can be no possibility for what they could call cheating.

How would you go about educating the public in a more positive manner, or do you think this is being done effectively now?

I think it is being done now, but I also think there has been just a little bit of a letdown throughout the psychic research recently. It seems they are stymied and don't know in which direction to go.

Have you ever been frightened by anything in your experience?

Yes, at that very terrible house outside Iowa City, Iowa. A light came floating down the path, down the driveway. That was the one time I was really afraid. I went back to the car and wanted to get away from there. I didn't tell you or the others why I was afraid, I just said I wanted to leave.

Can you say now why you were afraid at the Sumpter mansion?

I had the feeling that some violence was going to be involved – although spirits never hurt. I felt like there was something above us and beyond that I could not understand. It made me feel foolish to mention it at the time, but I had the sudden feeling that the energy we were seeing was something from another planet, like flying saucer energy. I have been afraid that something terrible would happen to me if I mentioned it, and it felt so absolutely overwhelming. I really knew that this was beyond spirit, because spirit just does not hurt.

I really have been deathly afraid that something would happen to me if I ever mentioned it, but I think I am getting over that. It was almost like the thing threatened me not to.

All I said that night to you was that I was afraid, though I wouldn't say why. I just wanted to get away. Normally, I am not afraid of anything, ever.

Yet you went back the second night. Did you feel it was a different energy then?

I wasn't afraid of it then. I felt that it was more calm, and I felt also that maybe I had a deeper understanding of it within me. It was almost like I was the only one who understood, and therefore the only one who could reveal it, so I felt the fear flowing through me. It was terrifying, like I was being run over.

You seem to feel happiest and most complete when you are helping people.

This is true, especially when I can see the good results. Once I worked on a case in which a young girl was married to a young man who had just been fatally injured in an accident. He died in a hospital. Well, this girl was working the ouija board, and some freaky person told her that they were going to cremate her husband when he wasn't really dead, and this made her quite hysterical. The mother of the young man sent the girl to me, and we had a very calming conference on her. I think I went into trance at that time, because when I finished she was saying to me, "I feel so good and so much better and different. I see everything in a perfect light." Then they left and two hours later her husband was cremated. I got a letter from her saying how much better she felt, and the mother of the son was saying that she felt the crisis was over.

This brings up a matter of ethics, Irene. Recently we heard of a woman who was very upset because someone had told her she was to die soon, and horribly. One of my associates, who does not claim any psychic abilities, told her what he felt was a justifiable white lie. He said he had a strong psychic impression that the woman was going to live for many years, and that the other person was wrong to tell her otherwise. The woman was much relieved, but our associate was concerned that he had done the right thing. Would you say he had done the right thing with this woman, or was he wrong?

Well, first of all, I think it was a psychic impression that your associate was getting. I am not trying to boost him at all, but when a person has this adrenalin of anger flowing through him, sometimes tremendous psychic impressions can come with it. I feel that in my most angry moments the greatest things come. Therefore, I do feel it was a real psychic impression.

I think, too, that this other person, who predicted death, was misinterpreting the impression received. I find so often that psychics do this. They don't seem to have the capacity to interpret the information that is revealed to them. What this particular psychic may have been seeing was someone in the past in that woman's life, or maybe a past life of hers, and not this particular time.

I feel that whatever comes the psychic should be able to tell it to the person, but diplomatically. In other words, I don't believe as a psychic that I have the right to interfere with any message that is revealed to me about a client. After all, that is what they come to me for. I would be more diplomatic about it, though, and I would indicate to her that maybe this death impression could apply to a past incarnation, a way that she had died previously.

It is easy to document your record of successes with your predictions because you print them in advance and everyone can check them to see that your score is very high. How would you rate yourself on your teaching ability?

The thing I really teach people is not how to *develop* their psychism, but how to become *aware* of their spiritual selves through bringing out their psychic abilities. This is sort of like a little proof that says, "See, you can do it. You have this tremendous God-spirit within you, and you just need to become more aware of it. If you need something physical to show you, then this ESP is it."

I don't take people through my classes to become psychics. I tell all of them that. It is for them to become more aware of their spiritual selves. So I can't say that my classes have been successful as far as developing new psychics, because that is not my intent. If they do develop, then that's great.

You have worked with hypnosis, haven't you? Do you feel that hypnosis could be a good key for developing psychism – or would you see a different application of hypnosis?

I am not a hypnotist myself, but I have employed hypnotists at various times to work with my classes. I have also worked in connection with hypnotists many times, and I feel that hypnosis can be very valuable in helping a person become more relaxed. Hypnosis can help a person get back to his natural abilities, sort of get beneath the surface of all the goop that has been placed in their minds, all that stuff that really has no value in life. I think that in that way hypnosis can be very helpful, because the more relaxed a person is, the more aware he is going to be of the spiritual person within himself.

How can average folks remove all that "goop" from their minds?

It is so difficult and takes such discipline, but they must sit day after day, taking the time to turn their thoughts away from the negative to positive mental attitudes. They have to feel grateful that they are alive and healthy, and they must declare this to themselves. They must decide that they are more aware of other peoples' lives and that they realize that all people are of the same blood. These are the kinds of things they have to repeat, because when you work something out, you've got to replace it with something. You've got to have something to take the place of the old, negative things like, "My friend did something to me, so I've got to get back at him."

How much to do rely on your guide in your work?

I feel that Kaygee is always with me. Occasionally, he does appear, and these are the times that I go into deep trance, deeper than my daylight trance, which I do with every reading. It's just a natural thing that when a person comes and sits before me, *wham*, I feel like I am half asleep. That just brings it on, and I start to talk.

Do you see that we are entering a period of transition and change?

This is absolutely true. I feel that the whole world is in a tremendous state of transition – not only people but nations, as well. I think we are sort of a quarter of the way through the tremendous spiritual awakening period that is ahead, where people are being revolutionized within. People are turning toward the mystical things in life now more than ever, because they are seeking God now more than they ever have – at least in many centuries, I would say. It is as though every soul seems to sense either consciously or unconsciously that some very dramatic era is right ahead and they want to be prepared for it.

Some have made the statement that part of the responsibility of those who are tuned in to this coming change will be to help others through this difficult period. These people feel that there will be millions of people totally unprepared for this because of their materialistic background. Edgar Cayce and others talked about physical catastrophes, but the psychological catastrophes could be even greater. Would you agree with that?

Well, I feel that the physical catastrophes of the earth changes are going to create the terrible psychological catastrophes, because people who have not been taught in their religions that there is going to be a spiritual awakening period, or a second coming, are going to be almost totally doomed. Unless they can in some way wash out all of the old – shall I say, erroneous – teaching and learn to accept that this is the time, they will be doomed.

I am not a doomsday prophet, because I don't see the world ending. These are the days, however, that the bride is preparing for the bridegroom.

Do you see a physical return of Christ?

I have never been able to come to the actual feeling that this is what will happen. I believe in reincarnation, and I believe it is possible, but there is something there that is holding me back from totally accepting it. If someone can enlighten me in this matter, I would be very happy to listen.

You don't see Jesus as the only Son of God.

I feel that he was an example to us, because the Divine Spark knew that man would not believe what he could not see. Jesus came to show all men that they can become the same as He was.

All men are Sons of God, then.

Absolutely. They are the same as he was, and Jesus was just here to show us this. It's too bad that a lot of men have changed Jesus' thoughts and his ways.

I feel that the organized churches are failing, because we are becoming aware that God is within us, and that we ourselves can communicate with that energy – or whatever we wish to call it – and we can know the Truth.

CHAPTER TWO

How to Choose
a Psychic Sensitive

[Author's Note: The following words of solid, constructive advice regarding the selection of a psychic sensitive were prepared by Irene Hughes for an earlier publication.]

Maybe you're troubled and filled with fears; or you've lost a loved one and you cannot seem to face life as once you did; or you have an urge in all reverence to satisfy yourself about the assertions of such Christians as Sherwood Eddy and Leslie Weatherhead that biblical accounts of spiritual communication are duplicated in kind today. You've heard that a professional sensitive might help you.

Your most prudent course is to obtain personal recommendations from friends whose judgment you trust. Having obtained the name of a sensitive, with much doubt and perhaps embarrassment, you make an appointment. What do you do now?

HAVE FAITH – AND RELAX

Most important to you, in order to get the best help available through that sensitive, is to have faith – faith in yourself, and faith in the sensitive. You are going to your appointment skeptical but expectant, relaxed, and courteous. To get best results, prepare yourself by taking some time to be alone in quiet thought and prayer. Do, above all, be relaxed!

Don't try to think of any particular answer or message that you want. Instead, come knowing that the sensitive is a spiritual person and that, aided by prayer, he probably will be able to help you. No one can assure you a satisfactory reading.

WHAT TO TAKE WITH YOU

Be on time for your sitting. Take with you to the sitting a tablet, spare pens or pencils, and, if possible, a tape recorder with tape to run well over an hour. To use the recorder, you need the sensitive's permission, as the machine distracts and annoys some psychics. Be prepared, if the gadget is forbidden or if it fails, to take rapid notes in great detail. Messages may come helter-skelter from several excarnates and you cannot possibly trust your memory to unscramble what is uttered. Accurate notes are essential if you are to check up on details.

Hold the microphone close to the sensitive's lips. When he is channeling, his voice often subsides to a whisper. At the same time, his hearing is dull. Hence be sure that your own voice always is strong and clear. Keep your hands from your mouth.

In chatting with the sensitive before the sitting proper, conceal every fact about yourself, your business, or your connections.

A VARIETY OF TRANCE STATES

Now we are ready for the reading. Delay turning on your tape recorder. There will be long minutes of silence as the sensitive sinks by meditation and perhaps yoga procedure into trance or semitrance. When the sensitive starts to speak, turn on the recorder.

If it is a "daylight" reading, in which the sensitive is not in full trance, he – in his own personality – will relay sentences and interpretations to you. If the sensitive is in trance, a completely different personality – a "control" or "guide" or "gatekeeper" – will be in control of the sensitive's body. This personality will identify himself as "Fletcher" or "Owen" or "Chief Silver Cloud" (names not always connected with his life on this plane), and he will mediate the conversation. The procedure, so far as you are concerned, is rather like communicating with a bunch of friends who telephone to congratulate you, but catch you in the bathtub, and your wife relays – mediates – what your friends say, and what you say.

The sensitive may either lie down during the reading or sit in a comfortable chair. Some psychics move about the room, shaking hands and gesturing, in a manner characteristic of the personality in control of the body. The voice and vocabulary commonly are those of the sensitive, but not always. Different controls with widely varying speech patterns work through George Daisley. On occasion, words or even foreign languages unknown to the sensitive pour from his lips.

BE POLITE AND FRIENDLY

The importance of your attitude toward these personalities cannot be overstressed. Be invariably polite and friendly, even if the man who murdered Grandpa seems to be there. Speak promptly when spoken to, just as you would if addressed by a guest at your table. Be positive and brief in your remarks, never negative, but never volunteering crucial information. For example, do not say, "I never heard of Fred Chamberlain." Say, instead, "Can you describe him?" Or, "Does he have a message for me?" The catch is that Fred may have been in first grade with you, but you have not seen him since then. Or he may have retired from Smith & Schmidt, Inc., before you began your apprenticeship there. Of *nobody* can you safely assert, "I have had no connection with him." If you do so assert, he'll hush.

Identifications constitute the hardest job for the sensitive and the most baffling problem of the sitter. Often names come as symbols – as a picture of the muscular arm on a package of soda for "Armstrong," or an item of yellow fruit for the name "Lemmon," or a dairy farm scene for an agricultural kinsman. At times, the sensitive "hears" the name, perhaps clearly, possibly mumbled. Why names are so much trouble is a mystery.

ENCOURAGE MESSAGES

Remember (or assume, for the purposes of your investigation) that the sensitive and the excarnates are trying to get information through to you, and that they are engaged on your behalf in difficult and baffling endeavors. Our communication between planes is less than perfect.

Part of the courtesy you must show is to stifle every sneeze or cough. It distracts minds on both sides of the line, somewhat as though a golf tournament spectator kerchooed during a putt at the eighteenth hole. Equally upsetting to the minds involved is a disposition to put test questions calculated to ensnare or discomfit the communicator. Since the whole experience is mental, a hostile mind availeth not.

HOW TO EVALUATE COMMUNICATIONS

Having considered how to encourage messages, let us now ponder how to evaluate them. Above all, don't try to discuss them with the sensitive himself. He will remember little or nothing of them. Moreover, anything you say will vitiate evidence that might come through at a subsequent sitting.

Remember that the world in which the sensitive works is one where present, past, and future are one; time and space do not exist. The communicator's method of transmission, largely in symbols and pictographs, has no grammatical indicators or tense. If he sees an event on Thursday, it may be next Thursday, or a Thursday in 1970, or even a Thursday in 1870. When predictions are given, there always is a chance that you, yourself, can change the situation facing you. God gives you free will. If you are told, for example, that you risk a particular traffic accident, exercise care and caution to forestall it. Let the premonition be an admonition.

Misleading exaggerations occur in mediating ideas because of the elimination of details, and, thereby, elimination of perspective. The communicator may see great confusion about you in your office. It may mean that several desks will be moved two feet each to improve the arrangement, or it may mean a general shakeup with transfers of personnel. After such a forewarning, just play it by ear at the office.

Another impediment to accuracy is coloration. Knowledge or emotions buried in the unconscious of the sensitive may emerge in the guise of messages or parts of messages from another plane. Clairvoyance, clairaudience, or telepathy involving only the earth plane sometimes intermingles with communication from excarnates. The skill and experience of the gifted sensitive minimize coloration, but they never quite eliminate the possibility that it has occurred.

WATCH OUT FOR SPIRIT PRANKSTERS

Occasionally, just as a prank, a strange excarnate will pretend to be your Great-Aunt Constance. The stranger knows something about Aunt Constance, but the giveaway is in her personality. If Aunt Constance had a Calvinist conscience, you'll know you're dealing with a masquerader if she advises some shabby maneuver.

Whether or not it's Aunt Constance, stand by your own conscience and your own judgment. Though discarnates have sources of information denied to you, they still are merely people, limited in knowledge, imperfect in judgment, human in motive. They are just members with you and me in one interrelated society. Weigh their advice as you would that of intelligent friends on this plane – seriously but not slavishly.

A good sensitive will not speak in general terms such as: "Everything is going to be all right. Don't worry." If such language is used by a conscientious sensitive, it will apply only to a specific situation; and the psychic will have received it from Spirit – otherwise it will not be relayed to you.

Saucer-eyed naiveté and trustful gullibility lead only to tearful disillusionment. On the other hand, if judicious investigation brings through one authentic evidential message from the Beyond, your world never will be so drab again. The sensitive is a channel. Make believe that the sensitive is a telephone; that, when it rings, you answer; that you must carry on the conversation with the entity that speaks to you on the other end of the line. The sensitive cannot speak for you. He acts as the wires and the instrument through which the vibrations flow, turning into symbols and words.

Olof Jonsson, the Swedish-born psychic who earned a reputation as a superman of the paranormal. Jonsson participated in the famous Moon-to-Earth ESP experiments conducted by Astronaut Edgar Mitchell during the flight of Apollo 14.

CHAPTER THREE

Olof Jonsson— Psychic Superman

When, in February of 1971, details of astronaut Edgar Mitchell's Apollo 14 outer space ESP experiment with psychic Olof Jonsson were released in *Life* magazine and in newspapers and news broadcasts around the world, thousands of people interested in psychical research began asking: Who is Olof Jonsson?"

As Olof Jonsson's biographer (*The Psychic Feats of Olof Jonsson*, Prentice-Hall), I was in a unique position to answer those queries.

Olof Jonsson is a psychic who has been widely tested by academic institutions and parapsychologists on both sides of the Atlantic. Dr. J. B. Rhine said that he had found Jonsson to be one of the truest sensitives that he had ever tested.

Jonsson is an incredible controller of psychokinesis who, under laboratory conditions, surrounded by scientists and medical doctors, has suspended in mid-air tables, chairs, and even living humans – solely by means of his "mind-power."

Jonsson is the astonishing accurate clairvoyant, who aids the police in locating missing persons and in determining guilty parties in crime cases.

Jonsson is the telepath who can read thoughts, cards, and objects with an accuracy that has astounded scientists and lay investigators around the world. Even with Jonsson in Chicago and parapsychologist Dr. O. Holmberg in Stockholm, Sweden, Olof has read 23 out of 25 ESP cards correctly.

Jonsson is the prototype of the hearty Norseman. He has a youthful face, blonde hair, and appears several years younger than his actual years. He is of medium height and build, the type of person you like immediately. He is now an American citizen, who worked for many years as a drafting engineer. Jonsson is a man of mathematics and drawing boards, not fortune tellers' booths or seance parlors.

At the age of seven, it was discovered that Olof Jonsson could will a bottle to move back and forth across the kitchen table without physically touching it. As he grew older, his powers of ESP increased. From 1946 to 1953, he was tested by some of the foremost European experts in the field of parapsychology. He was brought to wide public attention when he was called in to solve a series of bizarre murders in a small Swedish village. Because of Jonsson's psychic talents, the villagers were spared further maniacal savagery, but to Jonsson, a sick man had been needlessly destroyed, and he vowed never again to become involved in solving crimes of violence.

In 1953, Dr. J. B. Rhine issued an invitation to Jonsson to come to the U.S. The experiments of Dr. Rhine and his colleagues, conducted quietly and without publication, continued for more than fifteen years.

THE PROPER PSYCHIC LINK-UP

Jonsson seems to possess abilities that violate the vast majority of our known natural laws, yet he, personally, does not believe that his talents are "extra sensory" at all. Jonsson believes that anyone may develop his own psyche and the blessed Harmony that governs the Universe.

The first hint that an ESP experiment might be in the unofficial schedule for the Apollo 14 program came in an interview with astronaut Mitchell (*Chicago Daily News*, January 30, 1971.) Mitchell was characterized as the most intellectual of the astronauts and as an "amateur star gazer with a fascination for psychic phenomena." The article told of Mitchell's "insatiable appetite for exploring psychic mysteries," and the astronaut admitted that his interest in psychic matters often interrupted the few hours the space program had allotted him to spend with his family. Mitchell said that he could find no conflict between his curiosity for the unknown and the computers of Apollo 13. "I am completely unable to separate science from theology, from art, from humanity," he said. "Man is a total thing; everything is a total thing."

What had not yet been released was the fact that several months before the Apollo mission, Mitchell had asked a select group of parapsychologists to find sensitive subjects for an experiment across a quarter of a million miles of space. One of the sensitives the doctors chose was Chicago drafting engineer Olof Jonsson.

About two weeks before blast-off, Mitchell and Jonsson conducted a number of telephone experiments with the symbols of a standard ESP-testing deck in order to gain rapport. Jonsson says that these early tests were successful. Astronaut Shepard may have carried a golf club on board the space capsule, but Mitchell brought a pack of ESP cards along with him.

On February 3, 1971, Earth News Service of San Francisco broke the story of the telepathy tests. They quoted an insider who said that the test had been stimulated by "numerous reports of similar experiments in telepathy being conducted by Russian astronauts." A NASA spokesman officially denied that such tests were being carried out on the Apollo 14 mission, but during the astronauts' splash-down on February 9th, CBS news announced that while Mitchell had been in space, he had conducted some ESP experiments with a Chicago engineer.

On February 13, the wire services released Olof Jonsson's name and newspapers throughout the world carried details of the experiment. The release, date-lined Houston Space Center, emphasized that the experiment had been a personal project of Mitchell's, which had in no way infringed upon his assigned duties.

A MYSTIC OF GREAT DEPTH AND INSIGHT

As a witness to literally hundreds of tests and experiments with Olof Jonsson – and as his friend who has shared the confidence of personal triumphs and crises – I have come to resent those who suggest that the gentle Swede has been so conditioned to card-guessing, dice-rolling, and other experimental devices that he has become somewhat like the laboratory rat in a maze.

"Olof is the greatest in the world in the laboratory," some psychics have admitted, "but I do my best work with people."

The unspoken suggestion is such a statement is, of course, that Olof has become a mechanistic psychic robot, so programmed to perform for parapsychologists that he has surrendered a portion of his humanity.

I wish to go on record as stating that such is most emphatically not the case. To know Olof Jonsson well is to know a warm, considerate, almost saintly individual. He is a mystic of great depth of insight and feeling. He has much to share and a great deal to teach. Several men and women approached me after the publication of our book *The Psychic Feats of Olof Jonsson* to tell me how uplifted they felt after reading of Olof's concluding words in the volume.

I would like to quote the final paragraphs of that personal credo, then share with readers a discussion with Olof Jonsson the psychic engineer as a metaphysical teacher.

No man needs to be afraid of dying. The order of Nature, the Cosmic Harmony of the Universe tells us that in all forms of existence, everything has meaning, nothing comes about by chance. It is blasphemous to believe that man alone should be excluded from the orderliness and purposefulness of the Universe. The secret of life's course and death's chambers is found within each of us in the unknown levels of the unconscious, where lie many dormant powers.

The utilization of the powers, the "sparks of divinity," within each of us, should never tempt the wise to make a religion out of spiritual blessings that have been dispensed to all men. Rather, an awareness of the powers within should serve to equip the interested and the receptive with a brilliant searchlight on the path to Cosmic Harmony.

It is in one's own home, in his own little chamber, in moments of quiet meditation that a stream of the great light of Cosmos is best able to reach in and enrich the soul and open the eyes to the magnificent and tranquil gardens that lie beyond the borders of the Unknown. That which governs a man's life is neither chemistry nor physics nor anything material, but the proper spiritual link-up with the powers within his own psyche and the blessed Harmony that governs the Universe.

Summoned by scientists and politicians throughout the world, the globe-trotting Jonsson is seen here with former Philippines President Marcos.

Brad Steiger: Is psychism a natural human faculty, possessed by every human being to a greater or lesser degree, or is it acquired by mystical enlightenment?

Olof Jonsson: I believe that psychism is a natural human faculty possessed by every human being. There are cases of people who have had mystical experiences or revelatory experiences which have changed their lives and they had had a sudden dramatic development of psychic ability, but this is very rare.

Is it possible to teach the abilities you possess as a psychic-sensitive, or must each individual seek his or her own enlightenment and path to psychism?

Although I was born with these abilities, I do believe it is possible to teach the things that are required to achieve that state of mind necessary for receiving psychic impressions. The student must learn to eliminate all distractions from his mind.

Both Eastern and Western mystics and psychics are submitting to scientific examination to validate their psychism or paranormal abilities.

Will the scientific documentation of exceptional physical and mental abilities, such as you have consistently displayed, revolutionize our understanding of our human nature and that of our universe?

I think it is important to submit to scientific examination so that all may be recorded, even if we do not have adequate equipment to test all these abilities at this time. In all probability, there will be a better means of understanding and testing in the future, but it is important to record everything now so that we may be prepared with documentation for those who follow us.

We now know there are many people with these abilities. These abilities can be developed even if we cannot explain the abilities or the process scientifically. Psychic abilities may help us solve some of the problems we have today in various fields, such as medicine, the arts, our creativity. They may help us to live in harmony with our fellow man.

Do you believe there is unity in all matter and beings?

Yes, I believe that all things are a part of the great Universal Mind. All things, all men, all plants, animals, minerals. And I think people who are aware of this live in harmony with nature. This, I think, explains why some people have no fear of animals. They walk through jungles without being harmed. This accounts for people growing enormous-sized plants and vegetation, especially in areas where such things are not supposed to be able to grow. Some people realize reverence for the creative force in all things and benefit from it.

Is there a real hope that new and more improved attitudes towards mysticism and spiritual understanding of a universal nature are possible in the West under the present religious and educational institutions?

I do think there will be new hope toward mysticism and spiritual understanding. I do not think, though, that it will come from any one source of one group. The established religions are changing somewhat now. They are becoming more liberal in their views. We will still have to come a long way, but I do think that science will be responsible for changing the attitudes of the people in the mainstream first. Then I believe the religions will follow.

Did you have a "guru" or "master" who led you into your psychic heritage?

I do not have a guide, guru, or master. I feel the Universal Mind is my guide – through meditation. The information I get is from the Universal Source, much the same as "the river" Edgar Cayce talked about.

Do you believe there is intelligent life outside our planet earth?

I feel at times I have received impressions from intelligent life outside of our planet. I have the impression there are far-advanced civilizations beyond our galaxies. I feel that they have been close to us many times. I do know there are some people who are in communication with these "people."

What is your concept of God?

I do not think God is form as we understand it. God is beyond form. God is energy, but not as we understand it. I don't think we will ever understand the true nature of God until we become one with this Universal Energy.

Since we are a part of God, this part of us that is God-within sometimes will act, pushing aside our conscious mind. Many things happen to people which put them in contact with their Creator. Sometimes it is through an illness, an accident, or some other drastic means which brings them into contact with God. Other times, it is through conscious contact, as sought through prayer and meditation.

Please explain the force, influence, or power referred to as love.

I do not believe in love as a human type of thing. True love is beyond human emotion. It is an emotion that is reserved for God. it is beyond our personal attachments. Although we refer to our feelings for such attachments as love (and it seems to us as love), I do not think we are truly capable of understanding divine love until we have achieved a high, high state of evolution.

What is evil?

I do not recognize evil as most people think of evil. I will only say that I feel that evil is disharmony. It is the opposite of warmth and feeling of affection that we hold toward our loved ones.

What is our primary purpose as human beings in physical life?

Although everything has a purpose, I do not feel we can have any one purpose as a human being. I feel our primary purpose is not in the physical life, but beyond human life. We will not truly understand it until after we have left the physical life.

Do we retain our human personality upon physical death? Are we transformed into "cosmic energy" without human personality?

I do feel we retain our human personality upon physical death. We are transformed into energy, but at the same time we keep intact our memories of our earthly experience.

Have you ever had a formal religious affiliation?

I was born into the Lutheran Church in my native Sweden. I am not now an active member in any organized religion. I do not believe in organized religion. I feel that each person should be his own priest. I feel that it is up to the individual to be attuned to his Creator. I do not say that a person cannot benefit from church affiliation, but, for myself, I do not feel this is necessary.

Can an individual know for certain that the information he receives through meditation is correct and right?

When one receives information through meditation, there is also the feeling that it is right. His life should be guided by meditation and also by information received by the five senses. meditation alone is not enough. We are given many talents, and meditation is only one of the ways. If coupled with an academic learning, meditation should help the individual choose a path which he considers right for himself.

What is your concept of the human mind?

I believe the human mind is something apart from the physical body. I feel that the human mind is a channel where information is received from an exterior source. I do not feel the human mind is located in the brain, just as I do not feel other bodies, such as the astral body, are located in the physical part of us. Any more than one can put the soul in a test tube, I do not feel the mind can be put in a test tube. We are something beyond the physical body and the human brain. We are mind because God is mind.

Is the human species evolved through genetic improvements?

Although I feel we are evolving through genetic improvements and have made great strides in medicine, we also have to balance this with a type of spiritual evolution. We are also being awakened to things that have nothing to do with the physical. Both are important. I also think good health, good eating habits, and right attitudes of mind are necessary if we are to achieve more human intelligence.

Is there an increasing interaction between the Creator and human beings which is accelerating the awareness of, and adherence to, the spiritual principles taught by Jesus and other "masters"?

Every day, people are beginning to tell each other of their personal spiritual experiences. Before, they wouldn't talk about them. This seems to indicate there is more of a communication between the Creator and human beings. I think we are living at a time when the spiritual principles taught by Jesus and others will be something which is taught to everyone *personally* through his or her own awareness.

In a series of strictly controlled experiments in the Copenhagen laboratory of Danish parapsychologist Sven Turck,
Jonsson displayed his psychokinetic abilities by such
manifestations as this, in which he levitates a chair by mind
power alone.

*Do you see a future species of human beings who will possess superior psychic,
mental and spiritual abilities?*

I think that in a time to come man will enjoy a period of peace and
spiritual enlightenment. Man will be superior mentally, spiritually, and
psychically. He will also be superior physically. He will be guided to eat
what is good for him. He will not have problems with obesity. He will
develop his will to work in harmony with his Father's will.

Do you see a "superhuman" engaged in other than peaceful activities?

I do not think a human would be "super" if he engaged in other than
peaceful activities. I think such a race would not survive for any length of
time, although I think it is possible for it to happen, just as the legend of
Atlantis said it did. We understand there once were such types of "super-
men" but they ended by destroying themselves and their civilization.

*Do you see an event occurring that will elevate man to a higher spiritual and
mental stage of development?*

I feel we will see in our time a terrible war that will probably destroy a
great portion of the population of the world. After this will be a period of
peace where man will develop to a higher spiritual and mental state. But it
will take something terrible to awaken man first.

Olof, it seems to me that you envision a purposeful universe, a divine plan.
Yes, a divine plan that in the end will be harmonious.
Harmony seems to be your favorite concept.
Yes, harmony is God. When you are in harmony with the cosmos, you feel completely satisfied.
Are there beings, entities, masters on other planes of existence that may guide us in achieving cosmic harmony?
There are forces in the universe, minds that can help us gain information about the true meaning of life. I believe that there is a dynamic force and that intelligences are associated with it.
Who are these intelligences?
They could be entities from other places in the universe. Perhaps they are the souls of those who have died on highly evolved planets, who have left their radiation in the universe, and their intelligence remains as a force for good and for spiritual evolution.
You may interpret these intelligences in any way that is most compatible with your own psyche – as an Indian, as a wise old man, as a holy figure – but they are bodiless forms of benign intelligence. These intelligences may cloak themselves as Tibetans and astral teachers because the human brain will more readily accept an entity that looks like a human being, rather than a shapeless, shimmering intelligence.
You do believe firmly, then, that there are beings somewhere in the cosmos who are interested in guiding us and helping us achieve harmony and unity?
Yes, and I believe these beings have the ability to absorb our actions and our thoughts so that they may know better how to direct us toward cosmic harmony. These beings avoid language and work with us on an unconscious level. The phenomenon of telepathy affords us proof that language means nothing to the unconscious. We do not think in words, but in ideas and feelings. What language does God speak? The feelings and the harmony communicated between the unconscious levels of self comprise the one "language" that all men understand. That is God's language.
What, in your opinion, is the most important benefit that one can derive from a heightened psychic sensitivity?
A great calm and peace that suffuses one's soul and makes him harmonious with the universe. This sense of harmony places the minor distractions of our earthly life in their proper perspective and enables one to be serene and tranquil wherever he may be.

CHAPTER FOUR

There Is a Magic Genie Inside You!

Dorothy Spence Lauer of Glendora, California, became one of the nation's most talented clairvoyants. Mrs. Lauer possessed a high degree of ESP since she was a young girl. "My mother gave me sound advice regarding my ability," she related. "Live normally, and do not let this gift rule you. You rule it."

In *Search* magazine, noted editor Ray Palmer paid tribute to Dorothy Spence Lauer in an analysis of her gift of foresight: "Thus, we knew that Dorothy was predicting the death of the President (John F. Kennedy). In fact, she had warned us several times in the past three years that he would die. She was right about the Pope. She was right about several movie stars... We have been publishing the predictions of Dorothy Spence Lauer for nearly ten years now. During that time she has established herself as the most accurate prognosticator we have ever encountered."

Mrs. Lauer created her predictions of the future through an ability known as psychometry. "She holds an object that was handled or owned by the subject she is reading," an enthusiastic client explained. "By her unique psychic talent, she is able to receive future impressions." Mrs. Lauer believed that the world is entering a new age where ESP will be recognized as a normal faculty of the human mind.

"Distance makes no difference to ESP abilities," she said. "The person whom you wish to contact may be seated next to you or he may be 4,000 miles away; it is all the same to the hidden power of your mind."

"We each have within us the power of an Aladdin's lamp. Within each of us there lives a 'genie' awaiting our commands," Dorothy stated.

In Dorothy's own words:

There is nothing impossible. I know that sounds like a very strong statement, but remember I have tested these techniques over a period of many years.

I have noticed that when people meet me, they often look very skeptical. They just cannot believe that the things I speak of can occur. But little by little, subconsciously at first, and then later consciously, they begin to find these things in their own lives.

Later, I see these very same people having practically everything they want at their fingertips. But you see, they had not been using the genie within them as consciously as they should have for best results.

Some people need to have a visible means of attaining that which they desire. If you feel you need something like an Aladdin's lamp to rub, then go ahead and find some significant object. But you really do not need a physical crutch, because as you sit quietly and have this knowing power within you, you will find people coming into your life who will supply many of the things that you lack.

I am not going to tell you to sit quietly if you are a working person. You cannot sit home and not work. The genie within you would balk, and I would not blame him if he did. Once you have mastered the idea that you can bring into your own life and world the very things you want, you may rest assured that your genie will be working for you on the job or in your home.

THE MIRACLE OF BELIEVING

There have been times that I have had things happen to me that people have labeled as "miracles." I do not consider them as such, because I know they came about because of my own great belief.

When doctors decreed that I would never have any more children after the birth of my son, I told them that I would have a very beautiful daughter. Five years later, I delivered a nine-pound baby girl. Even up to the time of labor, the doctors were skeptical in regard to the birth, and some warned that the delivery would take either her life or mine. But I had no fear.

Had I taken the word of the doctors and given up the idea of having another child, I probably never would have had one. But to me this child, this daughter who was born to me, had been as real on the day that the doctors told me I would never have another child as she as on the day that they placed her in my arms. I had presented the problem to the genie, the knower within us, and I knew that this was to be.

ASK AND YOU SHALL RECEIVE

People go to church Sunday in, Sunday out, and they hear, "Ask and ye shall receive." They are told over and over again that their faith will bring them that which they desire. They hear this all their lives. They listen, but it just does not seem to penetrate their consciousness that much of the wisdom of the ages is written in the Bible. Regardless of the version you read, the Bible gives the promise of your faith bringing into your life that which you want.

If people would only stop and think, they would realize that they have everything at their command.

Many years ago, one of my clients told me, "Dorothy, I can't get anywhere just sitting here thinking that everything is at my command. I am going to go to an antique shop, and I am going to find a lamp that looks like Aladdin's lamp if I have to look from here to the end of the earth."

Strangely enough, she did find a lamp that looked exactly like the familiar Aladdin's lamp. She was very happy with the lamp. She came home and shined it up beautifully until it glowed. She put it in a very conspicuous place in her living room, and everyone who entered the room commented on her Aladdin's lamp.

After she became adept at practicing the techniques I gave her, she came to realize that she did not really need her "magic" lamp. She kept the lamp in the parlor, however, because it was what had prompted her faith into realizing that the power was within her.

She admitted to me that many times while she sat there rubbing the lamp with a little piece of blue felt – no ordinary cloth was used because it did not seem fitting – she would think to herself, "I must have this; I must have that. So be it."

She arrived at the point where she would end each request with "So be it," which, strangely enough, is a pronouncement that many mystics use, because when one says, "So be it," it is as if one had declared, "It is done."

Everything began to come her way. Everything, no matter what it was! She had found a wonderful mate, she had a beautiful car, beautiful home, and many times she would write to me and say, "I feel very guilty that I know this and I can't tell people about it, because most of them would look at me and think there was something wrong with me – just as I did when you told me about this, Dorothy."

A PECULIAR PROMPTING FROM A GENIE

One day the genie within me seemed to prompt me to walk down a certain street. Yet the street was too far from my home to walk there comfortably, and I do not drive. My neighbors were all out, and I thought, well, if I am supposed to travel to that location, the way will be shown for me to go.

A man whom I had telephoned three or four weeks previous to this date suddenly decided to come to give me an estimate on some work I had wanted done in my home. This man had had no intention of coming when I called him nearly a month before – why should he come on that day?

When he arrived at our home he explained that he had felt as if his phone had rung and he received an impression of my voice. "I must go see what work Mrs. Lauer wants done," he thought, "but I have to go right now."

I said, "Well, that's fine." I did not go into detail with him, as I did not feel he would understand what I was talking about.

"Before you give me the estimate," I said, "would you kindly drive me..." and I gave him the name of the street.

He was very obliging. I knew that I had to go to this particular street, which was about ten to fifteen blocks from my home.

I felt that what I would see would have something to do with my daughter, and as we drove down the street, I saw my daughter with three other teenagers, their arms all around each other, laughing. Evidently they had played hooky from school and were going to an ice cream shop.

You can imagine the astonishment on my daughter's face when she saw her mother riding down the street in a car with a strange man, then stopping and telling her to get into the car. She looked so flabbergasted! Although she had seen many psychic demonstrations before, she just could not believe it. However, that girl never played hooky from school from that day on, you can rest assured on that!

I had received an inspiration to go to a specific location. I did not sit down and ask the genie within me how I was going to get there. When I released that initial thought, I knew from that moment on that it would reach somebody, and it did.

THERE'S A POWERFUL INTELLIGENCE WITHIN US

There have been times when I have gone to events at which there are door prizes. Once someone had, oh, I think it was a $10.00 gold piece. I was not too interested in having this gold piece, but I thought I would try the genie within me on the prize. Sure enough, they picked my ticket out of the fish bowl in which they kept all the names.

I mention this so you may see that from a $10 gold piece to going somewhere that would prevent my daughter from playing hooky, the genie within works in a most strange and wonderful manner.

This is such a powerful intelligence within you; yet it is apart from you as a human being.

You have to be extremely careful in regard to certain people whom you may meet along life's pathway, who, knowing that you have this faith, may want you to use this force for them in the most unscrupulous ways. If you knowingly take advantage of someone, you yourself will lose twice as much as that which you have cost another. You must realize that you need to have your consciousness on a high plane. You cannot use this power with debased thoughts. You cannot use this force to hurt others.

Ever since I was a little girl, I have used ESP. My mother often said to me, "No matter what you want, Dorothy, you have it. It's almost as if paths were open to you in such a manner that you always achieve your wishes." And I would reply, "Well, mother, everyone can do this. I just don't know why you grownups don't use it."

HELPING OTHERS WITH ESP

I do not use the genie within me just for my own self. If I know that a person is a good person, who does not want to hurt anyone else, I am more than happy to help him with ESP until he himself can take over and do it on his own.

I have had the most skeptical people come into my life and offer me fees for getting this or that for them. In spite of their skepticism, I have often obtained their goals in such a dramatic manner that they considered it magic. If it is magic, then I am not aware of it, and I certainly do not call it by that name. This power is within each of us.

DO NOT LIMIT YOUR GENIE'S POWER

The genie within us has often been accused of not working unless one uses certain words. Some metaphysicians say you must use only special ritualistic words in order to obtain results. No other words will do; they have to be these "magic" words. I do not believe that there are any perfect words, any "magic" words, because here again, you see, one would be placing restrictions on that genie within you, which is the very thing you should not do.

Let us say that you awaken some morning and feel exceptionally unhappy about the day. You are filled with foreboding. This usually means that something will happen that day that will possibly make you a little sorrowful.

But if you rub your "magic lamp" or call upon the genie within you, you will gain some benefit from the day, regardless of what takes place. Somehow, some way, there will be a lesson learned. There is an old saying that goes, "You have to relive an experience until you learn thoroughly not to make that same mistake again."

People who are very religious often ask me if I do not think that these techniques go against God's law. I definitely do not, because of the fact that one is using these psychic methods for good. If one were ever to use these mental formulas in the wrong manner, the law of retribution would take over, regardless of what religion you practiced or whether or not you attended any formal church at all.

WRITE YOUR "WANTS" ON A BLACKBOARD

People have reported to me that they have received pay raises, they have received gifts, they have had many things brought to them so suddenly that it was hard for them to conceive that such power had been lying dormant within them all the time and they had never used it. They had not used this power because they had never learned how.

You do not have to have any formula to call upon the genie within you. All you have to do is set forth the thought. I have told many people that the best way to do this is to picture your thoughts written with white letters on a blackboard. Then it is as if someone would take the blackboard and put it out of sight. The reason I say this is that once the idea is projected through the genie, you should relax and know that it is to be.

I am still in awe of this wonderful power within. I do not know why more people do not use it. They profess faith; they profess that they are living a good life; and perhaps in their estimation, they are. But they are allowing the very essence of themselves to lie dormant and, therefore, they are not getting out of life all they should.

Every time you condemn someone or judge them, you are also putting the genie within you in effect, so that you will bring into your own life the very experience for which you may be condemning another. Stop and think before you condemn a friend. Haven't you, at some time or other, been in the very position in which the person whom you are condemning finds himself? Nine times out of ten, you must answer "yes" to that question.

Remember that the genie within you is at your beck and call. Use it wisely, use it carefully, and there will be no need for any disappointment.

You will also find that whenever something extra good is going to happen to you, you will feel a stillness, a quietness about you. This is the genie within you telling you to expect the good that will take place that particular day.

Naturally, there may also be days when the genie will warn you that something of a negative nature might occur for which you must brace yourself. You must not look upon this as bad news, because you will be prepared to handle whatever situation you are faced with in the most extraordinary manner.

CHAPTER FIVE

The Psychic Bloodhound

Joseph DeLouise was five when his psychic abilities first manifested themselves. His family then lived in Sicily.

"I told my parents to dig in the ground at a particular place. When they did, they found several coins worth $3000. We used the money to come to America."

Joe told his mother that an old man had talked to him, telling him where to find the money. When the youngster finished his description of the man, his mother realized with shock that her son was describing her own brother, who had been dead for thirty-five years. There were no photographs of this uncle that the boy would have seen.

Since that time, Joe's extrasensory awareness has multiplied to the point where he has given aid to "thousands of people." According to DeLouise, "I think I've saved about twenty-five people from committing suicide by telling them that things would improve if they would just hold on."

THE TERRIBLE COLLAPSE OF A BRIDGE

DeLouise first achieved national exposure when, on November 25, 1967, he stated over radio station WWCA, Gary, Indiana, that a major bridge would collapse. A large number of deaths would occur, making national headlines.

"In three visions within the past two days I have seen this disaster occurring and watched the cars pitch into the river," Joseph stated.

December 15th, three weeks later, headlines around the nation carried the story of the collapse of the bridge across the Ohio River at Point Pleasant, West Virginia, while rush-hour motorists plunged to their deaths.

Dating from the Point Pleasant disaster, Joseph DeLouise's predictions have been equally impressive, and sometimes equally grim. He correctly foresaw the earthquakes that rocked Mexico in July of 1968, an increase in the world price of gold, the election of Illinois governor Richard Ogilvie, DeGaulle's 1968 landslide victory at the polls, the death of Ho Chi Minh, and a "tragedy involving the Kennedy's around water."

Aside from his public predictions, DeLouise continues to amaze his friends with his remarkable knowledge of their personal lives. In one instance he commented to an acquaintance that he saw her apartment flooded. Within days she came home to discover that she had neglected to turn off a faucet in the bathtub before leaving that morning. Not only was her own apartment flooded, but so were the three floors below.

A PSYCHIC BLOODHOUND

DeLouise has also garnered attention for his work as a "psychic crime buster." His work on two notorious cases, the "Zodiac" killer and the Sharon Tate murders, both in California, was of great assistance to the police investigations in that state.

"The fatal attack on Sharon Tate was a thrill murder," the sensitive reported to the Long Beach, California *Independent Press-Telegram.* "Their joy was killing so it didn't matter if they killed five or ten or fifteen. The more they killed the more joy they received. Also, they have no conscience. They don't feel sorry about it at all. On the contrary, they are excited about it."

His further impressions detailed a man weighing 160 pounds, with darkish-blonde hair. The other he saw as shorter, with dark hair. "One of the suspects could be in an institution in Texas, either a mental or drug institution, or in jail," he added. "There will be a break in the case on September 14 or 15."

Police authorities later admitted that it was precisely on these dates that they first encountered the now infamous hippie "family." Charles Watson, 6-foot, 2-inches, 156 pounds, light brown hair, was arrested in Texas. Charles Manson, 5-feet, 7-inches, dark brown hair was taken into custody as the leader.

DeLouise said that a girl by the name of Linda would be important in

Joseph DeLouise's many accurate predictions first earned him the title of "Chicago's psychic hairdresser." After chalking up a series of impressive "hits" on such crime cases as the Sharon Tate murder, DeLouise was able to concentrate full-time on the exercise of his paranormal abilities.

the case. He also felt that black magic and drugs had been involved in some way with the murders.

DeLouise's "Linda" turned out to be Linda Kasabian, the family member who turned state's evidence after her arrest and whose testimony helped to convict Manson. The bizarre family did practice strange rites based on perversion of occult practices, and they were heavily into the unrestrained drug trip.

At the time, Joe told me: "If the truth behind these murders ever really comes out, there will be a terrible black eye for Hollywood. Several big names will come out of the case if it is allowed to progress. A lot of Hollywood has been playing with black magic without knowing the problems that they have been bringing on themselves."

FLOWERS OF EVIL WAITING TO BLOOM

The rumors still persist. There have been assertions made by many "insiders" to the Hollywood scene, as well as various counter-culture groups, that the seeds planted by Charles Manson have not yet been thoroughly uprooted, that there are many flowers of evil waiting to bloom.

When the Manson case came to trial, one of Manson's girlfriends came to Chicago to beseech Joseph's help in locating Ronald Hughes, the lawyer for the "family" who mysteriously disappeared during the trial. Such a request appealed to Joseph's sense of poetic justice, and he flew to California.

Once on the West Coast, DeLouise found that the negative vibrations of the Manson people caused him great inner confusion; but he was still able to receive a clear mental image of Hughes lying dead in a mountain culvert. When the police followed through on DeLouise's psychic lead, they found the attorney's body only fifty yards from the spot Joe had pinpointed on the map.

Joseph went on from the Manson case to assist the San Francisco Bay Area police with their infamous Zodiac killer, a mysterious sniper who goaded police and the press with announcements in the newspaper prior to his murders. Zodiac has never been captured, and the case remains open. DeLouise feels that although the deadly sniper continued his slayings for years, there will be no more crimes due to Zodiac's deadly aim. "I get the strong impression that Zodiac is dead," Joseph says.

PROVING ESP CAN FIGHT CRIME

Joseph DeLouise: I don't really know if it matters if I am actually on the scene of the crime or not. It helps to touch objects – psychometry, you know – and gain impressions. But whether I am on the scene or back in my office, I try to visualize. When I close my eyes or stare a wall, I see words, faces, places, just as if I were watching a movie. I think if you set your mind in action and go back and visualize the crime, the impressions will come.

Once a psychic becomes confident enough not to be frightened of being right or wrong, he will be able to do more and more to raise his accuracy. I give people just what I feel. I don't stretch things one way or another. I just have to give what I get.

Brad Steiger: In other words, you try not be become emotionally involved.

Right. I never listen to other people's impressions of what happened, because that sways me. I have to walk out of a room when people start using logic, because logic doesn't always work. At least it didn't work for them or they wouldn't have called me.

Joe, do you want to make a particular specialty of working with crime cases?

If I continue to work with criminal cases, I would like to be called in with no publicity, no attention directed to me. I don't want to become self-conscious because I know people are rating me.

I feel that psychics should be given a chance to work with detectives on certain cases in the capacity of consultants. Then, I feel, the psychics should just leave without ever knowing the results. I maintain that once a psychic becomes concerned with results, he will try too hard to stretch his impressions and he will not come up with specific things.

I feel that it is this obsession with immediate tangible results that prevents the average person from developing his ESP abilities. He becomes afraid of giving his impressions, because he is afraid of being wrong. ESP cannot be developed with the fear of failure in mind.

We have bloodhounds that can sniff an object and track down the owner without missing. I seriously believe that humans can become "bloodhounds" if they allow certain subtle clues to trigger their powers of ESP – and if they learn to project and visualize.

Do you consider yourself a psychic bloodhound?

Definitely, more or less. There is only one difference. I can go back in time, whereas a dog can't. You could give a good psychic a crime that was committed two thousand years ago and he could probably go back to it.

What is it within you that can go back?

I don't know. I start seeing pictures. I can turn them on fast through meditation. I have been working on this for over twenty years.

I can see pictures when I am asked questions. I feel that once you have developed confidence and the ability to bring forth the rapid pictures, you have got it! Psychics who have to sit down for hours and meditate, and still get nothing, aren't completely developed. If you are properly attuned, you can call for the pictures almost instantly.

I say that with experimentation and co-operation, ESP can be used in crime detection. Maybe we are just at the frontier today.

I want to think that I am a part of proving that ESP can be used to aid the police in fighting crime.

RECOGNIZING THE SPIRITUAL SIDE TO LIFE

Joseph DeLouise feels that man has been placed on Earth to gain perfection, but that he cannot gain that state until he recognizes that there is a spiritual side to life.

"I feel that it is my mission to dramatize the spiritual side of man by reaching out into time and making predictions. My ability to do this opens the possibility that there really is no time and space as defined in materialistic terms."

De Louise has found that he obtains similar results whether he is sitting in his office or at the scene of the crime. He admits that it helps to touch objects, and thereby psychometrize, but in either case, his chief method is visualization.

"When I close my eyes or stare at a blank surface, words, faces, and locations appear just as if I were watching a movie. Sometimes these pictures are symbolic. Sometimes my impressions don't come in pictures at all; I just seem to know."

If blockage of some sort occurs, DeLouise uses a crystal ball to remove the obstruction. He also will utilize the crystal ball as a focal point on which to concentrate his psychism for deep meditation.

CHAPTER SIX

We Have the Power to Alter the Course of Events

Dr. Ernesto A. Montgomery, who holds a doctorate in psychology, was born in Jamaica on October 2, 1925, of royal Ethiopian parentage. He attended schools in the West Indies and later came to the United States for college studies in Chicago and Indiana.

After leaving college, Dr. Montgomery served with the British Armed Forces and with police departments in Jamaica and Dallas, Texas. During his work in law enforcement, Dr. Montgomery used his powers of extrasensory perception to assist in the apprehension of criminals.

A PERSON WITH A SPECIAL GIFT

"Since I was five years old I have been known as a person with a special gift," Dr. Montgomery stated. "During my tenure with the Dallas Police Department, I made predictions that a president would be assassinated in that city."

The prediction came true several years later when President John F. Kennedy was killed at Dealy Plaza in the Texas city.

A Dallas newspaper published an article about Dr. Montgomery, commenting on his remarkable ESP ability and his practice of faith healing. "I was invited to join a hospital in Dallas and, as a staff member, I did faith healing for their patients," he related.

In 1961, Dr. Montgomery journeyed to Los Angeles, California, where he organized the Universal Metaphysical Church.

"I predicted the assassination of President Kennedy, Dr. Martin Luther King, Senator Robert Kennedy, and the Sharon Tate murders," reported the black seer. "Prior to each of these events I tried to warn the subject of their impending danger."

Dr. Montgomery also believes that Senator Ted Kennedy would have been assassinated if he had attended the 1968 Democratic Convention in Chicago.

"I warned the Federal Bureau of Investigation and Senator Kennedy's office of my forecast," Dr. Montgomery stated. "I believe my warning was helpful in the decision Senator Kennedy made to stay away from the convention."

FORESEEING THE CLOUDS OF WAR

As a ten-year-old boy in Jamaica, Ernesto astonished his schoolmates and teachers by predicting the start of World War II.

"I was attending the North Street Congregational School in Kingston," he recalled. "I did not fully understand my gift of prophecy at that time, but I knew instinctively that the war would start and that the United States and England would be involved in it.

"When royalty visited Jamaica I was called upon for predictions and counsel," Dr. Montgomery stated. "Former Prime Ministers Winston Churchill, Anthony Eden, and Princess Margaret have received my predictions and advice. The predictions I made for them proved true."

During his career as an officer with the Jamaica Police Force, Dr. Montgomery reported that he was granted a study leave in 1957 to observe practices of police agencies in America.

A PRESIDENT WILL DIE IN DALLAS

"I was welcomed to Dallas by Police Chief Curry," he related. "That same month I informed the Dallas police authorities that a President of the United States would be killed in their city. They were skeptical, and I pointed out the exact spot on a city map where the assassination would occur.

"A photograph was taken and published," Dr. Montgomery continued. "This picture showed me pointing out to the police officers the exact spot on Dealy Plaza where John F. Kennedy was later assassinated."

During this trip, Dr. Montgomery also predicted that a major railroad disaster would occur in Jamaica. "Unfortunately, this prediction proved true in August, 1958," Dr. Montgomery remarked. "A Jamaican excursion train jumped the tracks killing 600 people and injuring another 1,000 persons. It is still considered to be one of the world's most terrible train disasters."

A slim, handsome man with a quick grin and a broad smile, Dr. Montgomery believes that man has the power to change the course of events.

FREE WILL CAN CHANGE EVENTS

"Human movement and the element of time and space can change events," he explained. "The free will that God bestowed upon man can change the events of the future and prove a prediction to be untrue. When a prediction is concerned with death or disaster, I am always thankful that events are changed by man so that I am considered in error."

In addition to his ministerial work, Dr. Montgomery holds healing services. He is also known throughout the Western states for his healing work sponsored by other churches, groups, and organizations. Dr. Montgomery is also the executive director of the Youth Opportunities League, which assists young people in a variety of ways.

One of his favorite enterprises is a "help-hot-line" for people who are troubled or are in need of help and guidance.

MEDITATION: A KEY TO AWARENESS

Dr. Montgomery particularly believes that meditation is the key toward developing greater awareness, and he lectures frequently on his own method of transcendental meditation.

"As long as the various planes of mind are not completely functioning, or operating effectively – the unconscious mind, the conscious mind, the superlative mind – then the individual must suffer," teaches Dr. Montgomery. "Transcendental meditation, if understood in its entirety, is the key to the most complex of problems. Anyone can use it for the complete eradication of particular problems."

Along with Dr. Montgomery's enthusiasm for his method goes a strong dedication toward helping others. "I am now willing and able to travel to any part of the world to demonstrate transcendental meditation. Because it works. I have done it; I have seen it done. I know what it can do for people.

"The sooner psychics and people of philanthropic moods organize themselves to explore this area thoroughly the more benefit it will be to everybody. The time is ripe now – the people are hearing us."

Bertie Marie Catching's steady string of psychic successes has earned her the reputation of being one of the top clairvoyants in the United States.

CHAPTER SEVEN

Bertie Catchings: Texas' Remarkable Psychic

Bertie Catchings was born on May 5, 1927, in the little community of Harmony, Texas. Her parents met a tragic death when she was eighteen months old, and Bertie Marie Cotton was raised by her grandparents.

In December, 1968, Bertie appeared on the *Women's World* television show hosted by Carolyn Jackson. "I presented Carolyn with envelopes containing 116 predictions," she related. "When these were opened later in the year there were ninety accurate predictions."

Her prediction that Texas would defeat Tennessee in a New Year's Day football game was the first forecast to prove true. She also foresaw accurately that the U.S. would be successful in landing on the moon and that two or three men would be on the mission.

Since that time, Bertie has made hundreds of successful predictions, been instrumental in the solution of major crimes, and has located dozens of missing people.

HOW BERTIE RECEIVES HER PSYCHIC IMPRESSIONS

Psychic impressions begin when I look into a client's palm. I usually give palm readings and psychic impressions. As I study the lines for characteristic traits and give general information about the lines, I begin to tune in and many of my "psychic senses" begin to operate.

Sometimes several of the senses give information at the same time. I am very busy giving the information which is taken down in writing or recorded by the client, or the client's friend, who must write very fast if the information is taken in writing. I do not pretend to interpret the information and would rather not be interrupted until I have finished.

Then, I will ask the client if the information has meaning to him. If it does, then the information is usually something that has happened in the past or the present. If the reading has no meaning, then it is something that will happen in the future, say within three years, but usually, within a few days, weeks, or months. I do not know about time for sure except in some instances when something is very clear.

The information comes so fast, usually, that it may be like watching six different TV programs at one time, and listening to a conversation of several people, and traveling on a fast train where you see, hear, taste and smell the many different things along the road as the train whizzes through the country.

So, you see what difficulty is present to me, a medium, to give all the information that comes in the various true perspective.

There are many psychic senses. I learn about new ones now and then. For some, there is no vocabulary to describe them. I am familiar with sight, sound, odor, touch, taste, thought communication, aura lights around the person, vapor waves above the palm and body, cloud formations above the palm and on the palm and sometimes any place on the body. Or, symbols on the walls or floor that form letters or words or images. The images are sometimes very still or they are moving very fast. It is like a game between the images and me to see if I can guess what the clues mean.

Sometimes the images are something that would have a meaning to me. If so, a voice or thought communication alerts me to give an interpretation rather than say exactly what I see. However, sometimes these assistants don't always get through to me or I'm not sure and then I don't know if I should say what it means to me or what I have seen.

This is one reason that I like the client to go over the notes and ask questions. If I can remember the image I will give both interpretations and maybe the client can figure out what it means. Sometimes soft, spirit lights appear in the room near or behind the client. The spirits receive priority attention and the other channels of information fade out until the spirits are able to be identified by some clue.

One night, an orchid light formed the shape of a short woman and the smoke formed a large white letter "S" on the light. The client identified the spirit as her mother, Susie, who had passed away.

THE MODUS OPERANDI OF A PSYCHIC READING

Sometimes the readings are so exhausting that I have to limit the readings or not give any for a while in order to regain my energies. This woman started off by saying, "Now, I don't want to hear all that junk that readers usually give. I have given readings myself. I read cards and I know what it is all about."

Then I began to read: "I see a boy." I began to smell alcohol. "The boy drinks alcohol. No, no! He has something wrong that is like alcoholic problems. The boy has diabetes. I see you giving him shots."

Then all of a sudden a clear bottle about four feet tall was sitting on my table, and the odor of alcohol was so strong that my throat was on fire and my eyes were burning and I began to cough. My hands went to my throat, for I felt that I was choking on the fumes. "You must be a nurse, but you must give shots all the time."

"Yes," said the women. "I am a nurse and I have a boy who is a diabetic and I give him shots."

"I see an old man in blue overalls with white hair who is in a barn. A pitchfork is falling from the hay above him. It has struck his head and his hair has turned blood red. The people are running from the fields. There is a tree with water around it. A woman fainted." Then I stopped.

"I never saw this, but this did happen exactly this way to my grandfather," my client said. "My aunt saw it and told me about it many times. She is the person who fainted."

I did not feel friendly vibrations in her presence, yet I was able to give some very clear impressions. One of my friends, who has observed my work, has remarked, "Bertie, when you really want to, or when you have your back against the wall, you really come through!" This same friend gets a little provoked at me because I do not give her especially good readings. However, when she brings a friend from out of town over for a reading, she will say, "This friend wants a reading at this time and that is all I can tell you because the friend would think I gave you clues." Then when the reading is finished, the client usually turns to my friend and says, "Now really, how much did you tell her about me?" This puts my friend in an awkward situation and she doesn't enjoy the amusement as much as I do.

THE TERRIBLE SOUND OF A PSYCHIC SCREAM

One night, I heard a psychic scream about 10:00 o'clock. It was like the death scream of a woman. I was washing dishes when I heard it and cold chills ran all over my body. Who could it be? The thought communication said, "It is a woman close to you who lives alone." Well, needless to say, this really frightened me. I figured out that it was one of two women. It was either my aunt or it was a friend. The telephone rang. My aunt had called for a long friendly chat. By the time the conversation was over, I was calmed down and decided that maybe the psychic scream was just my imagination.

The next morning at about 8:00 o'clock my friend was involved in an automobile accident. She was standing on a street corner when an automobile knocked her off the curb, and she did scream once, very loud. I had not warned her before it happened. I felt that my psychic vibrations should have been working better; or, maybe Bertie Catchings should have been more on the ball and have done a better job with the psychic information given to me. Fortunately, my friend did survive the accident.

THE SEMI-TRANCE STATE

During a reading, if I slip into a semi-trance, I don't always remember what I have said. If a number, for instance "8" appears in a reading, I know that something is going to happen that will involve an "8." I usually have a feeling as to whether it will be either good or bad, maybe a message, or that someone will come into that person's life. But it is difficult to know more than that except in special occasions. The "8" could be on the 8th, the 18th, the 28th, 8 minutes, days, weeks, months, years. So, it is difficult to pinpoint this information except when the client returns and tells me what happened.

VOICES IN THE NIGHT

Sometimes I am awakened at night for no apparent reason, and a nice voice will talk to me. I am told things that are going to happen or things that I must do. I am used to these things. They don't bother me. Except if there is great trouble. When trouble is on the way, I get ill and feel as if a dark spirit or cloud is hanging over me until the event has happened, is finished and done. Then I am all right again. When I give a reading or sit near a person who has pain, I usually feel the pain myself to some degree. This is the reason that I like to have a living plant near me, flowers, ivy, or just wear the color green. I feel that somehow it is protection for me that wards off some of the ill effects of bad vibrations.

A GIFT FROM GOD

I attribute my ability to be a gift from God. I believe that I was selected for several reasons: (1) Because of prior lifetime experience and cooperation with the power; (2) because my condition of personality and situation caused me to be an attentive subject; (3) because as a child I often prayed that I might please God and that I might be used in His service in whatever way He chose for me. (4) It could be because now, as always, I feel humble and take no credit for my talent except to admit that at times I am an obedient listener who sometimes tunes in.

I feel that the Higher Power expects more from me than I have produced. Before this Power I am in awe and know that I am nothing except what the Power gives to me. To others I would suggest to let the Power come to you when it will, but be listening with all your knowledge, your heart and soul, and perhaps you will hear the soft whispers of wisdom and be taught by the great Masters in the ways they feel you will best serve all purposes.

USING PSYCHIC POWERS TO GAIN GREATER WISDOM

My psychic powers have prevented me from many errors and have helped me to gain greater wisdom. The power has saved my life many times. What is wealth without life, except spiritual wealth? Why with my gift am I not wealthy? Because psychic education is best learned when the medium has problems to solve, and my life has been filled with problems – many of which I have solved with the aid of my psychic powers. This education has helped me to help others.

I was very young when I first discovered my powers. It did not come all at once. A person usually grows toward higher advancements. My psychic world has never been frightening. It is the one place where I can go when earthly things are frightening. I was introduced to it in a nice way that was most pleasing. My relatives didn't know very much about my activities as my two guardian angels warned me against discussing these things with earth flesh people.

Anyway, when I was growing up, children had great respect for their elders and they spoke only when spoken to. When I became too forward with suggestions I was corrected. I did not begin to use my psychic information for their benefit very often. My relatives always thought that I had a vivid imagination and anything that seemed "way out" was considered to be my imagination. My grandmother, however, would listen to my experiences whenever I told her about them.

Sometimes I can slip into a crowd unnoticed, but often there are people who instantly stretch out their palms with questions like, "Tell me what I am fixing to do? Will I get any money soon?" If these people were not so serious I would be amused at their attitude.

They think that I am a constantly available faucet of knowledge and that all I have to do is open my mouth and the right answers pop out. There is a lot more to it than that. It takes effort, energy, and some concentration. If I tried to tune in on all the questions tossed at me, I would have trouble walking from one side of the room to another. I am human and have human problems of my own which I must take care of before I am able to take care of trivial things. There are some things that people are not supposed to know. But when they come to me at the proper time and place, then I am always happy to work with them. At parties when I do entertaining, I have set aside that time and I have conditioned myself for that purpose. But, when I am on the way to the grocery store, or to pick up a relative at the bus station, I don't have the proper frame of mind to suddenly stop every thought that is in my mind and concentrate on psychic information.

SOME PROBLEMS ARE NECESSARY FOR GROWTH

I try not to abuse my ESP. The degree of need determines the results. When I have a problem that needs solving, I try to consider all things. Is this problem necessary for spiritual growth?

I also use mental telepathy. If I have more people coming to see me than I can handle, I send out messages which delay them from coming or have them not come at all. They usually call me and apologize, and I know that it really isn't their fault at all.

If I need something at a given time, it usually shows up.

When I am in danger, when I have a great need, there are Powers that take care of me without my asking. Sometimes they tell me about things when I call on them, sometimes they work out things for me without letting me know what is going on. Through prayer I find out a lot of good information.

KEEPING THE ENERGY HIGH

Some people drain my psychic energies; others increase the energies. Lively flowers, green plants, soft light, and comfortable circumstances are helpful. I give my best work before eating. It is best that I don't drink coffee or tea. It is all right for me to have fruit juices or water before I work.

PREDICTING DISASTERS

I have tried to stay away from negative information, and I only try to attract positive things. But when I am tuned in and the channels of communication are wide open, I am going to pick up this information whether or not I ask for it.

It isn't easy for me to turn off my psychic power and it is not easy to keep it off. Things slip in that I don't really want to know. There has to be a balance in all things, and there are times when I need to rest. Of course, the spectacular elements of the future do cast intense rays and when there is disturbance in the weather, some of the strangest information is picked up.

THE OTHER SIDE

When the flesh is dead, the soul is free and becomes more alive than in flesh. The spirit is often near a loved one, especially when it escapes from its body through a sudden death of the body. The spirit wishes to communicate with loved ones and let them know that they *are* alive and that they *are* well off.

They feel surprised and elated when they find out what has happened. They usually have so many friends over there, not only from this life, but also from previous lives that it is quite a reunion, quite a wonderful occasion, especially if the trip to earth and flesh has been a worthy one. When we ask to be born, we come here with missions; and if we don't try to accomplish them, then we don't have much to report or brag about up there. This is why suicide is so bad, because the spirit doesn't receive the great joy in the other world.

Flesh life to them is like a person going on a trip and when they get back they can tell about their adventures. If they have done many bad things or committed suicide, then they don't have an interesting report. In a way, it is like going fishing and catching no fish. Or telling people you are going fishing and then not doing what you said you were going to do. They have some pretty high standards on the other side and some strict rules. Many souls are given work assignments on the other side. In a sense, the job on the other side is a bigger business than running Earth.

THE KARMIC LAW

The law of compensation is Karma. For each sorrow or pain we cause another we must pay in a lifetime when lessons of understanding for soul growth will be most impressive. Also, the Karmic law provides credits, and a person may be the recipient of many nice compensations.

At birth, when the infant breathes its first Breath of Life, becoming a conscious being, the soul or mystical birth occurs. A soul who may have considered occupying a rejected body (through abortion) would later select another body if it desired to be born.

Sometimes a soul will change its mind at the last moment. If another eager soul isn't standing by, the child will be an unexplained stillborn. A good reason for the nine-month period – besides the natural obvious one – is for the souls to decide which one will take over the body. If a soul absolutely needed to be born and it was the will of God, then that soul would be born, regardless of pills.

The soul is immortal. At so-called death or transition, the soul is born into another plane, a spiritual plane.

WHEN PSYCHIC PREDICTIONS MISS

Sometimes the predictions were made in haste; sometimes the psychic wasn't conditioned for making predictions. Sometimes TIME is off, and it will happen later. Sometimes the psychic who is asked to give world predictions is one who does better with personal predictions. I am sure that there must be psychics who pick up on world information far better than I do. And we don't know everything or even as much as we should. We often pick up information on subjects not related to a project because extra information comes through.

THE MASTERS

The Benevolent Brotherhood of Masters are not earthly Masters but are Cosmic Masters, who personally instruct a psychic student who is truly prepared and found worthy of these instructions. They are a Holy Assembly. Some work on the Cosmic Plane. Some are on the Earth Plane working on psychic assignments. Divine illumination cannot be properly described with earthly vocabulary.

ASTRAL PROJECTION

I usually do not travel alone and do not seek this experience unless an invitation is extended by someone in the spirit world who is familiar with the traveling conditions and other matters. To go alone would possibly be dangerous, as well as there are so many spirits floating around these days who are on "drug trips" or have been attracted toward the earth's plane.

I will tell you about my first experience. It happened that day long ago when I was a child playing in my grandmother's garden after a summer shower when a rainbow touched the ground and bathed my body. My grandmother was working among her flowers in this garden. She had been praying, which she often did in her flower garden. I thought I saw a shadow or someone standing behind her, just before the rainbow came. Then my attention was attracted in another direction.

Two angels appeared out of the rainbow. They were dressed in white garments. One of them was named Mary, whom I was told would be my personal guardian angel in the future. When they started to go back into the rainbow, I wanted to go with them. I reached out toward them, calling and asking to go with them. They came back and each took one of my hands and helped me to get out of my body. The sensation was something like removing clothes, only I felt very light and seemed to float a few inches off the ground with the slightest effort.

They each had a piece of material, like a scarf which they draped around me and tied with a silver cord. Then, they took my hands, and we went into the rainbow and upward as though in a path of light. We came to a place so cool and refreshing, an emerald sea, with a beach of sparkling sand. Then on, upward, toward the light until we reached a crystal cathedral with round doors and many beautiful steps.

There were others around the cathedral, both young and old, and men and women in bright robes of red, blues, and gold.

Then I saw Him, the shadow in the garden. Only his robe was bright red and his face was like a great light. He lifted his arm and pointed a long finger at me and said, "Let no harm come to this child lest you know my wrath."

Then his arm made a sweeping motion that seemed to take in the whole Universe. His voice was like the sound of many waters, the roaring of an ocean, but I felt peace, calm, and greatly protected, and we went back into the light and were soon in my grandmother's garden. They helped me get back into my heavy body. Their scarves were waving as they floated upward and out of sight.

The rainbow was gone. The angels were flying away, and nothing was left but the faint tinkling of bells that too soon blended into silence.

After that experience, I kept hoping the angels would come back; and I jumped around in the flower garden trying to get out of my body for many days after that. It was a long time before I learned how it was done.

I have been back to the cathedral many times. I usually wait for an invitation. Recently, while there I was given a large golden cross which was covered with scarlet roses. A warm light came from the cross and engulfed a great area with its splendor. The cross was very light – and it was alive.

FORESEEING A CHILD'S DISAPPEARANCE

In a publication I released in 1972, Bertie Catchings recorded the following prediction: "I see a child who will be lost in the United States, among trees and hills. Many will think the child is not alive and the search party will be discontinued. But the child will be found alive near water, a large stone and a tree. An intelligent dog could find the child. The letters O, K, C, and W seem to be involved. The letter J and the word 'Northeast' appear important."

Bertie had received this premonition while deep in meditation. In her original notes, she also wrote down the name "Kevin."

On June 4, 1971, shortly after submitting this prediction for publication, Bertie was on a radio program at KPRC in Houston, Texas. Again she felt herself moving westward, where she could see a small child wandering about in the woods. She could see a search party scattered throughout the northeastern section of the woods, but the child was sitting on a rock near a stream, further south. Bertie relayed this prediction over the air, concluding that a tourist or a ranger would find the child and all would be well.

July 18, 1971, eleven-year-old Kevin Dye accompanied his family to a Christ United Methodist Church meeting near Bear Trap Meadow, a huge bluff which towers some 3,000 feet above Casper, Wyoming. Kevin wandered into the heavy spruce and pine forest in the middle of the afternoon. By 6:00 P.M. one hundred persons were combing the area in search of the missing boy. Dogs were employed in the search as well.

Immediately upon learning of Kevin's disappearance, Bertie knew that this was the child that she had seen in her vision. She called Kevin's father, explained what she had foreseen, and assured the worried man that Kevin was alive and would be found. The boy had disappeared on Saturday; Bertie told Mr. Dye that Kevin would be found four days later, on Wednesday, at about 4:00 in the afternoon.

The Dyes clung more and more tenaciously to these words from a stranger as the days passed and Kevin was not found. It was assumed by most that the boy was no longer alive.

Then, early Wednesday morning, Michael Murphy, a member of the Rocky Mountain Rescue Team of Boulder, Colorado, found Kevin sleeping quietly in the morning sun.

As Bertie had predicted, Kevin was found near water and near rocks. He was found in four days. The "O" Bertie had seen in her original prediction referred to Oklahoma, where Kevin and his family had lived prior to coming to Wyoming. The "K", of course, stood for Kevin, and the "C" and "W" clearly indicate Casper, Wyoming, both the scene of Kevin's disappearance and his present home.

The only thing that Bertie missed was the time Kevin was found. She had indicated four in the afternoon, while Kevin was actually found early in the morning. One would suppose that Kevin's parents were hardly disappointed that their son was returned to them hours earlier than forecast.

THE CHALLENGE OF LOCATING THE MISSING

Other times, it is plainly not so easy to locate missing people. As Bertie Catchings has found, people sometimes disappear to escape their families or their problems. These people do not want to be found.

In cases of missing persons, Bertie said, she seldom works directly with the police. She usually works with a family member, a family friend, someone connected with the news media, or an individual who for some reason is extremely interested in the missing person.

"It's a little difficult to describe how I get accurate impressions," Bertie explained, "because we are working with something here that is nebulous. Sometimes impressions are correct; sometimes not. When I give information that turns out to be accurate, then, of course, everyone knows that I was right. If I come up with information that is apparently incorrect, then no one – not the people involved or myself – can really prove it.

"For instance, I might say that a person is alive, but when he is found he is quite dead. No one will ever know if that person was really alive when I said he was, and then was killed or drowned or something afterwards."

DON'T BE AFRAID TO STICK YOUR NECK OUT

"I am saying this for the benefit of all psychics who do this type of work. I do not think that psychics should be discouraged when it appears that they have been wrong. They may not have been 100% right, but they do not necessarily have to be 100% wrong, either. The only way a psychic can learn is by sticking his or her neck out on a limb by giving all the information. Otherwise, if the psychic gets some feedback at a later date he might find himself saying, 'I thought that was too silly to mention' or 'I gave so many other names, yet the right one was on my list and I didn't mention it.'

"If the psychic has a big ego problem, or if the people involved in the case are hard critics, then it might bother the psychic to have some misses. But really, a psychic is just like anyone else working on a case. Everyone tries to do his job the best way he can, and no one really enjoys working on a case that involves crime. If a psychic wants to help, though, and learn more about what he is doing, then you simply have to state all your impressions and hope they can be proved accurate."

When Bertie is consulted by a family member over a missing person, she begins to pick up little things about the person's personality. She feels there are images that "sort of hang" within a person's aura, because of some sentimental closeness or other importance.

"I begin to pick up all these little things about this boy. That he liked music; his favorite sports figure was Joe Namath; he has an eagle on the wall in his room with the word 'panther' on it. If I keep tuning in like this, and if I cannot feel too sensitive or silly, then it might be that in a little while I would pick up some important information like a ticket stub or a key. Now, I might not know that these things are important, but a detective, more familiar with the case, might.

"A psychic is put in a peculiar situation when he starts saying, 'I see the name John. . . I see a football. . . I see a picture of a blonde-headed girl on the table.' People are inclined to dismiss these as general things and think the psychic has no ability."

PSYCHICS ARE SOMETHING LIKE TELEVISION
SETS – WITHOUT BUTTONS

"But a psychic doesn't have a button that you can just push and suddenly see everything you want to see. A psychic is like a computer sometimes – you have to warm it up a little, then sort of sit there a few minutes and tune in on the person.

"Giving a reading is like walking over to a television and turning on a particular channel. Now, just because there is a ball game on Channel Four doesn't mean that there's nothing else on television. There might be an opera on Channel Five or a movie on Channel Twelve. So it is with psychic detectives. At the particular moment you might be just picking up one area of this person's life, and it might go on like that for hours and days. Then again, if you come back the next day, it might switch to another channel or another subject – the one that relates to the case."

Bertie turned on the right "channel" immediately when a friend of hers, Mrs. Coursack, called her. The woman, a journalist, lived in an apartment complex which had been robbed.

Bertie immediately told Mrs. Coursack that some of her tape decks had been stolen. Bertie then described Coursack's son, the car he drove (warming up briefly on another channel), then described several people who worked on the premises. One of them was responsible for the crime, she said (bulls-eye).

In another instance, a young woman from Dallas phoned Bertie over two very valuable rings which were missing. The woman was convinced that her maid had stolen them, and she had already called the police, detailing her suspicions. Authorities were to accuse the maid that day of the theft.

Bertie had been out when the woman called. Her message was one of several on Bertie's desk. Yet Bertie reached for that message first, called the woman, and told her that her diamonds and emeralds were in a jacket pocket in the closet. The woman found her rings and was able to call the police before they arrived to question the maid. This saved quite a bit of embarrassment for everyone.

CHAPTER EIGHT

John Catchings: Psychic Sleuth Par Excellence

Diantha Dickens was trying her best to keep troubled thoughts from her mind. After all, if it were not for the fact her eighteen-year-old son, Michael, was such a good and dependable boy, she wouldn't be so worried that he was late getting home.

She had fixed one of Mike's favorite dishes, cabbage goulash, for dinner. Mike knew that before he had left for work. Also he knew that one of his best friends from his high school days was coming to visit for the weekend. It wasn't like Mike to be late and not to call her and explain the situation.

Mike had graduated from Corsicana High School [Texas] and had attended Navarro Junior College for one year. He was a good Christian boy who had never caused his parents any problems.

The telephone rang, offering her the promise of Michael calling to explain his delay. Mrs. Dickens forced her voice to remain calm, struggling to conceal her growing fear when she heard Mike's friend announcing his arrival in town.

"Mike isn't here yet," she explained, trying her best to sound unalarmed. "Sometimes he works late. I know he's been riding to the job with Mr. Ferguson, and maybe they've decided to keep at it until the job is finished. Don't you worry, though," she reassured Mike's friend. "Mike is expecting you, and I've fixed cabbage goulash!"

Mike worked as an electrician at Ferguson Electrical Company in Ennis, Texas. On that morning, August 1, 1980, Mrs. Dickens assumed that he had left for work as usual at about 7:30 a.m. She was a schoolteacher, already in her classroom at nearby Rice, where her other three children were pupils, but several neighbors had seen Mike leave the house in his 1978 yellow Datsun, and he had waved a cheery "good morning" at his grandmother, who lived in a mobile home nearby. In the farming country outside of Corsicana few comings and goings were missed by the rural residents, and she had already been informed that Mike went to work right on schedule.

A GROWING CONCERN

By 6:30 p.m., she was becoming very uneasy. Mike never wanted her to worry, never wanted to cause problems for anyone.

Mrs. Dickens kept thinking that he must have had an accident. There were a lot of little creeks in the farm country where they lived, and she kept picturing him lying hurt in a ditch somewhere, perhaps unconscious, unable to call out for help.

When 7:00 p.m. came and still no Mike, she could no longer control her natural anxiety for her son, and she telephoned the home of Steve McCarty. He also worked at Ferguson's and maybe he would know what had delayed Mike and why he hadn't called her.

Steve's wife answered her call and told her that Steve had not yet arrived home, either. She thought there was a softball game after work.

Diantha Dickens did her best to satisfy herself that Mike was having such a good time playing softball that he had broken his own rule about always calling home to inform his mother of his whereabouts.

Then, at 9:00 p.m. Steve McCarty called her and asked if she had yet heard from Mike. When she answered that she had not, McCarty replied with words that chilled her very spirit: "I hate to tell you this, Diantha, but Mike didn't come to work today at all."

Later, Mrs. Dickens told Dorothy Fagg of the *Dallas Times Herald*, "I think I knew in that moment that something really bad had happened. This was not like Mike. He always called if he was going to be late. He never wanted to worry me. But I didn't think of anything except maybe he had had a wreck."

NOTIFYING THE POLICE

Diantha Dickens did not express her fears to the police at that time, but Michael's employer, Ferguson, called both Ellis County and Navarro County police after McCarty had telephoned him with the information that Michael had set out for work that day as usual.

Then there was nothing to do but wait. Diantha knew that her husband Jerry would be in that night around midnight. He was a trucker on a long haul, and she did not wish to alarm him by contacting him through the highway patrol.

When she did at last telephone the police herself, they did their best to set her mind at ease. They explained that they received hundreds of calls every weekend about missing teenagers, and most of them showed up in twenty-four hours.

The official lack of urgency did little to pacify Diantha Dickens. After all, they did not know her Michael. They did not know what a fine Christian young man he was. He would never thoughtlessly frighten his mother or cause anyone unnecessary alarm. He would never play hooky from his job.

When Jerry Dickens arrived home at midnight, he was met by a houseful of neighbors, a tearful wife, and three distraught children. All their friends were trying their best to give them emotional support, and it helped that their neighbors cared so much for them.

During the next days of anguish and suspense that followed, Diantha feels that it was her work as a schoolteacher that enabled her to keep her sanity. The kids at school were considerate of her feelings, and her own three children, 17-year-old Mark, 14-year-old Molly, and 8-year-old Mitzie – were extremely supportive.

By now the police were becoming seriously concerned. Michael Dickens did not fit the pattern profile of a runaway. Texas Rangers were called in on the case.

MICHAEL'S YELLOW DATSUN IS SEEN

Three days after Michael had been missing, William Arthur Lee, 21, an acquaintance of Michael's who had a minor police record, was arrested as a suspect in the teenager's disappearance. Lee had been driving Dickens' yellow Datsun around the country, and his story was that Michael had given him the car to use.

Lee spent about two weeks in the Navarro County jail, but the authorities were unable to hold him on the charge of an unauthorized use of a motor vehicle since Michael Dickens could not be found to testify that he had not given his permission to drive the Datsun. Jerry Dickens filed a complaint, but since the car belonged to Michael and he was not present to confirm or deny Lee's story, the suspect was released on a writ of *Habeas Corpus*. Besides, Lee and another suspect in the case had both passed polygraph tests which had established their lack of involvement in the case.

A SUSPECTED MURDER – BUT NO BODY

Navarro and Ellis County Sheriff's Departments instituted a massive search of the creek-laced farmland. In addition, the Dickens family and their friends and relatives, went out on weekend after weekend to comb the same areas and the nearby wooded regions.

False leads and clues bombarded both the police and the Dickens family. Stories about bodies in unused wells and deserted farmhouses began to haunt them. Reports from those who claimed to have seen Michael alive and well in other parts of the state tormented them.

Weeks passed, and the Dickens family was becoming desperate. Several people suggested that they contact a psychic. Diantha was not *that* desperate, she told those well-wishers who urged her to traffic with the "occult." She was a sincere Christian, and believed that crystal balls and that eerie stuff should be left alone.

By mid-October, however, Diantha felt that she could no longer go to school. She felt that she could no longer work. The nightmare had become too much for her.

TIME TO BRING IN A PSYCHIC SLEUTH

It was about this time that a social worker at the Rice school, Donna Wright, talked to her and told her that she had a friend who had been helped by John Catchings, a Dallas psychic sensitive. Diantha decided that she had nothing to lose by at least hearing what Catchings would have to say about her missing son.

After two abortive attempts, Mrs. Dickens made contact with John Catchings on her third try.

Diantha Dickens remembers that he was very calm, very brief, different from what she had expected. "Will you help us find our missing son?" she asked.

"I'm sorry, Mrs. Dickens," he said softly. "I don't like my feelings about this at all. I am sorry, but I think he has been killed. I feel that he was buried close to home in a dry creek bed."

The next day, Diantha Dickens and Detective Ron Roark of Ennis brought Catchings a map of the terrain and several objects that had belonged to Michael, including his senior class ring.

A VISION OF WHERE THE BODY LAY

"As soon as I held Michael's senior ring," John recalled, "I could see a vision of where his body lay. I could see a trail leading up to the house to the suspect, William Arthur Lee. I could see where the trail and the creek bed intersected. And I could see something that looked like a shoe. And then I saw a foot or a leg showing, and I knew that this was the grave of Michael Dickens."

Catchings took the map that Detective Roark had brought and circled a three mile area where he believed the body to be.

"Although that area has been searched many times," John told the detective, "the body is there. If you find that intersection with the shoe that

I have described, you will find the body in a very shallow grave. He was buried in haste."

Before the detective and Mrs Dickens left his office, Catchings said again that Roark would be the one who would find the body.

The day after their visit with the Dallas psychic, Roark went alone to the area that Catchings had indicated on the map. He searched for quite some time, but he found neither the shoe at the intersection nor Michael's body.

Diantha Dickens put in another call to John Catchings. "He asked if Roark had taken anyone with him to search," she recalled their conversation. "We said, no, and he replied that if Roark were to take someone with him and look again, they would find the body in the area that he had marked."

That afternoon, Detective Roark returned with two other officers to the oft-searched area about fifty yards behind William Arthur Lee's house. Roark remembers that they were virtually on the heels of a larger search party that had gone through the dry creek bed that same day.

"When I crossed over this gully, I found this tree right in the middle of the creek with all these tires around it," Detective Roark said.

For the first time in all his searching, the tires piled around the tree just didn't look right to him. "When I moved one of the tires, there was this thong – or a sandal-like shoe. I started pulling the tires away, and then I pulled the log off and there was his heel. I got his shoe and pulled. Michael Dickens' body was underneath."

MICHAEL WANTED HIS BODY FOUND

John Catchings later said that he had received the strongest impressions from Michael's senior class ring. "My strong feelings were that Michael was dead and that he wanted his body to be found. My gut feeling was that he had been hit on the head, tied up for awhile, and left unconscious."

Detective Roark spoke freely to the press: "Catchings said we would find the body within 100 yards of the place where the suspect lived. Well, we found it about 50 yards from that fellow's house.

"Catchings said that I would be the one to find the body first, and I was.

"He said the shoe would be there...but it was not Mike's shoe. It was a thong up on top of the debris.

"And a funny thing, he told us about a path leading from the creek to a house. It's there all right. But the number of times we had searched that area, I had never seen it before.

"Catchings also said he thought the boy had been struck hard on the head and then tied up. We don't know for sure that was true, because there wasn't a skull fracture, but the body had been stabbed twenty to thirty times in the back.

"But Catchings sure led us to the body."

The Dickens family agreed with the psychic impression that told Catchings that Michael wanted his body found, but Diantha told Dorothy Fagg of the *Dallas Times Herald* that she was now trying not to feel sorrowful or bitter. "We were blessed for eighteen years with having Michael, with knowing him, and we know now where he is – because he was a Christian. It's hard not to ask why, though."

On February 26, 1981, six months after the disappearance of Michael Dickens, William Arthur Lee was arrested in Dallas and charged with murder. Lee's indictment was made possible because of an informant who told sheriff's deputies that Lee had boasted to him of his committing the savage attack on Michael Dickens.

Tommy Witherspoon of the *Corsicana Daily Sun* quoted Navarro County District Attorney Pat Batchelor as stating:

"All the evidence that we had up to the time we got the statement from our informant was developed about the time the murder happened, but it wasn't enough to get the case to the grand jury. We could not tie Lee to the killing. We could get him for stealing a car, but that's all. And we couldn't have even gotten him for that, because the owner of the car was not around to testify, and we could not disprove his explanation of how he got the car. The law requires us to do that before we can get a conviction.

"Basically, we were not looking to convict Lee for car theft, but for murder. Sometimes it takes time to get the evidence in cases of this nature."

It might be added that in "cases of this nature" it certainly does help to call a psychic detective in on the job.

THE EPISODE WAS TRULY "INCREDIBLE"

Shortly after I learned of John Catchings' remarkable demonstration of psychic ability in regard to the Michael Dickens' case, I telephoned one of my contacts on the *That's Incredible* television show and arranged for a segment to be filmed which dramatically illustrated to a mass audience just how effective a psychic detective can really be. The episode proved to be very popular with the audience of *That's Incredible*, and it was repeated on the ABC network.

THE MAKING OF A PSYCHIC DETECTIVE

What does John Catchings remember as his first psychic impression?
"The major one occurred on July 4, 1969, when I was struck by lightning!

"Now, I don't feel that this bolt of electricity from the sky changed my brain cells or anything like that, but since my life was spared, I saw that near-fatal experience as a calling. That lightning bolt told me that I had been born for a reason. I have a purpose in life. I must devote my life to doing helpful things for humankind. So, I became a psychic as a serious professional."

Since his mother, Bertie Catchings, had gained a national reputation as a psychic sensitive, John decided to sell his home in San Antonio and to join her in Dallas. He came to be her business manager and a part-time psychic as her assistant. He knew that he was fresh to the field and that he had a lot to learn.

"Mom was very busy with readings by mail and with telephone calls, so we teamed up with our abilities so that we could better service those in need. Eventually, I began to attain more confidence in my own abilities, and I went out on my own."

John found that it wasn't easy, trying to make a living as a professional psychic. Tammy, his daughter from a first marriage, is a handicapped child, and she required several involved and expensive operations.

John Catchings was an apt student of his mother's example of how to live a spiritual life and her instructions on how best to develop psychic talents. His abilities as a "psychic sleuth" are sought by law enforcement officers all over the world.

"But we managed," John laughed, sweeping his arm around to indicate the supposed expansiveness of his small office. "And as you can see, I am now living the life of luxury. I drive an old car with 50,000 miles on it – and I have two other heaps that don't run. The secondhand furniture in this house is nothing for anyone to write home about, either."

John leaned back in his chair and gave expression to a rare moment of undescribed emotion. A large, bearded man, he is often described as "bearlike," but one would have to say, "teddy-bear-like" tonight.

"I'm going through the economic crunch, just like everyone else," he smiles broadly. "But I love this work. It's exciting and interesting. It is also my purpose in life."

Has he ever thought of using his powers for any other purpose?

"I choose not to use the word 'power.' 'Gift' is a misnomer, also, in that it suggests a certain amount of selectivity involved. I feel that everyone is born with this talent. It's a matter of degree and a matter of practice. 'Ability' is a much better word.

"But, anyway, no, I have not considered using my abilities for any other purpose, and I'll tell you why: If you become emotionally involved, and the money becomes too important to you, you will begin to lose your objectivity; and, consequently your psychic abilities will begin to deteriorate."

Barbara, his attractive wife, spoke up with an addition: "Another reason is that his mom and I frown on anyone abusing psychic ability toward financial gain for self. We feel that, in regard to psychic ability, if you abuse it, you'll lose it."

Researchers have long noted that psychometry, the ability to gain information about someone through the handling of an object that once belonged to him, is a popular technique employed by psychic detectives. When did John Catchings first know that such a technique worked for him, as well?

"Actually, outside of handwriting analysis, there is no much else available for the psychic detective to use. When I hold an object that belonged to the victim or the missing person or a suspect, my mental pictures begin to clear up.

"I don't always need an object, of course. In the case of Michael Dickens, I just heard the mother's voice and I was able to see the body in its shallow grave.

"Psychometry is useful because of the vibrations that are somehow left in the object. It seems that all things collect these vibrations, and it depends on the psychic's abilities how well he or she can pick up on them."

RESPECT FOR MOTHER'S WORK

While some psychics have told stories of rather difficult childhoods wherein they were ridiculed or persecuted for their unusual abilities or beliefs, John insists that he experienced what would have to be labeled as a "normal" childhood.

"I played football too much and didn't study enough. I could just never seem to sit down and do my homework. The only ridicule I received as a child was for not having good enough grades. I managed to make it through high school and about 30-hours credit at the college level.

"When I was a kid, my goal was to be a pro-football player. Even today, you'd better not mess with me when the Dallas Cowboys are playing on television."

Even as a small child, John respected his mother's psychic work. He understood that she was sincere and that she was extra-sensitive to everything.

"My mother and I have always been very close. Even when we are apart, I can feel her presence or her vibrations. Most often these impressions just tell me that she is thinking of me."

John is well aware that there are many charlatans who utilize their psychic abilities for their own personal benefit.

"But I really don't know if you can ever really use psychic ability to perform truly evil deeds. I do believe in the presence of evil. I feel that if you believe in good you have to believe in evil.

"I've been heckled by religious extremists who said that I was working for Satan. That hurt my feelings a bit and it was certainly unpleasant to hear, but you just have to roll with the punches when things like that occur. When they found out that I was responsible for finding murderers, rapists, and thieves, they began to realize that they had no call to make such accusations toward me."

NOBODY GETS 100%

What advice would John give to those men and women who might wish to seek out a reputable psychic for consultation?

"I would never see a psychic who claimed to be 100% accurate. Nobody is that good. In my opinion, that is an immediate indication that you are about to be ripped off.

"I would never see someone unless I knew ahead of time exactly how much it was going to cost me.

"I would never see a psychic sensitive who would not permit me to record the reading.

"Try always to see a psychic sensitive who has established some kind of credibility in his or her community.

Does he encounter a certain amount of skepticism toward his work, regardless of his high profile accomplishments and excellent reputation?

"There is a basic cynicism toward this field, which I believe to be issuing from the element of suspicion. It is difficult for most people to put faith into something that cannot be touched or made visible on a mass level. Many men and women simply do not recognize the practical aspects of psychism.

"And, of course, there is always the element of fear. Even today, psychic abilities and their functioning are largely relegated to the area of the Unknown, because people are generally discouraged from inquiring about these aspects of the mind. Too many secular and clerical authorities still decree psychics as ridiculous or evil."

ANGELS AND GUIDES

John Catchings acknowledges his ability to concentrate, his determination, and his strong sense of how to deal with things the way they are as his greatest strengths. *His greatest weakness?*

"My deep need is to be loved. I know that this is my weakness and that people can exploit that weakness. My wife Barbara has to look out for me, because I'll do anything for anyone – and people will tend to ask too much of me most of the time."

His mother readily admits to having a spirit guide. Does he have such a contact on the Other Side?

"I do believe in guardian angels and spirits who try to help us the best they can.

"Sometimes I will think about people who have passed on, and I will feel their presence trying to help me. Like Michael Dickens. 'You know, Michael,' I will sometimes say, 'I solved *your* mystery. Now help me solve *this* one!'

"Every now and then I sense my aunt and my uncle giving me little pieces of advice, too."

John has come to understand that an essential aspect of his mission in life is to put together an effective psychic detective squad and to utilize it to investigate difficult crime cases. He can foresee the day when major police departments will include a division of psychics on their staffs.

A solid family life is important to the Catchings, and they – Bertie, Barbara, and John – feel that it is possible for psychic sensitives to have strong marriages. They also recognize that, as with anyone else, psychics must work at the relationship, and that "working together is tough for most couples."

"I believe," John responded, "that in order to be psychic you have to believe that you are doing the right thing. I feel a psychic must be spiritually aware, that he or she must be honest, considerate of others, and just plain as good a person as he or she finds it possible to be. You must believe in a source of strength outside of yourself, and you must believe that what you do is the best you can do to help others."

CHAPTER NINE

Great Britain's Extraordinary Seer

John Pendragon, Great Britain's extraordinary seer, was acclaimed by many to have been the most gifted prophet and clairvoyant of his time. When he died, January 25, 1970, he left behind him an incredible corps of friends around the world who loved him deeply and mourned his passing. Strange to say, the largest number of these friends had never met him, but had carried on faithful correspondences with him over the years. These correspondents nurtured the bonds of true affection, even without the reinforcement of physical contact.

Recognizing me as a friend and collaborator, several of those closest to Pendragon wrote to me when he died.

"He died in his sleep most peacefully," wrote George Louis Pasteur, an imminent spiritual healer, "after some ten years of acute illness and disease of the prostate gland and kidneys, coupled with a cardiac illness and other complications. It was sad to see his workroom so empty and bare where his soul had worked and striven to acquaint mankind with his knowledge of Metaphysics and Astrology. Without doubt he will be greatly missed by me and I know by your very good self, and readers in the U.S.A."

Another friend, Dianne Richman, wrote to say that she had scolded the psychic eight months previously for not resting. "I said he was working himself into the ground. He took no notice, of course, and carried on... he felt he was 'working against time,' which of course he was, if one takes a fatalistic view and thinks one has an allotted number of days and cannot hope for borrowed time."

PUTTING PROPHECY ON THE LINE

Pendragon's paranormal achievements read like an encyclopedia of psychic phenomena. As a prophet, his predictions amounted to a verifiable 85-90 per cent accuracy. He took great pride in laying his psychism on the firing line by printing his impressions of the future well in advance of their actual occurrence – and challenging other seers to do the same. The irrefutable evidence of the printed page always enabled him to walk away from that firing line unscathed.

Pendragon was also adept at gazing into the earth and clairvoyantly determining minerals and buried objects. He was very sensitive to maps, and he was often successful at locating both minerals and missing persons by studying a map of the suspected area. On innumerable occasions, Pendragon demonstrated his ability to describe the interior of a house and its occupants by merely placing his finger on the little black dot representing the house on a large scale map.

In addition to the exercise of Pendragon's psychic abilities, an enormous amount of wordage flowed from the seer's typewriter. He contributed "Pendragon's Panorama" to British *Fate* for several years. He also wrote the monthly "Occult Question Time" for *Prediction* magazine until Stella Truman assumed authorship in 1968. His published books include *Pendragon, Cupid and the Stars, The Occult World of John Pendragon,* and *The Weird, the Wild, and the Wicked.* And, as if the above were not enough, he managed to comply with the voluminous requests for psychic assistance that came to him through the mails.

Pendragon's massive knowledge of metaphysics was the result of long hours spent in study. How, then, did he come by his psychic abilities?

A "NATURAL SENSITIVE"

Pendragon was what is known traditionally as a natural sensitive. This means either he was "born" with his abilities, or that neither he nor the society surrounding him was ever able to suppress his innate psychic ability. At this point in our research into the development of psychism, the reader may take his choice.

As is the case with many "natural" psychics, John Pendragon's growing years were characterized by a series of personal crises. At barely three months of age he contracted infantile dysentery, and for a long time, he was fully expected to follow the thousand other babies who died in that summer's epidemic.

However, through the solicitous care of Lizzie, the Pendragon's domestic, he survived the disease. Lizzie provided young John with much of his childhood care, sheltering him from the fixed notions and narrow attitudes of his parents.

John's parents, Thomas and Alice Pendragon, were not suited for each other at all. They were married when Thomas was thirty and Alice thirty-seven.

Their incompatibility played havoc with their child's sensitive nature. John's mother was extremely possessive toward him, and as a consequence, she would not allow him to be alone with his father for any length of time.

"Incredible as it may seem," Pendragon wrote in his autobiography, "I cannot recall, but with one exception, ever going anywhere with my father unless my mother was present. If father announced that he proposed to take me for a walk, Mother either prevented my going or insisted on going too."

Such stifling possessiveness could scarcely be anything other than very detrimental to John's psychological health.

The intense strain of being brought up under these circumstances resulted in very little security for the young boy. He could sense scant love directed toward him from either of his parents. Moreover, further vagaries of his parents served to isolate John from acceptance by his peers.

If Alice was morbidly worried over John's safety, Thomas, his father, more than matched her with his economical binges. Forever afraid that they did not have enough money, Thomas tightened the purse strings to the point of the ridiculous. As a result of Thomas' warped concept of thriftiness, John was forced throughout most of his childhood to wear an odd assortment of ill-fitting clothes which were frequently hand-me-downs from both sexes. His peers made no effort to hide their playground scorn of the bizarrely attired boy.

But Thomas' reluctance to loosen the purse strings had even more far-reaching effects upon young John. Thomas was determined to secure for his son a free education. Such was to be had only from the ill-equipped, out-of-date church schools, therefore John was enrolled in one of them.

"This particular establishment," John related, "was staffed by a weary team of frustrated sadists. What the boys suffered at their hands was duly passed on to the smaller and weaker of the student fraternity. It was a case of survival of the fittest."

John's nervous home condition scarcely qualified him for the survival category, and the clothes did little to help. Thus his physical misery was socially compounded.

TUNING IN ON PEOPLE'S "SPRINGS"

Throughout this time the boy was unknowingly conscious that he was psychically sensitive.

"It is very difficult for me to state when clairvoyance became part of my life, but I was certainly manifesting it as early as five years of age," John has stated.

Frequently vocabulary would fail him when he picked up impressions from people. He just "knew" about them, without being able to put into words what he knew. Most often, the information was medical.

Quoting from *Pendragon*: "... I had no medical knowledge in those tender years. In common with most other children, I had some toys that were driven by clockwork. I knew that a spring was the basis of clockwork and that when the spring of the toy broke it would not work. Consequently, it is not surprising that I visualized the human body as being motivated by a clockwork mechanism.

Young Pendragon caused a great deal of consternation among his elders by earnestly pointing out that this friend's tummy "spring" did not work, and that relative's leg "spring" was broken. The difficulty these childish medical impressions caused the budding psychic convinced him at an early age to keep them to himself.

OLD MOORE AND THE ZODIAC

The only encouragement he received came from Lizzie, his staunch friend and ally. Lizzie had an extensive collection of *Old Moore's Almanacs*, and John took great delight in gazing enchantedly at the Zodiacal symbolism.

On one occasion, as John sat with Lizzie and flipped through the pages of an old issue, he came upon a picture of Emperor Wilhelm II of Germany.

"One of his arm springs doesn't work," the boy exclaimed.

"You and your springs," was all Lizzie could reply, with a shake of her head.

At the time the child had no idea that Kaiser Wilhelm had a withered arm.

One day the rustling of the pages through an old almanac elicited an unknowing prophecy out of Lizzie.

"Old Moore tells you what's going to happen," she remarked. Then she turned to her small charge. "Perhaps one day when you grow up, you'll be able to tell people what will happen, as Old Moore does!" She had no idea her unconscious shot in the dark would eventually prove true.

For a while, the fate of her prediction looked rather bleak. The idiosyncrasies and incompatibility of Pendragon's parents put such a stress upon the child that his clairvoyance deserted him almost entirely at the age of ten. It did not reappear, except for occasional, dramatic flashes until after he was twenty-five.

In the meantime, his health took a turn for the worse, and in his early teens, John suddenly found himself out of school for eighteen months because of ill-health. This period proved to be very valuable to him.

emotionally, and its significance to his psychic growth became increasingly more pronounced as these abilities later developed.

PEACE IN THE GARDEN SHED

The long vacation was not wasted. John spent every day the weather permitted in the open air. He devoted much of his time to a shed in the garden, where he taught himself the elements of carpentry. He picked up a smattering of botany, ornithology, and entomology, aided by books from the local library. He frequently took long walks into the country, accompanied always on these expeditions by a puppy given him by a generous neighbor.

In future years a medium friend of Pendragon's was to psychically see this time in his life, describing to him the wonderful freedom and the marvelous shed. "Here was peace," she remarked to her friend, and Pendragon admitted that it had been so.

"Those school-abandoned days gave me some kind of spiritual growth I find it impossible to define," he told her.

When the time came for the young man to enter a profession his erratic education caught up with him – to his disadvantage. His father was determined that his son would become a chemist. Yet even at this point Thomas refused to pay for the necessary books, and only grudgingly allowed John to attend a commercial training college so that he might catch up scholastically with other boys his age.

Such a course of cramming only resulted in the deterioration of Pendragon's health. His formal schooling came to an end when the family moved to London.

As John gradually grew into autonomous adulthood, his parents were forced to admit that they had long lost any influence they might have had over their son. With relief, John abandoned the study of chemistry, in which he had never had any interest, to indulge in a long suppressed desire to enter the field of commercial art. He went to school in the evenings to study art, and supported himself during the day as a salesman.

THE TALENT LONG DORMANT

In the mid-1930s, Pendragon became a commercial artist. Then, in the latter part of that decade, his clairvoyance began to return to him in a highly intensified degree. Throughout this time, however, Pendragon continued to live at home, despite the increasingly oppressive atmosphere. Finally, the constant strain of his living conditions overtook his fragile health.

He became obsessed with the need to be in London, and he remembered running to a railway station crying, "Must go to London. Hitler's going to invade us! We're going to be bombed! Must go to London!"

A man of great wisdom and wit, Pendragon wryly urged caution in the development of psychic abilities for their own sake. He always stressed the seeking of higher spiritual values.

Though he could recognize friends, his parents were unfamiliar to him. His mental grip on things had slipped to the point of a kaleidoscope of clairvoyant impressions, coupled with a confused comprehension of reality. His health was so feeble that at five feet, nine inches, he weighed only ninety-six pounds. He was voluntarily committed to the psychiatric ward of a hospital.

Pendragon's neurotic breakdown, as unfortunate as it was, seems to have been the final stop which, once it was pulled, unleashed the full flood of his psychic abilities. As health and balance returned, Pendragon gradually became aware that something had happened to his "conscious pattern," as he called it. The psychological "jolt" he had received had activated a talent long dormant.

John best described this event by saying that something had wiped the window clean between himself and other people. His thought processes translated themselves into pictures. When he looked at a person he would free associate impressions of that individual, and these impressions would manifest themselves visually. Most fascinating to the psychic was the ability to see, in an adult, the child he had once been.

TEACHERS FROM THE INNER PLANE

With the onslaught of these paranormal abilities, Pendragon found himself surrounded by phenomena. His deceased maternal grandfather, whose presence he had felt at moments of crises during childhood, reasserted itself, guiding him to a better understanding of his psychism. Numerous teachers from the inner plane presented themselves, taking their leave when their "work" with Pendragon was completed.

Finally, after years of study, John Pendragon made the decision to become a professional clairvoyant.

Unlike the popular misconceptions entertained by many people, clairvoyance – as well as other psychic abilities – cannot be turned on and off with the same ease with which a light switch is flipped. Thus Pendragon found it essential to have a piece of the client's handwriting or a recent photograph in order to establish a firm contact. He also liked to have a client's full birth date, for in the event that any "blockage" occurred, he would cast a horoscope to prime the psychic pump. Such a blockage can be caused by either the client's obstructive vibrations, or the sensitive's own lack of receptivity.

To secure accurate predictions concerning public figures, it was Pendragon's habit to work from press photos. If none of these were available, he would write the name on a piece of paper and concentrate upon it until an image was formed.

The great accuracy of his predictions caused Pendragon to receive more than his share of people asking the proverbial question, "How do you do it?"

To understand the methods of prediction, however, it is necessary to explore the manifold meanings of time. How could the psychic "see" events in the future? Could any of these events have been avoided?

"I do not believe that the future is 'fixed' on some sort of moving belt that men call 'time,' and movement of time brings the event out of the future into the so-termed present," John often replied. "For if that were the case, there would be no free will, and we would have to take whatever came along on the belt."

To illustrate this concept of Fate, Pendragon was fond of citing the analogy of a man who is "fated" to travel from New York to San Francisco.

"Fate dictates that he *must* go to San Francisco and to no other place," the explanation would go, "but Fate does not bind the man as to the route he is to take or the means by which he is to travel. The man may travel by air, by rail, by road, or even by sea via the Panama Canal. He may dawdle about or hurry. The important thing is that in all these things he has made a choice – free will – but he *must* reach San Francisco."

Pendragon, then, believed in predestination only in a very broad sense. Perhaps those individuals with positions of national prominence have been destined to play their particular parts, but the seer felt that Fate plays a much smaller role in the life of the more common man.

Yet still the question of "how" has not been answered.

"How am I able to view the future?" John used to echo. "I cannot honestly say that I know how to do it, but I do know that I have been doing it regularly since childhood."

Such an openly disarming reply has frustrated more than one seeker of knowledge. John was, however, more definite in his concepts of time. From these concepts, the more enterprising reader can attempt to piece together some of the methods of prophecy.

Quite simply, Pendragon believed time to be a condition created by the mind while on earth, to facilitate an understanding of space. As such, time and consciousness interlock. To explain this concept, Pendragon developed the following example, taken from his autobiography.

"Let us suppose that one has a very long table, and at intervals of two or three inches a very small object has been placed. First, for example, a button, then a matchbox, a pin, a bean, and so on, until 50 or more objects have been spaced out down the table. Now the room is plunged into darkness.

"A person who has no knowledge of the objects on the table enters the darkened room. (In effect, he is born.) He is handed a tiny, low-powered flashlight with a beam sufficient to illuminate only *one object at a time*. He directs the beam on the first object – a button. The beam of light represents his consciousness. For a second, he recognizes and appreciates the object that he has illuminated. Then he moves the beam on to the second object, and at the same time, the first one "vanishes" into darkness again. Object one, by "vanishing" has moved into the past. Meanwhile, object two, being illuminated, is in the present, whereas object three and all subsequent objects are in the future. Finally, after he has illuminated each object in turn, he reaches the last one, and his illumination – his consciousness in a "beam sense" – goes out. (The moment of physical death.) Then somebody enters the room and switches on a big light over the table, and the examiner discovers that he can see *all* the objects at the same time. In short, his tiny beam of consciousness has been exchanged for a greatly enlarged one...

"Now that we have reached this inadequate comparison, we might add that a clairvoyant has a second tiny lamp which he can direct upon objects far down the line. The non-clairvoyant... on the other hand, has to direct his little beam on each object in strict rotation. No such limitation is imposed upon the clairvoyant, who can direct his second beam both backwards and forwards."

Pendragon was convinced that, reverting to the briefly mentioned time-belt theory of time, that it is possible for us to determine by voluntary action just what we will encounter on that belt. In other words, Pendragon believed that the future was "psychoplastic," or capable of being molded by thought. In this way a prognosticator can be proven "wrong."

A seer may pick up a certain pattern, or set of conditions, that he can psychically see will lead to one conclusion. This conclusion then becomes a "prophecy." If the client is sufficiently forewarned, however, he may be able to take steps to avoid the "future" as seen by the psychic. If he is successful, the prophecy falls more easily into the category of a warning.

In some instances – and this John firmly believed – no amount of precise warnings will be able to avert a specific tragedy. This observation brings us full circle, depositing us once more on the doorstep of Fate.

John Pendragon's experiences taught him that Fate operates most inflexibly in the lives of those who govern, guide, or render service in some way to large numbers of people.

On May 4, 1965, Pendragon reported seeing a vision of Mrs. Jacqueline Kennedy with a man surrounded by a large number of ships. When the time came to release his predictions in 1968, he recalled this earlier impression, stating that, "I forecast the remarriage of Mrs. Jacqueline Kennedy. Her second husband may be a naval man," Aristotle Onassis was not a naval man, but he did own a mighty fleet of ships.

This prediction is an excellent example of a problem common to all prognosticators. Pendragon's image was a true one; but his interpretation of it missed. This occurs frequently, particularly in those cases wherein the prediction is received pictorially, in symbolic form.

Five months before the tragic assassination of President John F. Kennedy, Pendragon composed the following letter to the White House:

"... The President may make powerful enemies among his own people, and I would not rule out the possibility of an attempted assassination or worse if he is caught off his guard. There may be a strange turning of the Wheel of Fate, for it is just a century since the American Civil War was raging with unabated fury. President Lincoln was shot by a madman, Booth, in April, 1865 ...."

A FINAL TALK WITH JOHN PENDRAGON

Brad Steiger: You became world famous after you made the prediction of President John F. Kennedy's assassination several months in advance of the terrible occurrence. How do you gain your predictions of world figures?

John Pendragon: I usually work with the press photographs of public figures, or if I do not have a picture of a certain individual, I write the name on a sheet of paper and concentrate on it until a "picture" comes. I like, if possible, to have birth data, but this is not always necessary.

I had neither photo nor birth data when I forecast President Kennedy's assassination. Neither would have been necessary, for I was overwhelmed with the forcefulness of the precognitive image which I had of the President's approaching death.

I know that in addition to publishing your prediction of President Kennedy's assassination you also tried to contact him by letter. If he had heeded your warning, could he have been saved?

He might be alive today, unless he were *fated* to die at that time.

Do you feel that everybody has the potential to become psychic?

Well, I believe that everyone may have latent psychic abilities, But again, there must be something that makes one person a psychic sensitive and the vast majority of other people apparently "non-sensitive."

What do you think that "something" may be?

If I knew that, I should become a wealthy man selling a psychic development course!

One thing I have always believed, is that while the stresses I experienced resulted in my becoming a psychic sensitive, the same stresses might, in a slightly different man or woman, have resulted in that individual becoming an artist, a musician – or a madman, a drug addict, a drunkard!

I also feel that there is a correlation between the creative person and the psychic person. I studied art for many years, you know. Perhaps if the stresses had been a bit different and my cerebro-nervous system (and possibly my etheric system) had been otherwise constructed, you might be here today interviewing me for the beauty of my paintings, rather than the accuracy of my predictions.

In metaphysical literature, we read of an astral body, an etheric body, an etheric double, a spiritual body, and a soul body. What is your opinion of these many "bodies"?

In my opinion, man has a physical body, a spiritual body, or soul, an astral body, and an etheric body. I liken the physical body to a base from which the others operate. I would not say that they permeate each other, since each can act independently of the other.

The astral body can travel of its own accord while man is asleep and can visit places and return. In this way, a man may be able to describe scenes and conditions in parts of the world where his physical body has never been.

Many experimenters say that the astral body is attached to the physical one by a cord – rather like the umbilical cord between mother and child – and that this cord is connected with the head of the physical body. I agree with Dr. Alexander Cannon, who wrote that the astral body has no extremities, is more or less egg-shaped, and emits an orange ray.

And what about the etheric body? Is that just another name for the astral body?

The etheric body is one through which contacts are received on the channels that supply us with guidance, spiritual and inspirational. This is the body that receives our impressions, refreshes our memory of the past, directs our emotions, and is the center of our spiritual awareness.

It is from the etheric body that the radiations known as the auric colors build up around the physical body and enable those who are physically sensitive to see what the state of this realm of being denotes. It is exceptionally helpful in health diagnoses and in all psychological aspects of the person. It is also the most important adjunct to the earthly body, as it is the reservoir from which the mind draws much of its substance.

You have always been a stickler for professionalism.

If a career psychic wishes to be truly conscientious, he will find that one of his most difficult tasks is to bring the credulous down to earth. The wide-eyed believers outnumber the hard-backed skeptics ten to one.

A conscientious seer must allay the fears of the apprehensive, yet he must make them realize that he has no magical power to wave a wand over them and change their conditions in the twinkling of an eye.

In short, the professional seer, the career psychic, must at least endeavor to attain the patience of Job and the wisdom of Solomon!

That sounds like a tall order, indeed.

I have always felt that much is given to the able and conscientious clairvoyant, but, believe me, much is expected of him.

I have never made private forecasts concerning the results of sporting contests of any kind. I do not fill in people's football-pool coupons, or attempt to foresee the results of any kind of gambling activity.

In my opinion, psychic powers should be used to aid men and women in trouble, not to attempt to obtain large sums of money from the troubled and confused.

I believe that everyone has *latent* psychic abilities. Yet there must be something that makes one person a "sensitive" (a word I prefer to "medium") while the vast majority remain apparently "non-sensitive."

I think that emotional, mental, and physical stresses, in certain rare instances, produce psychism. I was one of those rare instances.

Since psychics throughout the ages have been telling man about the afterlife, why do people remain so afraid of death?

If we reincarnate, as I believe we do, we may receive a glimpse beforehand of what will happen to us in our coming earth-life. We may see what suffering lies ahead of us in the body's rebirth. When we enter death, nature may draw down the blind, so to speak, and we may have difficulty recalling the happy things we have experienced in the interim of waiting or perhaps during the last time we had a body.

Furthermore, nature has given us the law of self-preservation. If we did not have the fear of death to encourage us to preserve ourselves, we should allow our physical bodies to be destroyed before it was our time. It is the fear of death that keeps us locked tightly in our physical bodies until such time as we have learned the lessons of life and worked off some of our Karma.

THE CREATIVE AND THE PSYCHIC PERSONALITIES

Pendragon and I often discussed at great length the similarities between the creative personality and the psychic personality. The psychically sensitive possess talents of a sort that are beyond the grasp of the average man. But then, so does the artist, poet, or musician.

If one's talent for sketching has never progressed beyond kindergarten fingerpainting, if one's proficiency on the piano has never surpassed "Peter, Peter, Pumpkin-eater," if one's gift for prosody has never eclipsed "Roses are red, violets are blue," then how extraordinary must seem an Andrew Wyeth, a Van Cliburn, or a T.S. Eliot.

Creativity must find an outlet, and whether it be in composition or in clairvoyance may be only a condition of circumstances or environment. Is the feat of dipping ahead in the stream of time really so much more extraordinary or extrasensory than the capturing of beauty on canvas or the capsuling of the essence of personality on paper? Are not the activities of mind which we now label "psychic" and "paranormal" only expressions of the limitless universe imprisoned within each of us?

"What is man?" the psalmist asked, and concluded that he was but a little lower than the angels.

Modern science has reassessed the ancient, plaintive query and concluded that man is no more than an arrangement of biochemical compounds, a cousin of the laboratory guinea pig rather than a son of God. Science, which has alleviated so many curses of the human condition, has levied a worse blight on mankind if its mechanistic magic deceives us into believing that we are trapped in the same cycle that imprisons the atoms of hydrogen and oxygen.

CHAPTER TEN

The Mystery of Zohar Science

The biography provided on the jackets of his books make Frank Rudolph Young sound like an ideal hero for a series of Doc Savage-type adventure novels. He claims to have descended from a line of yogis that dates back nearly one hundred fifty years, and from a chain of doctors and dentists nearly two hundred years long. Certain of his ancestors had been in close touch with the *cimarrones*, a secretive tribe made up of slaves who escaped the Spanish conquistadors to establish their own under-jungle cities in the wilds of Darien (Panama). The *cimarrones* were well known for their psychic miracles, and Frank inherited a treasury of never-before-revealed secrets from them.

I found out that Young never lectured, never made public appearances, and never granted interviews. Almost by accident, however, I contacted a source that published his shorter courses before they were expanded into books, and they arranged a "by mail" meeting for me. Although Frank Rudolph Young guards his privacy with a fervor I have never before encountered, he proved to be a most frank and courteous correspondent.

Brad Steiger: Why do you so oppose speech as a means of communication?

Frank Rudolph Young: The moment I meet anybody, I feel his thoughts shoot through my whole nervous system. Even if I don't read his thoughts – for I don't claim to be a mind reader – I feel intensely his reactions toward me, no matter how subtle they are. I also feel, as I associate with him, the "approvals" or "disapprovals" of his thinking, even when he is silent.

Everybody has this ability. Mine, though, is so much more explosive than most other people's that when I am in anybody's company, it repeatedly tightens or relaxes my whole body. When I converse, I feel it keenly in my vocal muscles, and it can make my speech too hasty or throw it into a stutter or shut it off   completely or into a stammer.

The more physically fit I am, the more keenly I react in this manner, because my nerve electricity is then popping with its highest millivoltage like a sprinter ready for the starting gun.

The few times in life when I drank to intoxication, while in college, I lost that super-keenness and relaxed all over without effort. But I also lost my psychic power. The other person became like a lamppost to me. I was no longer supersensitive to his thinking until he spoke and revealed his thoughts to me. Since people don't always tell you their exact thoughts, I extracted from my companion then only what *he* wanted me to know. To possess psychic power – psychic supersensitivity – you have to oversensitize yourself into the super-stutter state, like that of the medium in action.

Most, and perhaps all, mediums in the trance turn incoherent or speechless! Winston Churchill, Bernard Shaw, Moses, Aristotle, and other super-psychics and geniuses stuttered and stammered, except when they took extreme measures to restrain themselves day by day.

And you aren't at all interested in appearing on radio or television to discuss your work?

My book *Cyclomancy* broke the occult ice in this country – or in the world. Previous to it, all you heard scientifically about the occult was an occasional mention of the experiments of Dr. Rhine and a few other laboratory men. Once my book was published, however, the occult explosion started.

Cyclomancy demonstrated how the psychic masters achieved their powers and taught the reader how to do likewise. But it insisted that the average man should be satisfied to acquire but one hundredth or less of such powers, and that he would be so unusual that he would become a superman in practically anything he wanted to.

Why is such an unusual book out of print after four printings?

Simply because too many new readers found it too profound, too far in advance of their times. I had refused to simplify it before my publication, as my publisher had implored, because I didn't want every Tom, Dick or Harry to procure it just to try to get rich in a hurry or to bring others under their control and subject them to the enslaving powers of the "Psychic Harpoon" and others which I thoroughly described and showed how to master.

I preferred to keep this previously carefully guarded knowledge so deeply scientific that only the sincere student would concentrate on it and extract these far-ahead-of-the -time secrets, just as the alchemists concealed their fabulous secrets for centuries. *That* person – that *deserving* person –

could make a superman of himself (or herself) and truly attain wealth, health, body power, X-ray vision, and all the powers described, in exceptionally fast time. So, I had limited the numbers who would master it, and thereby favored those who were sincere.

I have been begged for years, too, by readers and students of my books and courses to open institutes across the country. I have resisted doing so for twenty-two years. Some students have been after me to do this for as long as fifteen years, and they feel disappointed and resentful because I have not done it.

What is your educational background?

I am the proud kick-out of two leading universities! My big failure was my *not* being kicked out of the third! I degraded my talents so much in that one, in fact, that I graduated with an A – average and earned a doctor's degree besides! I'll never live that one down! Colleges are little more than camera-mind institutions.

In Northwestern University Dental School, I was flunked in the first semester of anatomy. The semester's work was limited to the head, but I spent most of the time investigating the pineal gland on my own and insisting to the professor that it contained psychic powers which have, thirty years later, been attributed to it. (I passed the course easily the second time by keeping my mouth shut.) In the physiology laboratory, too, in my sophomore year, instead of concentrating on vivisecting the dogs, I secretly conducted psychic power experiments with brain waves.

So enmeshed was I in my secret psychic investigations already that I hardly did my work for the different classes. At the end of the term I showed up for only one examination, immediately handed in a blank paper with my name, and bewildered the examiner by shoving it under his nose and walking out. So they gave me the boot, with the postscript that I would never be accepted back. That was my proudest day. I had stopped being an academic zombie!

What made you think of brain waves, which were just being discovered then, as being linked up with psychic power?

Aside from my ancestral background, I had been researching the occult from a mere boy, right in the midst of the Voodoo center in the Republic of Panama, where I had been born of a Scotch-Irish mother and of an English-Spanish-East Indian father."

What did you do after being kicked out of the universities?

I was penniless, so I went into physique modeling for sculptors and did part-time bus-boying to keep myself alive while I proceeded singlehanded with my occult investigations.

A scout for Universal Studios discovered me, and I was urged to go at once to Hollywood. I was cast immediately into the leading role of a bullfighter, with elaborate plans to make me the big romantic star of the day, the successor to Rudolph Valentino. But to my impatient mind, the picture took too long to get started, and I was dying to sink my teeth back into occult research. So I walked out of Hollywood, lived in Los Angeles on odd, ill-paying jobs wherever I could find them, and spent the remaining hours rounding out my knowledge in the public library.

I was now using my own mind, my *creative* mind, my *individual* mind in full swing. My hidden powers swung into full use! I determined to read and master at least one book from each department in the library. I didn't read to memorize to pass examinations, but for *my own* curiosity, for my own tracking down of whatever puzzled me.

How did you proceed with your research?

I met leading psychics and learned secrets which they have never put in print. But my learnings were too scientific for them to follow, since my education had been strictly along medico-dental lines. Not only that, but my interest in history and politics remained insatiable after New York University.

Frank, you have sent me a most impressive list of predictions which you made well in advance of the actual occurrences. How can one be positive that he is making an accurate prediction when it is so easy to be misled by one thing or another?

By watching five important obstacles which constantly threaten to ruin the very best predictions:

1. WISH THINKING. A desperate wish for a particular phenomenon or result to occur. This wish fills you with dread that the opposite might occur and befuddles your prophetic acuity. When your mind subsequently receives the right answer, your dread refuses to accept it. And so, you predict *not* what your psychic power center perceived, but what you *wish* it had perceived.

2. LACK OF OBJECTIVITY. Too much knowledge of the wrong kind about what you are trying to predict, or knowledge of a misleading nature, or a kind that appeals to you most, will blind you to the truth of what your psychic power center perceives. Without your even trying to, as a result, you tend to mold the psychic impression you receive about it into what you presume it *ought* to be logically. As a consequence, you predict *not* what your psychic power center "received," but what you assume it *ought* to have received.

3. OVER-RESPONSE TO SUGGESTION. Suggestions by others either in writing (as from the media or in a letter), or orally (as from a speech or a conversation), or telepathically (as from another person's wish thinking), or in sympathy (as from your own emotions, pity, sense of justice, fervent desire to help other person, and the like) will saturate your psychic power center and alter the color of the prediction you receive in order to "fit it in with" the suggestion itself, or try to make the prediction came to pass.

4. STATE OF YOUR HEALTH. You predict most accurately when you are healthy and free of pain.

When you are in fine health and free of pain, you are at your most objective, at your most courageous to face the worst, and you are then less affected by tremulous wish thinking and less responsive to suggestion. Your sympathetic and parasympathetic nervous systems (your yang and yin) are perfectly balanced then, and you leave your conscious and subconscious minds less subject to one-sided emotions.

You are affected just the opposite when gripped with pain, terror of the future, discomfort, incapacity, and other sequelae of sickness, disease, or even of undiagnosable chronic health problems. All these plagues supersensitize your mind to the least impressions, particularly to those which comfort or flatter your ego and distort the accuracy of the predictions you receive.

5. MUSCLE TONE. To be healthy but without muscle tone is akin to being naturally intelligent but without the education to use it. Muscle tone reinforces the courage in your brain by adding the suggestion of a great physical power to back it up.

You feel much stronger than you really are, after all, if you contract your pectoral (chest or breast) muscles when you face trouble or disaster, than if you don't. When your "aggressive" muscles are maintained naturally toned, your whole body automatically backs up your psychic power (and your conscious and subconscious minds as well) *reflexively*, with the independent feeling that you *can* stand on your own feet, come what may. When any prophecy is triggered in your psychic power center, you then normally accept it like a philosopher, no matter what side it favors, and present it as it is, with the least distortion.

People who fail to predict with accuracy are usually handicapped by one of these five lacks.

CHAPTER ELEVEN

Merging an Ancient Philosophy with the New Age

Sybil Leek was truly one of the great women of metaphysics, and her death in 1982 marked an enormous loss for all serious practitioners of the esoteric arts.

Sybil and I celebrated two birthdays together – one in Hawaii, the other in Washington,D.C. – for our natal anniversaries were but a few days apart in February.

Before our first meeting in 1969, I had anticipated the *gran dame* of the paranormal to be a bit of a prima donna. I was delighted to find that Lady Sybil was charming, erudite, exceedingly friendly, and lacking in nearly all forms of overt ego expression. Throughout all the years that I knew her, Sybil Leek was filled with genuine humility and a continual wonder at the promise of life.

Sybil Leek was a Witch, an astrologer, and a psychic. After she moved to the United States, she became one of America's foremost advocates of scientific application to astrology, enlightened psychism, and a true understanding of Witchcraft.

BORN INTO THE CRAFT

Sybil was born in England into a highly unusual and wonderfully stimulating family. Her maternal grandmother was a very psychic lady and a lifetime follower of the Old Religion. Her father was an intellectual, well-versed in metaphysics, but more inclined to a scientific investigation of the field. Sybil's mother was a theosophist with an inborn affinity toward all children. Added to these were an assortment of aunts, cousins, and other extended family members. No one in the family was ever too small to be excluded from family discussions or opportunities to be taught the ways of the universe.

Under the combined tutorial care of her family, Sybil managed to escape the British public school system for many years. Each member of the family taught the child his or her particular specialty, as well as a diversity of other things. Sybil learned about herbs, witchcraft, astrology, the general field of the occult, and the mystical Kabbala. This unorthodox rearing was far from one-sided, however. Before the age of nine young Sybil had "read through the major classics." She had read the Bible, the works of Shakespeare, and many other volumes of Eastern religious and non-Western philosophies.

Most of all, though, Sybil learned from her grandmother. Long before and long after Sybil's rather brief career in the public schools, her grandmother was there to teach her the Craft of the Wise. She taught her the practical lore of herbs; she demonstrated the laws of nature, and she gave the young girl lessons in that most difficult area to teach to another: spiritual laws and their applications to daily living.

A PSYCHIC SCHOOLGIRL

Sybil Leek began manifesting her psychic abilities early in life. Around her own family this caused no problems, for psychism was a common household occurrence. Blurting out psychic impressions around others could sometimes prove troublesome.

On one occasion, while at school, Sybil was talking with one of the few teachers who understood the girl's innate abilities. Sybil told this woman that her aura showed anger every time she encountered one of the other instructors at the school. This harmless observation seemed to clear the way for a deeper, more troubling impression.

"Elise Barton won't be back next term. She'll have some trouble in her head and she will die."

Sybil continued talking to her teacher, explaining the uneasiness she felt when she heard others planning the next school term for this brilliant student. She told of the ugly gaps and distortions visible in Elise's aura, which boded ill health.

Sybil's teacher advised the girl to refrain from speaking these thoughts to others, especially the Barton girl. The instructor urged Sybil to be good friends with Elise, acting as if she did not know.

Elise Barton did not return to the school for the next term. She contracted meningitis and died the day before the term was to begin.

During her school days the resourceful young psychic also managed to confound two of her teachers and the headmistress when she thought of a clever way to escape her dreaded math class. By staring at her inkwell Sybil could give the appearance of considered attention while she really projected herself out-of-body and into an English class. This seemed quite agreeable to Sybil, who continued the arrangement until a perplexed headmistress called the girl to her office. How could she, the woman fumed, be present in two classes at once? Both the English and the math teachers were willing to swear an affidavit that Sybil was present in their classes.

The girl brightly informed her headmistress that it was a simple matter of astral projection. This was too much for the very proper lady to bear, and Sybil's formal education nearly ended there. The arrival of Sybil's mother and grandmother resulted in a reprieve for the girl, who did finish the term with honors in seven out of eight subjects.

A conciliatory headmistress informed Sybil's parents that a scholarship could be arranged if the girl were interested in a university education. Here Sybil's grandmother stepped in, and Sybil embarked, under her tutelage, upon a far different course of graduate studies. It was time for the traditional intensive training, passed from generation to generation, that would culminate in a new Witch stepping into the ritual circle.

THE INITIATION

Sybil's preliminary instruction was completed. She had absorbed masses of rituals, lessons, and lore. Then the phone call came announcing an opening in a coven in France, of which a distant aunt of Sybil's was High Priestess. The young initiate journeyed to France, to the *Gorge du Loup*. There, in utmost secrecy, Sybil was initiated into the world's oldest religion.

In her book, *Diary of a Witch*, Sybil Leek described briefly the oath of fidelity that every Witch solemnly gives on the night of his or her initiation.

"It is accepted as being binding forever, and no initiate can take it lightly. She accepts wholeheartedly all the tenets of Witchcraft – the acceptance of the Supreme Being, the knowledge that good and evil are equal parts of a human being, and that she must personally strive to outbalance evil with good. She must not debase the arts which she has been taught, and at all times she must be conscious of the need to be discreet, not only in her own life but with regard to any other members of the coven."

Shortly after Sybil returned to England the family moved to the New Forest, a large area that roughly extends from Southampton northward to the borders of Salisbury and nearby Stonehenge, and westward to Dorset. It was in this area that Sybil widened her lore of herbs, nature, and human psychology.

WITH THE GYPSIES IN NEW FOREST

To escape a suddenly fermenting plan to turn Sybil into a budding socialite, the newly initiated Witch decided to leave her house and bed and live in the woods with the Gypsies. For a year Sybil lived with these people, and as she respected them, they learned to respect and love her. She ate from their communal pots, slept on the ground, learned a few conning tricks, and vastly increased her knowledge of herbs. She communicated with her estranged family via telepathy. That is, whenever they wanted to get in touch with her, Sybil's mother or grandmother would contact her mentally – and Sybil would go to the nearest telephone. The system never failed.

At the end of this year's sojourn with the gypsies, Sybil returned to her parental home.

"You look very healthy," said her grandmother.

"You need a bath," her mother added.

"Did you have an opportunity to study *King Lear*?" her father inquired.

"After such a reception from my family," Sybil writes, "how can anyone say we are eccentric?"

A year of independence was enough to sever the economic ties binding Sybil to her parents. She opened an antique shop, one of her many diverse ventures outside the realm of the paranormal which Sybil successfully pursued in her multi-faceted career. She lived in the New Forest, and became a member of the Horsa coven.

Since the age of fifteen, Sybil had been in and out of various media jobs. Now, with the opening of the antique shop, Sybil began moonlighting as a roving reporter for Southern Television.

It was Sybil's task to provide material for the *Day by Day* program, a series using the magazine format of small documentaries, interviews, and highlights of the day. The show's producers were particularly interested in Sybil's contacts with the Gypsies of the New Forest, and Sybil was able to present several interesting and informative vignettes about her nomadic friends.

THE FIRST TELEVISED MEDIUMISTIC TRANCE

It was in December of 1963 that Sybil Leek's media relations caused her to be, very probably, the first person to be filmed in mediumistic trance. The incident began when Sybil was contacted by a parapsychologist Bennison Herbert. Herbert wished Sybil to accompany him to a twelfth century building on French Street, Southampton, England, which was reputed to be haunted. Sybil was to enter the trance state and try to determine the cause of the psychic disturbance.

The building had been used as a Theater Club for the past eight years, and during that time the actors had reported strange noises, disembodied footsteps, and the opening and closing of doors. Props had even been thrown around, causing several of the actors to develop severe cases of nerves.

Photo by Julian Leek

Sybil Leek was a great metaphysical teacher of warmth, humility and marvelous insight.

Bennison Herbert had contacted the BBC, asking that they come to interview Sybil after the investigation. The BBC team arrived at the same time as Herbert and Leek, however, and as the night was bitterly cold, all entered the building together.

Almost immediately Sybil began to feel herself slipping away from the laughing joviality of the others. The group reached an upstairs room of the old stone building and settled around a large table. Within moments Sybil was in a deep trance.

Sights and sounds beyond the normal senses surrounded the entranced psychic. She felt someone come in through the door, then felt herself seized from behind. Rough, thick hands tore at her flesh in an effort to remove her ear rings and necklace. Sybil, enraged, shouted at the woman standing in the doorway. The struggle ceased as the heavy table at which the group was seated suddenly rose into the air and traversed the room. Then, with vented fury, the table repeatedly threw itself at the heavy stone wall, chipping the surface. Finally, the table resumed its docile stability. A door slammed and something was heard running down the steps. Sybil came out of her trance and was told what had happened by Bennison Herbert, who had taken notes on all the strange happenings.

At this point the BBC crew could no longer contain themselves. They hastily set up their lights and cameras, hoping to catch more of the same phenomena. The crew was not disappointed.

The table began to move once more, traveling across the room to fling itself with renewed vigor at the ancient stonework. An incredulous sound man, weighing 220 pounds, tried to sit on the airborne table, only to be tossed off as if he were a featherweight. The table assaulted the wall with such force that it chipped a two-inch hole through the surface.

"If you have ever tried to make a mark at all on a Portland stone from the Dorset Isle of Purbeck, which Sir Christopher Wren used to build St. Paul's, you will realize what a feat this was," Sybil observes.

The footage received wide distribution throughout the south of England and generated tremendous interest. The tables were shown in almost complete levitation and the mark on the wall was quite visible.

Bennison Herbert, who was also with the Psychical Research Society, wrote a description of the seance for the Society's *Proceedings*. His research had shown that the building had been a storehouse for a wine merchant in the twelfth century. The lower depths had been vaulted with a well in the center. In the seventeenth century the place had been an inn, and the landlady had devised a system of robbing the guests with the aid of a servant. Apparently she had retained her mercenary ways in spirit form, and thus had desired the jewelry worn by Sybil the evening of the seance. She was concerned about the jewelry, which had been stolen by the servant and hidden in the well. This well corresponded to a place under the wall, which had been covered over in subsequent years.

THE WITCH OF NEW FOREST COMES TO AMERICA

Eventually Sybil Leek's productive years in the New Forest came to an end. The advent of publicity brought many visitors seeking the "Witch of the New Forest," and the attention irritated Sybil's landlord. In a fit of modern Witch-hunting, he refused to renew Sybil's lease, and she was forced to leave her comfortable abode.

It was at this point that Sybil decided that if she were to move, she might as well cross the ocean as move to the next hamlet. She came first to New York, where a series of residence changes made her increasingly unhappy. At this critical time, she received a call from psychic investigator Hans Holzer.

Holzer had a proposal for the witch-psychic. Would she like to team up with him on a series of ghost-hunting expeditions? Sybil liked the idea immediately, and the two embarked on numerous de-haunting sojourns, both here and abroad.

The two were often followed by an entourage of local – and sometimes international – press men, eager to sniff out a good story where they saw one. Frequently, movie cameras would roll while Sybil was in a heavy trance state, but this never deterred the medium from obtaining solid material, which Holzer would then try to substantiate.

Sybil never knew where their next jaunt was going to take them. Holzer usually investigated the cases brought to his attention, first affirming that the material represented a solid psychic case, worthy of being investigated. He would give Sybil none of this information, to ensure that her trance information could never be accused of being the result of suggestion. This system often embarrassed the psychic, for friends and newsmen might inquire about a certain case that Sybil could not even remember.

THE WITCH AND THE WITCH DOCTOR

Sybil Leek's intrepid spirit also led her on other excursions, apart from her ghost-hunting activities with Holzer. With Hollywood filmmaker Jim Newman, Sybil embarked for the Yucatan in April, 1969, with a complete film crew. The object was to find a witchdoctor whom Sybil had once met, and film the inland trek as a documentary.

The collection of people moved inland to the witchdoctor's tiny village. The company was plagued with unbearably hot weather and a series of uncomfortable mishaps that nearly broke the morale of the crew.

Finally the group arrived in the tiny village, only to learn that the witchdoctor was away for several days on an herb-gathering mission. The dismayed crew was ready to pack up and leave immediately for a comfortable bed, but something told Sybil to wait. She was rewarded when the tiny figure of the village witchdoctor slowly came into view.

"I came back to see you," the wiry man explained.

With the sound of the camera equipment whirring behind them, the Witch and witchdoctor settled down like two old crones, discussing the ways and means of their trade. The docile scene was interrupted once when a frantic woman rushed toward the doctor with her son, who had a bloody head wound. The doctor quietly placed his hand over the still seeping mess and held it there for a few moments. When he lifted his hand, the bleeding had stopped and the child toddled uncertainly toward his mother.

The doctor continued with Sybil as though the disruption had never occurred. Healing, he explained, was the part of his work that concerned him the most. Then he and Sybil talked of the herbs they knew, and of their miraculous uses.

When Sybil left the old man, she was overcome with a sense of his value and worth to his people. She wished she could spend infinitely more time with him, learning his life-gathered knowledge of herbs.

DEFINING THE OLD RELIGION

A Witch is one who strives for well-being, according to the oldest precepts in the world. If these precepts are followed, illnesses can be kept away, or driven from the body psychically. To maintain this state of well-being the witch seeks to remain close to nature, and to seek harmony in herself and her environment. She can raise her own psychic abilities by developing her mind "to a point where we see or feel no barriers of time and space, when the horizons become limitless. Then we are able to experience the conquest of the self, and influence others," writes Sybil in *Diary of a Witch*.

Sybil Leek was determined to aid in the understanding of Witchcraft. Unfortunately, she found some of the gravest misunderstandings in her adopted country. The press confused Witchcraft with black magic and Satanism, and an undiscriminating public was often more interested in losing its inhibitions than establishing inner balance.

Sybil was instrumental in bringing a greater awareness of a non-polluted Witchcraft to persons in this country who wished to form traditional covens, and she never ceased using her wit and celebrity to advance the truth about Wicca, the craft of the wise.

"ASTROLOGY IS MY SCIENCE; WITCHCRAFT IS MY RELIGION"

In addition to Sybil's many talents as a psychic and her deep immersion in the Old Religion, this remarkable lady had yet another major field of interest that was with her all of her life. As she states in the opening lines of *My Life in Astrology*: "Astrology is my science; Witchcraft is my religion..."

For Sybil, astrology lessons began when she was eight years old. From her grandmother Sybil learned the basics of astrology, with personality traits and psychology stressed; from her father she learned the painstaking technical aspect of casting a chart.

In Sybil's younger days the world of astrology was a glamorous one, especially to a girl in her circumstances. Every summer the family would vacation in the Riviera, and Sybil's skills were in great demand among the celebrities and nobility that would gather on the beaches. In return for her services, the girl often was given wonderful gifts of gratitude. Among her notable clients were the elder Aga Khan, Queen Marie of Rumania, and author Somerset Maugham.

On one occasion Sybil was traveling on a train from Paris to Avignon. In the compartment with her were two army captains. Sybil did a thumbnail horoscope for these two men, and for one of them she found herself saying, "If you had been born in another age, you would have worn the Crown of France." The man was Charles De Gaulle.

The advent of the war ended forever the sumptuous style of living that the Riviera had known, and although Sybil has nostalgic feelings for that particular time, her later life was to show her an even more exciting use for her astrological skills.

"It is wrong to think that astrology belongs to the past, for it moves with the times and always updates itself," Sybil has written. "But the updating is only as good as the astrologers of the age, who must look for new patterns in the astrological maze."

Sybil Leek became a major force on the psychic scene. Her rich and varied life consistently led her to prove the deeper meanings and interrelationships between all areas of metaphysics, and her vast experience prepared her admirably for the research and study to which she devoted herself. From such a vast store of personal research came a practical and insightful knowledge into Witchcraft, into psychism, and into astrology.

Brad Steiger: Sybil, much of America's first acquaintance with you began in the early 1960s, when you were being heralded as a "queen of the Witches."

Sybil Leek: Yes, but of course there is no such thing as a queen in Witchcraft. That's a journalist's term.

It was about that time when you received notice from the press for standing up and correcting an anthropologist who was lecturing on Witchcraft, wasn't it?

Yes, that was at the University of London.

Could you describe what was said that put you off that night?

Well, this man had been going around in England making the statement that Witchcraft didn't exist. I had heard him first over the radio, from my house in New Forest. Two visiting witches, from different states, were with me, and we laughed about it. He just went on without anyone saying anything to him, and he was just speaking a lot of nonsense.

Well, it was my birthday the same date as the university lecture, so I gathered together forty witches from various parts of the country, and we went to the lecture as part of my birthday party. The lecture did get a bit out of hand, but he didn't know he was informing a company of forty-some witches that they didn't exist.

I know I have a strange sense of humor, but I thought it was quite humorous. Finally, we devastated him, because the humor wore off, and all he really was saying was a lot of nonsense. So we went off to my regular birthday party.

Things have changed so in the last few years. Largely due to your efforts, Witches have "come out of the closet," so to speak. Yet people still refuse to believe in Witches while having no trouble believing in Christians or Buddhists. Why is there still this refusal on peoples' part to believe in Witches, especially as they are so popular in fiction?

I think simply because they *have been* so popular in fiction. People want to believe that they still are just fiction because others have this fear of Witches. If a giant came out of a storybook's pages and came walking down the street, people would be afraid of him. It is when a thing appears in life, when some fantasy becomes a reality, that people become frightened.

Do you think the fear is some residual holdover from the superb job of propagandizing done at the time of the Inquisition?

Oh, yes. The brainwashing was pretty well done; and we know now, with our great interest in psychology, that fears which are securely lodged into the subconscious will remain there and become quite terrifying.

Is there a term you would prefer to "Witch"?

No, I am quite happy with it. I know what it means.

It is so difficult to get away from the negative connotations connected with Witchcraft, though.

Only in America, where we have the idea of the old hag as Witch. But, you know, the personification of the Italian Witches in art and drama has always been quite pretty. When we speak of Witches we should always add that *Wicca* is the religion, and people have loosely translated this into Witch. And, of course, I believe the old fashioned saying: "Evil to him who evil thinks."

Words change, connotations change. For instance, I was in Paris last year in August, and whenever the word "American" was used, it was a dirty word. We know Americans are not dirty words, but to the particular people around those meetings there, it was a very bad word.

There seems to be a really concerted effort of certain fundamentalists to institute a modern Witch hunt. Do you think there is going to be a sort of fundamental backlash toward the metaphysical explosion?

Oh, yes. It is also a very good political ploy. Whenever you see dubious things happening in politics, the call goes out to hunt down a few Witches.

Are you concerned at all about this, that the persecution might begin again?

I have always been concerned about persecution of anyone, because I think tolerance and compassion are two of the things lacking in our very sophisticated natures. After all these years, we are still not compassionate, we are still not tolerant.

Well, then, suppose you were in a position of authority, and you could direct the education of the masses. What would you do to create a better climate for acceptance of psychics and Witches or whatever?

Well, I think we have to study modern philosophy as well as ancient philosophy. We have to realize that philosophy means a way of life.

Then I think that the greatest thing we could try would be to merge spiritual qualities with science. I don't mean merge religious dogma with science, but a merging of spiritual qualities into science. This is where we are going to get more tolerance, because the churches and science have always battled, and we don't want them uniting into one battle over other people.

There is a new look to the scientist of today, and a new feeling. Also, I think there are religious people who are not necessarily regular churchgoers. I think a liaison between these two, a liaison between spirituality and science would be one of the things I would aim at.

Would you, or have you ever consented to go into a laboratory and have yourself poked and prodded and wired up?

Oh, I was done like this for years and years in Europe. I was also called the "golden guinea pig."

The golden guinea pig?

Well, I have always had red hair and a fair complexion and these combined into a very golden look. All of my life was being swept up by other people proving what I *already* knew, and they were too *foolish* to know.

Did you come to resent it?

Yes, very much, because it was my life they were playing with. I regard myself as a teacher, and I don't like to do experiments time after time to provide fodder for another person's book. I don't resent this so much, but I do resent the attitude of the scientist coming to a psychic and putting him or her through the most terrible things while he is tied down in chairs. It is uncivilized.

Would they ever recognize your abilities?

Yes, they have always gone away entirely dumfounded. At one time there were about forty scientists altogether – and I confounded them. But then they became resentful at having been proved wrong.

And what if someone contacted these forty scientists. Do you think they would admit that you had these abilities?

No, I don't think any of them ever will. It's like what happens when a psychic helps the police. The police are madly keen to get help because they don't know where to turn. They are paid to do their job, and the psychic isn't. As soon as the case seems to be near breaking, the police forget they know you. I don't care two hoots about this as far as Sybil Leek is concerned, but I care about their attitude to psychic phenomena in general. I don't need to spend my time helping the police earn their dollar, which I am contributing to anyway, in taxes.

You acknowledge yourself as a teacher, but you don't really consider yourself a mystic.

I don't like that word. How do you define a mystic?

Someone who is devoted to the spiritual side of life, perhaps in a quiet way of going about the life of contemplation more than –

On, no, I am not a mystic then. I am made up of mind, body, and spirit. Obtaining a balance between the mind, body, and spirit is my aim. I like the joys of the flesh; I like the joys of the spirit; and I like the joys of the mind.

You think it is possible to keep a balance among all three.

Essential. It is essential to keep a balance among all three, because in this world we do have to function in the body, in a physical manner, and we have to function in a mental manner. We have neglected to function also in the spiritual manner. Bring your spirituality into the physical and mental, and you will see what life is all about. To me, a totally ascetic person seems to be a drop-out from living.

So you would not advocate to any of your students going to a cave and contemplating their navels?

That is hard to say. For some people this might be the way in order to get rich in spirituality, but I don't think so. I came to grips with mine so long ago. I do believe, though, that one should meditate, and I see that periods away from the world, the everyday life, would also maintain the body and mind and spirit in good condition.

What kind of meditation would you advocate for someone who is just getting into this?

Well, I think the essential thing with meditation is to not make it sound like it is taking you away from the rest of the people in the world. A lot of people judge meditation as if it is everything. Meditation should become a natural thing.

All methods of meditation recommend regular periods of meditation every day and that means never let up until the time comes when you are not conscious of how many minutes you have meditated. So many people practically plot it out, saying, "Well, I managed to meditate in ten minutes flat." Some days it is necessary to meditate for twenty minutes.

In time a person is able to meditate just as well at the top of a bus or in a car, as he can by quietly going into a room in solitude. In the end, meditation doesn't have to be solitary.

Your approach to witchcraft and the paranormal is a very practical one, isn't it?

Yes, I believe that it is a way of life, a lifestyle. Therefore life is involved, always. Of course, I believe in reincarnation. As we are in this life, we are paving the way for the next life.

What personal proof have you had of reincarnation?

I have always had personal proof of it. Take my own life. I am totally uneducated. I mean, I am *really* uneducated. There are very few subjects, however, which I can't tune in on. This may not seem like very practical proof of other lives, but I must have learned something from them. When the time arises, this little shutter of the past clears itself, and I see it very clearly. I see everything absolutely in the right and proper manner.

That is one way to prove it. The other is that three or four thousand ghost hunts that I did with Hans Holzer. This was purely a scientific investigation into psychic phenomena that led me to accept completely that death is not the end, and that the spirit is indestructible. It would be such a waste if it were not, and it makes more sense. It is more just. We are raised in logic, and what logic is it that a child should die at the age of two when a man could live three score and ten years? Logic is not the answer.

No, this is beyond logic.

I completely accept reincarnation. I could spend the rest of my life trying to *prove* it; but it is there, it always has been, and now let me get on with living. Let me live within the idea that the spirit is going to be indestructible.

You made an interesting statement recently when you said that you thought many professional psychics today were committing some of the same errors as some of the fundamentalists.

Oh, yes, they are becoming too wrapped up in themselves. Ego means an awful lot. I know people say I get a lot of publicity, but I have always had publicity, wherever I go. Frankly, the throwing away of the ego during meditation and trance work is very much easier for a flamboyant person to do than the persons who are tied up with themselves, wondering what their hair is going to look like while they are in trance.

There are two things that I think we all need, psychics particularly, and these are tolerance and compassion. I am finding many psychics who are intolerant. Everything has to be their way, while I believe that different things work for different psychics. What is good for them is fine, but my way of life works for me. If it didn't, I would change it. I am resilient enough to make a change.

Have you ever been frightened in your psychic investigations?

That's hard to say, for fear is a strange thing to analyze. I have done such reckless things in my physical life and been frightened while doing them, that I am sure I have done reckless things in my psychical life and been frightened. I have got tremendous confidence in myself in trance work, so that stops the fears. Once in Cincinnati, I think, I was frightened when I came out, because there was a silly woman screaming. I don't believe in these big displays of trance work just to amuse people.

So you would feel confident enough in your own abilities when you are in trance, regardless of how eerie you may feel. You would not feel fear.

Oh, I always feel I have tremendous protection.

What is it about your involvement with Wicca, or the entire area of the spiritual, that has made you the happiest, the most contented?

That's a blockbuster, isn't it? Well, I have evolved a system of happiness which has escalated as I got older. I think I am happy now that the occult sciences are coming into their own. I think we have a lot of things to sort out, but I am confident they will be done. I am very happy that the occult sciences are being studied more thoroughly.

What direction would you like to see these studies go?

I would like them to be a part of the regular educational curriculum, to be as much accepted as algebra. That would be very good and would take the kookiness out of the field.

To me, it is so sane, the occult sciences are so right. They don't need to be bolstered up by anything.

I am very much against people who use the occult sciences and are afraid to come out and stand up for them, legally, in their own right. They always have to hide behind a church or a foundation. Sure, it's the easiest way to get things done, so I suppose the end justifies the means; but I think the time has come how when the occult sciences are the occult sciences, just as medical science is a science.

Regardless of the name one gives to it – the Age of Aquarius, or whatever – do you feel we are approaching a time of transition right now, a bold leap forward on the part of spiritual evolution?

Yes, I do. I think this is inevitable every two thousand years. Every big cycle does have this big leap forward. How we use it is going to be so important. We don't want to be like some Stone Age man, jumping into the present age and feeling lost in it. This is why it is so important to have education in the occult sciences, because they are going to be needed much more.

Do you think this change will be happening to people regardless of whether or not they are prepared for it, or understand it?

I think to a certain degree. Of course, what will emerge from the species are the people who understand it more. It is just the same as the space age and the electronic age, both of which were bred in, or prepared for, this age. Boys and girls have suddenly appeared who are very adept to this type of work. Something has happened to this particular breed, and they can tune in and do these things with great facility. I see this as inevitable. Then when you get this feeling in the whole species, of course more leaders emerge, more dramatic things emerge on the individual basis.

Do you have any final comments?

Well, I would like to think I have contributed something to the occult sciences. I think the children will make greater contributions, more in the true interests of the occult sciences.

I hope psychics will stop battling among themselves. After all, it's the thing, not the person.

I think I've finally got my body and spirit together, and now I am living the enjoyment of that harmony. It's not imagination, either, not the person.

I think of myself as being a very ordinary person, living a very ordinary life, in which the supernatural is just the natural.

CHAPTER TWELVE

A Warning to Those Who Would Seek Occult Knowledge

Author's Note: Although Great Britain's John Pendragon had been a profes-sional psychic-sensitive for decades when I met him, he displayed remarkable caution toward the matter of psychic development without adequate study and preparation and without the proper attitudes of growth and awareness. Here are his words on the indiscriminate seeking of hidden knowledge.

There is no subject that provides such golden opportunities for the swindler and the get-rich-quick boys as occultism. This is because it is a subject that attracts neurotics and psychotics galore. Such persons are only too easily duped into believing all manner of nonsense, especially if it is inclined to be esoteric.

I first had my taste of the flamboyant flimflam of the bogus psychic when I was just a lad hawking cosmetics in the market place. The master of the occult billed himself as: THE GREAT ZHARA-ZHARZO – SPIRIT MEDIUM & AFRICAN MAGICIAN.

These words were emblazoned on a moth-eaten banner he displayed on his booth. The Great Zhara-Zharzo (privately known as Emmanuel Well-ington Lovejoy) was assisted by a pasty-faced Cockney called Alfred. Alfred had a resounding, brassy voice that out-trumpeted most of the other traders. His hawking often reached me above the medley of other voices that began with the famous "Raz Prince Monolulu, the recently deceased racing tipster."

The Great Zhara-Zharzo would retire to his large car and change into an African garment and – rather incongruously – a top hat. Alfred merely decorated himself with a fez. He needed no decoration, for his voice attracted the crowd.

In the center of the pitch stand the magician placed a small folding table and covered it with a piece of green baize, under which there was placed, by sleight-of-hand, a small object the nature of which eluded me for some time.

Alfred then produced a large dinner gong and beat upon it so lustily that the sound completely overshadowed all other sounds within a radius of 30 yards. the interest of the crowd was by then aroused and the people began to gather around the magician and his assistant.

"Ladies and gennelmen!" began Alfred, adjusting his fez more firmly on his head. "Friends! You are now about to witness one of the greatest and most astounding performances of the 20th-century. I 'ave 'ere beside me the Great Zhara-Zharzo, the famous Hafrican Wizard, who will, through his amazing mediumistic powers, bring a message from the spirits of the dead for each one of you, 'igh or low, rich or poor, it matters not, ladies and gennelmen! I 'ave at enormous expense brought this man from his native jungle where no white man but me 'as ever set foot and returned alive. I challenge – I *defy* – anyone to come forward and per-form the miracles that you are now about to witness. The Great Zhara-Zharzo has got power over one of the most deadly snakes in Hafrica. . . ."

Alfred tapped the colored man on the shoulder and made a few signs, since the Great Zhara-Zharzo apparently was incapable of understanding English when he was performing. The magician nodded, and the whites of his eyes flashed. Then, fumbling in the folds of his flowing garment, he suddenly produced a live snake about four feet in length. What kind of snake it was I do not know, but it was certainly not a cobra. He whistled softly to it, and it reared a little to his caress. Finally it slunk into the folds of his gown again to coil itself about his torso.

The crowd thickened and began to lap up Alfred's words as he continued his pitch.

"My friends, the Great Zhara-Zharzo will now give you a demonstration of 'is powers. Now you will observe that I have 'ere a perfectly blank writing pad. I'll pass it round, ladies and gents, for your inspection just to prove to you that there is no fraud or de-ception."

The writing pad was passed around, and the crowd convinced itself that the sheets were completely blank.

"Thank you, friends," continued Alfred, when somebody had handed back the pad. "Now, who wants a inspirational message from the spirits? Sixpence each."

The applicants, who placed their money into Alfred's fez, were asked to state the number of their house, which he carefully wrote on the bottom of each sheet of the pad. When 40 or more sixpences had flowed into the fez, he pocketed the coins and ripped the sheets out of the pad. "No fraud or deception, friends. Pages completely blank, as you still witness before God."

Gathering up the pages, he slipped them under the green baize cover of the little table. The baize had previously been raised some nine inches in the center by the invisible object.

Alfred then made more signs to Zhara-Zharzo, who stepped forward and proceeded to make passes over the table, muttering as he did so some sort of incantation in his native language. This he continued to do while Alfred diverted the attention of the crowd with a few sleight-of-hand card tricks.

Presently, the Great Zhara-Zharzo stood back and non-chalantly produced from one of his pockets a baby's skull (it may have been the skull of an ape, for I never saw it closely). An audible shudder when through the crowd. Alfred stepped forward and removed the pages from under the baize cover and – lo! – they were covered with writing! Here were the "messages from the spirits."

Alfred distributed them to his patrons, according to the numbers of their houses.

The recipients of the spiritual communion were visibly impressed and read the messages almost feverishly. Their wonder must have been great when they drew forth the sheets from their pockets and handbags on reaching home, for by that time, the pages were completely blank again. Such was the magic of the Great Zhara-Zharzo!

You will probably have guessed that the messages had been written in some kind of invisible ink, and the object under the cover was a small, carefully gauzed oil lamp, the heat from which caused the writing to reappear for a few minutes. To those not in the know, this magic could be quite mystifying. A regrettably high percentage of those who advertise themselves as practicing psychics are able to produce no greater bona-fide results than those achieved by the Great Zhara-Zharzo. Their approach may be a bit more subtle than that of the market-place medium, but their object is the same – to defraud their clients.

PENDRAGON ON NUMEROLOGY

I would not be so sweeping as to state that there is nothing in numerology, but it is a subject that has been so confused and rehashed that the result is practically worthless. There are several systems of numerology, and many of them do not agree on which number relates to a particular letter. Systems of calculation are also contradictory, with the result that it is possible to calculate one's "numbers" with more than one result, thus rendering the whole subject mostly nonsense.

Numerology can provide another field for the racketeer. I get pitiful and tragic letters from people who have spent large sums of money for their "lucky numbers" and have tried to apply them to football pools, races, and the like, with the result that they lost all they had staked. The only people who have made themselves rich with lucky numbers are the merchants who sell these "secrets" to a gullible public. The dupes do not realize that basically there are only nine numbers, so there is always one chance in nine of a particular number coming up. I know that some schools of numerology allege that there are numbers beyond nine – such as eleven – which should be taken into account, but their dogma is ruled out by others who disagree with them.

Nevertheless, I hazard that in the dawn of civilization certain numbers may have had a certain significance, but that original significance has been lost or buried under a welter of error. Yet we still have those numerologists who claim that *their* system is the truth. When people – no matter what they represent – tell me that they have the occult truth, I become more than usually skeptical.

OBSERVATIONS ON THE OTHER FORMS OF THE OCCULT

The number of persons who fall for the woolly-minded esoteric clap-trap of the self-styled professors, reverends, and swamis must run to hundreds of thousands. If anybody claims to be "in touch with the masters" or "receiving messages from the Christ sphere" it is as well to investigate their claims.

Such grandiloquent statements pander to the egoism of both the deceiver and the deceived. It is possible there *may* be such persons as "masters" in a discarnate sense, but the number of letters I receive from those who claim to have contacted them indicate that both masters and their chelas are three a penny! As far as I am aware, no master, either incarnate or discarnate, has ever favored me with his presence. The simple manifestation and recognition of the ghosts of my two grandfathers mean more to me than a whole truckload of colorful personalities claiming to be the twelve disciples.

A large number of alleged mediums emphasize their supposed contact with masters and other personalities, especially if the latter be *ancient Egyptians*. I would like readers especially to note that I am not decrying the probability that the ancient Egyptians and other civilizations had esoteric and other knowledge that escapes us today. Much that has been written about the esoterics of these civilizations is conjecture, fiction, with – here and there – a grain of truth. In certain extremely rare instances there may have been paranormal manifestations, either subjectively or objectively, of learned, discarnate personalities, but I feel it is wise to regard even these instances with discrimination.

I am sure that if I regarded as truth all the claims that mediums and others made about having made contact with wise personalities of the ancient world, I should come to the conclusion that the ether – or whatever term you may prefer to use – was simply jammed with kings, queens, and high priests and priestesses from ancient Egypt, Atlantis, Mu, Babylonia, and early China. One must never forget that the subconscious or unconscious minds are capable of producing all manner of impressions, pleasant or otherwise. We have scarcely touched the fringe of this vast subject.

THE UNCONSCIOUS DESIRE FOR RECOGNITION

There is within all of us a deep, unconscious desire for some kind of prominence and recognition. Unconsciously we all want to "be somebody" and to achieve great things. That is why thousands of people spend time and money hunting their ancestors in the hope that one of them may be a titled person or at least a figure of national or world importance. How much easier it is to claim that one is in touch with King Asoka, Cleopatra, Nefertiti, Shakespeare, St Paul, or even Jesus Christ Himself, either directly or via one's pet medium? So let us be analytical and discriminating. If my readers could have my mail for just three months it would be a revelation to them. The colorful and fantastic dreams and hallucinations of the schizophrenic are half-brothers of the visions of those who claim to be in contact with an etherial world.

ON DEVELOPING ONE'S PSYCHIC TALENTS

Many people have asked me what they might do to develop into seers and clairvoyants. They hope to induce some of the types of psychic sensitivity which I, and a handful of other folk, possess. My answer is always the same: Don't!

I am definitely against "development." If one has any marked psychic faculty, I feel it is best to let it develop itself. Everyone has *latent* paranormal powers, but quite likely nature – or God, if you like – intended these to remain below the level of conscious mind. If it were otherwise, nature would aid the development of the ability.

YOU CANNOT PRY OPEN A ROSEBUD

It is like nature unfolding a rose with sunshine. One cannot pry a rosebud open in an effort to make it bloom. So it is with the psychic gift. Many are ruined psychologically and sometimes physically by this effort to "develop."

Often I get letters, like this one from Miss M. McF., asking advice on special "clairvoyant diets": "I am trying to improve my psychic sensitivity by having a strict vegetarian diet, even omitting eggs or any form of animal fat. So far, however, it doesn't seem to make much difference to my achieving clairvoyance. Also, I get dizzy."

No one will achieve clairvoyance by half-starving himself; he will only get anemia, debility, and general ill-health. Clairvoyance, especially if one practices it professionally, entails considerable physical strain. It is important to have adequate vitamin B which is best obtained from brewer's yeast and plenty of food, especially animal protein. If nature had intended man to be vegetarian, she would not have given him the gastric secretions that digest meat.

I have also been asked if there are certain places that seem to inspire my paranormal gifts more than others.

I prefer quiet places, but really it matters little. It is rather like asking an artist if he can draw better in some places than in others. A true artist can draw anywhere, although he may have preferences.

ESP, DRUGS AND ALCOHOL

As to the possible stimulating effects of alcohol or any of the psychedelic drugs, such as LSD, I am a teetotaler, and I never take drugs of any kind. I understand the nature and the effect of the psychedelic drugs, but I cannot see that any such drugs would be helpful to a psychic sensitive.

SEX AND PSYCHIC PHENOMENA

Generally, I believe seership and marriage to be incompatible, unless the partner who is the sensitive is in complete harmony at all levels with his or her mate.

There may be a relationship between sex and psychic phenomena, as in the case of poltergeists. I believe that repressed sex can *cause* psychic phenomena. Psychics have much magnetism and a wide magnetic field. This often gives them a personality which some, not knowing otherwise, mistake for "sex appeal." It is just that something extra. Musicians often have it, and some artists, but as real sensitives are so few, I have not enough examples to determine whether they are generally more sexy than nonsensitives. It seems likely that they may be.

THE TWO-EDGED SWORD OF SENSITIVITY

Basically, I am highly nervous and alert (moon in Gemini at birth) and can get answers almost before the questions are put. I am prone to phobias that are deeply rooted as a result of my early life. I accept these and try to do my best within these limitations, knowing that others also have limitations, perhaps worse than mine. I have been much compensated in other respects.

Believe me, psychic sensitivity is indeed a two-edged sword. While it may seem fascinating to be able to foresee events, to be able to "see" over distances of thousands of miles, to be able to "see" into human bodies and in to the earth itself, there are extreme dangers of which the would-be sensitive is completely ignorant or, if not ignorant of them, he believes he lives such a good life that nothing evil can harm him. These people should take their heads out of the sand.

I do not doubt that the sufferings I experienced at the hands of my parents did much to sharpen my sensitivity, but I like to believe that the "sharpening process" also arose during those merry hours when I sat on Grandad Hazel's shoulders and sang at the top of my boyish voice to the tune of his fiddle.

Occultism is not a subject for everybody. Alas, it is the very people who should keep clear of it who wallow in it. Some folk escape via drugs, some via drink, sex, nervous breakdowns, perhaps religion; but there is a large percentage who flee earthly reality via occultism. And it is these tragic figures who need protection from the racketeers who would prey upon them and use them as a means of making money. I take the view so well-expressed in an ancient adage: "Those who know, do not speak. Those who speak, do not know."

CHAPTER THIRTEEN

Jane Roberts and the Teachings of Seth

In the early part of 1970, I was asked if I would write a cover blurb for a book by a new figure on the psychic scene, a young sensitive named Jane Roberts. The book was entitled, *Seth Speaks*. I was struck at once by the clarity of style and by the obvious intellect of the author, but I could not predict that the entity "Seth" would go on to dictate a virtual shelf of books and that Jane would become world-famous as a medium.

Jane and I shared many conversations about things paranormal, and it was in the summer of 1974 that I conducted a lengthy interview with her in order to fix a number of her thoughts for my own research. When she made her transition in 1985, there was sorrow for the loss of her physical presence, her psychical wit and her charm, but I knew that she had now entered the Great Mystery about which she wrote so beautifully.

On September 9, 1963, Jane Roberts had finished her supper and was sitting down to her usual evening session of poetry writing. Her husband Robert F. Butts was in the studio, three rooms away, working on his painting. Jane picked up her pen and stared at the blank piece of paper, waiting for the creative juices to start flowing. She had no reason to suspect that this night would be any different from others in her life.

All at once she found herself in the throes of an experience she could only liken to a drugless trip. "Between one normal minute and the next, a fantastic avalanche of radical, new ideas burst into my head, with tremendous force, as if my skull were some sort of receiving station, tuned up to unbearable volume," Jane wrote later, describing the experience. "Not only ideas came through this channel, but sensations, intensified and pulsating. I was tuned in, turned on – whatever you want to call it – *connected* to some incredible source of energy."

The startled young woman had no time to call out to her husband, but her pen began feverishly to cover the page before her with a multitude of thoughts and feelings traversing her being. Consciousness and reality were all turned around, and the revelations she was receiving seemed to be invading her body, taking up permanent residence. Feeling and knowing became one and the same thing, and the importance of intellectual knowledge paled before the mighty sensation of wisdom gained beyond the power of reasoning.

At the same time all this was happening a small part of Jane seemed to be remembering that this same scenario had been enacted the night before in a dream, but it had been forgotten. Somehow, the two experiences were connected.

When time and space again became the familiar limitations of her world, Jane found herself giving a title to the barrage of words that had flooded the paper: *The Physical Universe of Idea Construction*. The title fit the hastily scribbled notes, but none of the material fit into Jane's previous convictions regarding life and the human psyche.

This revelatory experience turned Jane upside-down, and eventually led to a series of dramatic events that forever changed her life.

Following the experience she began to remember her dreams in great detail, an ability she had never before had. Two of the dreams were precognitive, which had never happened to her before, either.

Jane and Rob were intrigued and bought a book on extrasensory perception. Perhaps this could explain the bizarre occurrences that the revelatory experience seemed to have unlocked. They did not realize it, but the purchase of this book was another link in a chain that was inevitably leading them towards the extraordinary.

Jane, a poet and fiction writer, had been expressing discontent over her chosen subject matter when Rob picked up the ESP book. He jokingly suggested that she try nonfiction and encouraged her to write a layman's approach to psychic development.

Jane's interest in the field had already been piqued, and Rob's suggestion challenged her. She would write her editor and propose a book on extrasensory perception. The idea was to devise a series of experiments to test whether an ordinary person could develop his psychism. Jane would use herself as the guinea pig. To her surprise, Jane was told the project had been accepted.

THE FIRST EXPERIMENTS

The couple decided to begin the experiments with a ouija board. Their landlady found an old board in the attic for them, and with a little embarrassment they dusted it off and began.

The first two times they tried to move the planchette, nothing happened. Neither Jane nor Rob was surprised, for they had little faith in the board's capabilities. On the third try both were amazed when the planchette started to tremble underneath their fingers, then slowly move across the board.

The board spelled out answers to their questions, and the two discovered they had contacted an entity calling itself Frank Withers, who claimed to have lived in their New York town of Elmira and died there in the 1940s. He gave his nationality as English, and told them he had a wife named Ursula Alteri who had been of Italian descent.

Jane and Rob still could not overcome a feeling of foolishness, so they were surprised when this information actually checked out via town records. They tried the board a few more times and contacted the same Frank Withers, who gave them reincarnational material which proved impossible to verify.

THE COMING OF SETH

On December 8, 1963, Jane and Rob again sat down at the ouija board, for what they supposed would be another semi-interesting evening with the almost taciturn Withers. Instead, they received longer responses denoting a far greater intelligence. When addressed as Frank Withers, the entity rather drily responded, "I prefer not to be called Frank Withers. That personality was rather colorless."

Jane and Rob shrugged at each other, uncertain as to how to regard this. At least the sessions were beginning to produce some humor. Rob inquired as to how the entity wished to be addressed and was answered:

"You may call me whatever you choose. I call myself Seth. It fits the me of me, the personality more clearly approximating the whole self I am, or am trying to be."

Furthermore, Seth stated that Jane and Rob had other names which more accurately represented "the sum of your various personalities in the past and the future." His name for Rob was Joseph, his name for Jane, Rupert.

The session lasted until past midnight, and at its conclusion Jane and Rob stayed up discussing the situation. Jane was convinced that Seth was a part of either hers or Rob's subconscious. She could not accept the idea that

Seth might represent a separate entity who had survived death.

The couple conducted two more sessions, with Jane growing increasingly disturbed. She had begun to anticipate the board's replies. Rob would ask a question, and each time Jane would hear the answer in her head before the board could spell it out. The answers came faster and faster, first in complete sentences, then in complete paragraphs. The board seemed clumsy and slow in comparison.

Finally during a session on the night of December 15, 1963, the compulsion to speak grew to an intolerable level. Jane was determined to fight off this development, but she found her curiosity growing stronger. Then Rob asked a question and the board began its regular, laborious spelling out of the answer. All at once it broke off in mid-sentence.

In *The Seth Material*, an account of the birth and development of the Seth phenomenon, Jane described what happened next:

"I felt as if I were standing, shivering, on the top of a high diving board, trying to make myself jump while all kinds of people were waiting impatiently behind me. Actually, it was the words that pushed at me – they seemed to rush through my mind. In some crazy fashion I felt as if they'd back me up, piles of nouns and verbs in my head until they closed everything else off if I didn't speak them. And without really knowing how or why, I opened my mouth and let them out."

There were many more changes and surprises to come in the ensuing years of contact with Seth, but for now the most dramatic event had occurred. Seth was no longer restricted to the board and began to express his own personality more clearly. Unhampered by the board, the material turned with increasing facility to complex subjects that first attacked, then changed the Roberts' total response to the universe and their own role within it.

A POET AND A PAINTER – AND THEIR FRIEND

There was nothing in either Jane or Rob's early lives to which a psychical researcher could have pointed and reached the conclusion that a psychic was in the making. Jane had never manifested any extrasensory abilities that she could remember prior to Seth's arrival.

Jane began writing poetry as a child, and her creative process was very similar to mysticism although she did not know this at the time. Other than this, there was nothing to indicate that the bright young girl would grow to a psychic of substantial ability. Her parents were divorced, and Jane lived with her invalid mother in an Irish neighborhood. They were always extremely poor, and mother and daughter did not enjoy a close relationship. A poetry scholarship got Jane to college and out of her relentlessly poor life.

Rob was a product of what Jane calls "social Protestantism." His family was middle-class American, and they were not steady churchgoers.

Neither Jane nor Rob would have picked themselves for the highly unusual work they now found themselves doing. Regardless of how it happened, they sat for two weekly sessions since 1963, and the Seth Material came to cover several dozen looseleaf notebooks.

At first Jane was reluctant to give in too much to Seth, and she insisted on keeping her eyes open while she paced around the room. Later, she liked to sit in a rocker while in trance, and though she went through a period of closing her eyes for a couple of years, she returned to open eyes, though half-lidded. Seth usually announced his presence by taking Jane's glasses off and casting them to the floor or a nearby piece of furniture. The volume of his voice went through various stages of development. It was resonant and conversational – although the first time it boomed out at extraordinary volume Rob was a bit taken aback.

Rob's role from the first was that of scribe and querente. Though they once used a tape recorder, Rob maintained meticulous notes. He recorded changes in Jane or Seth as he took down Seth's words verbatim, and he had the pleasure of conversing with Seth, something that Jane at times wished she were able to do.

Both were tremendously affected personally, with the lessons learned through the weekly sessions spilling out into their everyday lives. Rob, a painter, benefited through what Seth terms "inner visual data" and even received a few art instructions via this unorthodox "friend."

Jane saw her latent psychic abilities flower under Seth's tutelage. She received specific instructions from Seth on how to develop these talents, and she evolved in areas of telepathy, clairvoyance, and precognition. Of particular interest to her were her out-of-body experiences (OBE), which sometimes occurred under curious circumstances while she was in trance and Seth was present.

TESTING SETH

Early in the sessions, the Gallaghers, good friends of the Roberts were taking a vacation in Puerto Rico. Seth was asked to demonstrate his own psychic abilities by checking in on them from time to time, providing information which could be checked for veracity when the vacationing Gallaghers returned.

In the midst of a session when Seth was giving impressions of the Gallagher's trip, Jane suddenly found herself in the back seat of a cab, staring at the thick and stubby neck of the driver. The vehicle took a sharp turn and Jane was thrown to a corner of the cab.

While all this was occurring, Jane's physical body was seated comforta-bly in her Elmira living room, and Seth was giving impressions similar to what Jane was undergoing. The return of the Gallaghers confirmed this episode as correct. It was especially memorable to the vacationing couple because of the extremely sharp turn made by the cab driver.

Another OBE occurred in response to a letter written by two brothers in California, who wished to test Seth's abilities themselves. They asked that the entity describe their home. Jane was against the idea, but Seth seemed unperturbed. Shortly after the beginning of a session, Jane found herself hovering in mid-air overlooking what was obviously a neighborhood in Southern California. Back in Elmira, Seth was describing what Jane was seeing, though she was only distantly aware of his voice.

In this instance, Seth spoke in the first person, as though he were personally surveying the scene. Actually, it was Jane's consciousness that had separated itself from the body. She found she was able to shift her position for a better view, and from this better vantage point Seth was able to describe the areas surrounding the brothers' home in great detail.

The information received that evening was sent in a letter to the two California brothers who wrote back, confirming the accuracy of the infor-mation. They later signed an affidavit which the Butts' placed in their files.

Jane steadily became convinced that Seth was not a part of her subcon-scious, though he made use of it during their contact. For a long time the fear that she was only listening to a clever part of her own consciousness inhibited the sessions, but Jane felt that her constant probing and question-ing ultimately contributed to the scope of the sessions. Never once did she stop and say, "This is it; this is what's happening," and thereby halt her own progress at that point. By constantly opening herself up to new ideas and possibilities regarding Seth and the material he presented, Jane believed that she had helped to widen the range and quality of information that was imparted.

CREATING REALITY BY THOUGHT AND EMOTION

Essential to an understanding of Seth is an awareness of his basic teachings. His approach to reality helped to free Jane and Rob from the time/space continuum to which they thought they were chained, and Seth's concept of the personality is not only challenging, but sheds light on the nature of his relationship to Jane.

Central to Seth's teaching is the premise that all reality is created by thought and emotion. Specifically, what a person thinks and feels forms his surrounding reality.

This process of reality-building is not static, however. It is dynamic. Therefore, reality is constantly changing, and it follows that a conscious awareness of this process can change any reality for the better. Man is not at the mercy of past events. He cannot blame his parents, his church, his schooling, or any other person or event for "making him the way he is." In ignorance he may have made himself an unhappy person, but with conscious awareness he can make himself a happy, productive individual. *Because man makes his own reality, he can therefore change it.*

Seth has also developed an extensive theory of personality. It is scarcely a ten-words-or-less theory, but it begins by attacking the supposition that the conscious personality called John or Mary or whatever is one person. John or Mary might be personality manifestations of the same source entity, even though they exist concurrently in physical reality.

THE ETERNAL NOW

It is impossible to extend Seth's concept of personality without drawing in a familiar metaphysical concept, that of the Eternal Now, the Specious Present, or other terms which specifically refer to a reality freed from the limitations of time. According to the precept, there is no past, present, or future – all exist as one. Time is but an arbitrary system imposed upon this three-dimensional, physical reality. It is a reality construct that personalities on this plane have created, but they are not bound to it anymore than they are bound to their other creations.

In terms of this concept of the Eternal Now, one source self may be manifesting itself in several dimensions at once. Each personality would operate under the artificial limitations of the plane which it inhabits, and depending upon the degree of development, would be aware or unaware of these various aspects of itself operating on other levels.

These concepts of time and personality intertwine particularly in the phenomenon known as reincarnation. According to Seth, all lives, or incarnations, on a specific plane are lived simultaneously. This does not rule out "past" lives, but it does require a different approach to the subject.

An individual, acting according to the laws of his particular plane of existence, will either see these lives simultaneously, or fit them into that plane's existing time structure. On this plane, because of the division of time into past, present, and future, it is convenient to perceive these various incarnations as neatly arranged into these three categories of time.

THE MIND IS THE BUILDER

Seth's belief in mind as the builder expands the concept of personality in a unique way. Since thoughts and emotions create reality, then dreams, too, have a separate reality. When a person dreams of himself, he is seeing a fragment of his own personality. Furthermore, this idea extends to other areas. In particular, it extends to an area which Seth calls the probable self.

"According to Seth," Jane explained, "each of us has counterparts in other systems of reality; not identical selves or twins – but other selves who are part of our entity, developing ideas in a different way than we are here."

PROBABLE SELVES

Probable selves are likened by Seth to distant relations, who are not as close to us as our reincarnational selves. To further explain, Seth proposed the metaphor of a tape recorder. An individual is the master tape; it has numberless channels. Each channel represents "a portion of the whole self, each existing in a different dimension, yet all a part of the whole self... When the stereophonic channel is turned on, the selves then know their unity. Their various realities merge in the overall perceptions of the whole self... Ultimately the inner ego must bring about comprehension on the parts of the simultaneous selves. Each portion of the whole self must become aware of the other parts."

To add further fascination to this concept, Seth suggests that with any given event there are a number of ways to experience it. To man's ego, it is perceived as a physical event, but each probable way to apprehend this event will be explored by every probable self, according to its own time system. Specifically, if a person has a choice between three possible courses of action, he must choose one and then realize it. The other two possibilities will be experienced as well, but not in physical reality. These probable actions are definitely perceived, however, and "it is such experience that makes up the existence of the probable selves just as dream actions make up the experience of the dreaming self," according to Seth. Seth also maintains that all layers of the whole self continually exchange information on a subconscious level.

In these terms, Jane Roberts may then have been a physical manifestation of the personality Seth; she may even have been one of his probable selves. She could have been part of a completely other whole self, separate from the whole self of which Seth is part.

Jane was aware of all possibilities, and she was constantly seeking more. She continually attempted to better understand the relationship she had with Seth and to explain the nature of their contact.

It is difficult to place Jane Roberts in a category, for she herself refused any attempts to analyze either her trance abilities or the phenomenon of Seth in the old, traditional way. Perhaps she was right, too, in this insistence, for the material that Seth imparted through her was of a tremendously high quality, not often seen in more traditional examples of mediumship and spirit guides. It will be fascinating to see how the material is evaluated as the years go by.

A CONVERSATION WITH JANE ROBERTS

Brad Steiger: Jane, since you have become either a willing or unwilling medium, what do you now consider yourself to be? Are you a writer who has had some kind of growth attached? Are you a channel, a medium? In your mind, how has your life changed since Seth came on the scene?

Jane Roberts: I am afraid I can't give an easy answer. In the beginning I was quite curious, amazed, and shocked, as you can tell from some of my writings. It took me some time to realize that all of this is highly connected with creativity in the highest type of fashion. Now I just try to think of myself as a person who has these various kinds of abilities.

Do you think there was anything in your early life that prepared you for this?

Yes, but I didn't realize this when the Seth Material started. I have written poetry since the time I was a child and was always, as far back as I can remember, highly involved with this feeling of mystic communication with the earth and with everything around me. I never considered myself psychic, though. I wasn't familiar at all with even the way the term would be used.

You didn't separate things, in other words.

No, I didn't. From my later experience I can tell that an awful lot of the inspirational type of poetry I did was a stepping stone to what I am doing now. I'd be working two or three nights in a row on a poem, while in an altered state of consciousness. I didn't know, I thought that all writers and poets did this. I think that it is just a short step from that kind of acceleration of consciousness into this other kind of thing.

What about someone who would look at this phenomenon from a more skeptical point of view? They could feel that Seth is only an extension of the creative faculty and that you are like Edgar Bergen and Charlie McCarthy, or that Seth is simply your alter ego.

Well, it's according to your definitions, I guess, because I don't see Seth the way many people do. I try very hard to keep it extremely open. You know, I am writing a book for Prentice-Hall now that will probably be called *Aspect Psychology*.

Can you say a little bit about that?

Actually, the whole idea for the book has come from my own questions about the nature of personalities such as Seth. From my own experience and from letters I've received from people I think it's clear that psychic experience hasn't been given a framework in our country. People need this kind of framework to use in order to examine their own experiences. They've either had to go spiritualistic and say, "Yes, these are spirit guides walking around and talking to me," or the psychiatrist said, "Look, these are hallucinations and you really need help."

This kind of thing has been going on for centuries. It is a part of our heritage that we haven't any accepted framework that people can use to explain the true dimensions of their experiences. Hopefully, *Aspects* will be providing that kind of framework, at least in which questions can be asked.

I have never thought of Seth as a spirit guide in the way that most people do. When I say that, though, the usual response is, "Oh, yes, he is just a part of you." But none of us knows what we are yet, only what we've been told. I think the entire range of the self includes so much more than we are usually aware of on the conscious level, but we can find out. I mean, it is possible to move through the dimensions of your own being.

You probably dislike labels, but if someone pressured you, how would you describe yourself? In view of what you have just said would you call yourself a medium?

I just don't know. I accept the term in that this is what people say. I think Seth is something besides what I am, for example.

But not in the sense, then, of "Seth comes to guide me and Seth tells me what stock to buy and Seth tells me what to wear today."

I wouldn't think of asking those kinds of questions. And I don't let my students use him as a crutch.

In the class situation, does Seth come as a resource person, from time to time, in addition to teaching?

As a resource person in what way?

Well, you don't let them use Seth as a crutch but you let them ask questions.

Oh, yes, they ask all kinds of questions.

Like, "my mother-in-law says I shouldn't do such and such and is she right?" Do you let them get into mundane matters like that?

They don't ask questions like that.

They stay more on the higher, more philosophical kind of questions?

Well, Seth has just finished another book called *The Nature of Personal Reality*. The idea of that book is that we form our own reality right down to daily events through our beliefs. Lately, then, some of the students' questions have been along the line of, "I have this effect in my life, can you help me see what the belief is behind it? Or, "What do I do from here?" Seth might then tell them a method or a way of finding this out for themselves. So if I were thinking of a term, something I would consider myself as, I know the term I would use, but it wouldn't make much sense to other people. The term is "Speaker."

As you define Speaker in Seth Speaks?

Right, even to some extent as Emerson would define it. It is someone who tries to ferret out the secrets – if you want to call them secrets – of the universe, and translate them in some fashion.

Do you ever feel resentful that you were chosen for this? Obviously, there is some process of selectivity here that may be too subtle for us to fully understand.

Well, not the "why me?" type of thing, but in the beginning I certainly did wonder what the hell had happened.

What about your husband? How does Rob relate to all of this?

He is great, absolutely fantastic.

Do you think because you have been together before, or maybe your sex roles were reversed before?

Yes, and not only that. The way our abilities work together is really wild. I don't think we could have the Seth books as they exist without Rob. For example, details drive me up the wall. I can get really accelerated and turned on with the idea – I always have – that we each have a consciousness and we can do all kinds of wild things with it. I don't want to be hampered; I just want to go.

You would find it laborious, then to take notes.

Oh, Rob does that.

Obviously, Rob must have been open to this before or it would have blown his mind.

Neither of us knew a damn thing about it, so in the beginning we were both very cautious. We watched to see if my personality was all right or if I started doing strange things.

People will write to me and want to know if I sense Seth's presence or if he is around me all the time. Well, if I had seen or felt him around while I was doing other things, that would have been it. I didn't encourage that kind of thing and I really don't now, either.

Some who have been at your sessions have said that they have never seen Seth arrive. They look away, turn back, and he is there.

I think some students have seen him come.

This is an interesting kind of overlap, as it deals with some of the ways we apprehend reality. Would you consider the poltergeist as one of the aspects of our plastic reality?

Oh, that's a good thought. Yes.

It is a similar situation in which objects are seen in motion when they land, but they are never seen to take off. Do you think there is some kind of connection here?

I don't know. Many people do sense Seth when he is coming. I think there are different kinds of acceleration that some people can pick up in terms of sound. They don't hear it, though, they feel something quickening. Poltergeist activity could be the same kind of thing.

Yes, but the poltergeist is probably some externalization of an aspect of personality. Are you saying, then, that Seth would be an externalization of an aspect of your personality?

No, you missed me. It's easy to do, because I don't know exactly what I meant. It's like there was some kind of an acceleration that I sense with Seth, and in various altered states of consciousness there is a certain kind of speed that you can't verbalize, but you can feel. Now, the same kind of speed could be behind whatever force it is that moves the objects, or whatever.

As far as the Seth thing, I can explain it for now according to personality aspects. For the *Aspects* book – which is being written in altered states, by the way – I am making up some words and getting by with others, so now, instead of "entity," I use "source-self." The idea is that our entire reality exists outside of the three-dimensional field. I am trying to explain it in terms of two things; psychological reality, or psychic reality; and energy.

The source-self would be energy that identifies itself. As it strikes the three-dimensional field, it comes into a wave formation in terms of energy. Then, as it strikes the field, it changes to a particle type of thing, which would be the physical body, the physical self. Thereafter it acts as a particle, which I then call the focus "personality," because it is focused in physical reality. This source-self, though, being energy, radiates out in all directions in other realities of which we are unaware. Therefore we would be an aspect of that source-self.

Now, there would be other aspects in other kinds of reality and to me Seth would be one of those aspects. I think those aspects become the basic components of our personalities, as we know them.

There are persons who from time to time claim, with psychiatric substantiation, that they are twelve personalities in one.

Right.

Is this really that unique? Are we all twelve or however many personalities in one?

Right. I think that these are like basic components, but that some people can isolate them. I also think they represent something entirely different from what we think they do. Consequently, to call Seth a spirit guide is to me like putting him down. People don't understand it, though. They think I am putting him down by saying he is not.

We know so little, and when we try to think in terms of a Seth or anything like that we project our limited ideas into them. We also project these limited ideas into things like life after death, but when we do that we think in terms of good and evil. We also think in terms of one personhood, where there may actually be something like multi-personhood. These are the lines along which I am working right now.

Thomas Edison believed that the "soul" was like a swarm of bees. How to you regard that?

Right, okay.

Then we might have a bee from this person and a bee from that person, and so forth. Is that what you are speaking of?

I'm not sure when you put it that way, but sort of, I suppose. However, I think a Seth is in a terrific position, as far as we're concerned. I have to deal with physical reality in very definite terms, while he does not. I believe he is a strong enough portion of the source-self, in whatever terms, so that he can explain some of the reality that we don't understand. If he is free enough of our dimension, yet close enough so that he can explain, we are better able to understand.

Why do you think he bothers?

Probably, because I bother.

Is there an identification with the role of teacher?

Well, from the time I was a kid and writing this poetry, I was always trying to reach further than you could go, to find things out. I became a young adult, looking around and saying, "God, what a mess." The early poetry and science fiction that I did was all extremely pessimistic. It began to look as if nothing made any sense at all. We were at the mercy of our pasts and couldn't get free of it, so people were really in pretty rough shape. I think I wanted to understand so badly that my need somehow accelerated certain portions of my consciousness, allowing me to pull in this thing, but I think that the need or the impetus had to come strongly from me, I really do.

So there would be something about you that attracted something like Seth.

Yes, yes.

Like magnetically pulling it to you?

Right.

Suppose you were suddenly the recipient of several million dollars, and with your desire to study the paranormal, you put together a foundation or institution. What direction would you like the research to take?

I've never been turned on by the idea of a foundation, mainly because I like to work solitary. Rob and I are really very private-type people. I couldn't think of setting up something like that.

All right, then, you are behind the scene and you hire doctors and researchers. What direction would you like them to take in their study?

I don't know if I would do it that way. I think I would try to get a bunch of people together, regardless of what they were in, who were fairly intelligent – not gullible – gifted intuitively and intellectually at the same time. I don't think I would work with trying to scientifically prove anything. I think there are plenty of people already doing that. Instead, I think I would try to teach people and see what they could do.

Do you think our present researchers are going about it in the proper way?

Let's put it this way: I think they are going about it the only way they can with the beliefs they've got.

To me, the most important thing of the Seth Material is that we make our own reality. I think, then, if I did have a foundation, the biggest thing I could do to help people would be to show them how their thoughts and feelings form the world, form their daily family life to the nation and the entire world. I think that would be the most liberating thing anybody could ever do – if it would be done. It would free people from all other kinds of areas and would be far more important then scientifically proving to some scientist that out-of-body travel is legitimate.

Whatever you do on the outside isn't going to make a damn bit of difference unless you change the thought pattern. Seth goes into this even further than on the individual level and deals with it in *The Nature of Personal Reality.*

For centuries people have been negatively creating reality constructs. It is time to learn to make positive reality constructs.

Right. Seth even goes into the matter of how your emotions can cause the weather. Say you have a certain emotion, and there are certain hormonal changes in the body. Therefore certain chemicals go into the air, and your feelings then become part of the physical atmosphere. The atmosphere is formed *en masse* by this chemical give and take between us and what we would call space. Buildups occur, and balance is kept between the exteriors formed and the interior emotional storms. That is, you might have a population with a strong racial problem. They might have a riot, but they might instead have a flood.

This is the whole idea of the Seth Material, and to me it is the most important part. It frees the individual.

It is more important to you than making a glass move across the table?

Yes.

You are a creative person. How do you feel about someone else having jumped into your mind, used your body, and written another book on its own?

You see, I don't look at it that way.

Do you think you are being physically or emotionally drained, for example, the way Fletcher was with medium Arthur Ford?

It is all the way the person regards it, I think. With Ford, it could have been his ideas about Fletcher that caused the drain.

Some spirit guides seem to ignore the way a medium may feel, but Seth is very considerate of your physical well-being, isn't he?

Yes, but again I think that is because I look at it in a different way. For example, I am refreshed after a session, and I can have a session go on for ages. But again I think it is because I don't feel used.

I think my abilities as a writer are extremely important. Without them Seth couldn't do as well as he does. That is the reason we work so well together.

He uses you as a tool, then? Perhaps he is not that gifted verbally, or he is not gifted in getting the message down?

No, because in the first place I don't think these personalities exist in a realm where, well, to say they are equipped verbally is meaningless. I don't think they deal with words. I think they deal with kinds of concepts that we translate, and they might be translated automatically by using all the creative ability I've got on an unconscious level. This is in response to something that is not originally verbal, though. I do think that what we think of as creativity is just the tail end of something that is fantastic, and I have tuned into that whatever it is.

The interplay is interesting, though, because Seth did not choose a shop girl or an illiterate person to come through.

Well, let's put it this way. I get a lot of stuff through the mail that is supposed to be automatic writing – and it's absolute rubbish. I've gotten letters from a woman who thinks she is hearing from Socrates, and a nine-year-old kid could do better. It's just trash. But I do think that in each way every person tries to tune into this revelatory knowledge. I do think that according to whatever abilities you have built up in yourself you are able to interpret it, but a lot of that depends on you.

To me it still means that this ability has been in me and I just didn't know it. I think this kind of experience does enable people to bring out their abilities if it is done correctly.

What kind of element within our educational system do you think is most needed in order to create a more positive attitude?

It goes back to what I said before. Kids should be taught that they create their own reality. My students try to teach their kids this, and they are really doing a pretty decent job of it.

Kids know this intuitively, don't they?

Right, but instead they are taught, "No, it's not you, it's these other elements." Or they are taught, particularly in religious terms, that they were born with original sin and they are bad right off the bat. They are taught not to use their imaginations, really, to just crush the inner self. I think this is terrible, and particularly wrong in terms of illness. There, if you create your reality, then you create good health or lousy health or whatever it might be because of your beliefs. If you start telling a kid that he'll get sick because there's a virus going around, then he'll react to this miserable suggestion.

Do you feel, as so many people do, that we are entering a period of transition? Are we on the brink of a spiritual, evolutionary leap forward?

I don't know. I hope we are. This is difficult for me, though, because I believe all time exists at once. Therefore anything we do in the present automatically changes the past and therefore the future. This means you are asking questions from different levels.

I do not believe that there is any point where all of a sudden Earth is going to be holy, blessed, true and great, and everyone's consciousness is going to fly like wings, without any effort on peoples' part.

Do you believe, however, that there is a group evolution as well as an individual evolution taking place?

Yes, yes.

And that maybe that is what we are talking about when we speak of all being part of one?

Yes. Perhaps I am overstressing my reaction, though, because people talk so blithely about the Aquarian Age. So yes, and I do hope, particularly, that the young kids now can start really doing things with their consciousness. And even though kids get into a whole lot of trouble with a whole lot of occult nonsense with all these cults, they are beginning to look inward and do things with their consciousness. Despite the trouble with drugs and things like that, I think the generation of kids who are now in their twenties will make a big difference, I really do.

Do you see any specific dangers coming up for these youths?

No, I guess not. I don't even know if I see any particular dangers in the cult thing. If they weren't doing that, they'd be doing something else. Also, there is one thing that gets me in trouble with the rest of the field (and I don't really care, because I think it is so wrong): I personally do not believe in good spirits, bad spirits, devils and all. This, to me, is hogwash. You read a book and it says how to work the ouija board. It also says to look out because bad spirits could come through on the board. I don't know how many letters I get from people who get these "evil spirits" just because they believe they will.

If someone has hated his father for years and won't admit it, then the ouija board can suddenly tell him, "Your father is going to die tomorrow," or "Kill your father," or some other stupid thing. Instead of realizing that these are natural hates that he has buried inside and wouldn't admit to, he has read a book telling him there are evil spirits around. Naturally, he then thinks it is an evil spirit telling him to kill his father.

I think that people who warn the public away from ouija boards and the like by saying that there are evil spirits who are going to possess them, do more harm than any evil spirit would ever think of doing.

What about The Exorcist theme?

I haven't read the book and I don't intend to. I gather, though, that it is based on the ideas of possession as they have been understood and misinterpreted through the ages.

It is a fairly Roman Catholic interpretation.

Right. See, I think we are so fantastic in our spiritual and biological nature that we are so much more than we realize. With revelatory knowledge, I mean, information and knowledge that wouldn't ordinarily come with regular consciousness. The question is, "Where does it come from?" Now regardless of where it comes from I think we could personify that source with our ideas of what is great, honest, true, good, or whatever, and this might be extremely necessary. Otherwise, we probably couldn't get the information.

When you say, though, that this is from a definite other source, a spirit guide outside of me, then you are saying that humanity as a whole cannot get this information. It is not a human thing to do; it is not within our capabilities and it is always outside of us. I don't believe that. I believe that it is created in the deep sources of our being – say our psyche or our soul.

For example, Seth many times calls himself a "bridge personality." When he comes through, he is formed by parts of my psyche and parts of his psyche. There is also a representation of something else, that can't really be represented. The only way it can be represented is the way it is received.

Then Seth is both outside and inside?

Right.

Then there is a realm or a dimension where there are external personalities – external to us, that is – with whom we can come into contact or reach out and touch?

Yes, but I don't believe anybody knows the *extent* of the external or internal quality. That is one of the things I am trying to do right now. There are about ten levels that I can recognize and tune into and get different types of information from. Now, many of these give me creative products. They are each different, though, and in them I perceive things in a different kind of fashion. It is a different inner kind of feeling I get in each, and that is what I am just studying. I try to do them and then afterward write down what I can about the different kinds of perception; that is, what you get, why you get it in a certain way, and so forth.

The lines between daily life and creativity are really funny. It was that sort of thing that led me to *Personality Aspects*. Last year I was working on a book, with two chapters to do, and all of a sudden I got an outline for six or seven more books, plus the whole concept for *Aspects*. I am convinced that *Aspects* came to me because of my need to know. Had I accepted anyone else's interpretations along the way or happily said, "Oh, yes, Seth is a spirit guide in the same old way," then I don't think I would have been led onward to this kind of thing. I think my intellectual questioning is as important as the intuitive part of me. They work together in an odd fashion.

In balance.

Right, though again I don't think I would have gotten the material for these other books without being my particular self.

There is, then, that process of selectivity or interaction that we perhaps cannot fully understand or articulate.

And it is, again, the importance of the individual.

Do you receive any harassment from your community for the work you do?

No. For one thing, I make a point of not using this material to set myself apart from others and say I am different. Also, our best friends are reporters on the local paper, and they always give me great coverage. We enjoy Elmira. Anybody who thought we were kooky probably wouldn't let us know, either.

Oh, one of the interesting things about our class is that people who have this spiritualistically oriented background usually don't like the class. It drives them up the wall because we don't meditate. We keep the lights on, and we drink wine. I stay away from that "Sister Jane" type of thing, which can be played to the hilt, you know.

The main point I try to bring out is that all people have these abilities, and they can bring them all out themselves. Some people go from psychic to psychic to psychic, trying to find the answers to their problems – when the only real answer is that you have to trust yourself. The more you look to somebody else for *the* answer, and are given it by them, the more the other person builds himself up at your expense, and the less capable you feel.

CHAPTER FOURTEEN

Spirit Guides and Apports

Joseph Donnelly of Sebring, Florida said that his psychic talents first manifested themselves in 1917. "Prior to that time I had witnessed intermittent phenomena," he related. "In order to delve into the then seemingly puzzling questions, I attended evening classes and seances with many mediums."

Donnelly was born in New York City in 1899 and, after college, took the New York State examinations and received a degree of Certified Public Accountant. Several thousand people filed for the open competitive civil service examination in New York City, and Donnelly scored number one on this test. He served the City of New York in an executive capacity for fifteen years, resigning in 1950 to continue his career as a public accountant. "I retired in 1963 and moved to Florida," he declared.

Donnelly studied mental telepathy, breath control, hypnotism, occult subjects, and many religions.

"I know and have sat with hundreds of mediums throughout the United States," he said. "In my own experiments I have experienced clairvoyance and clairaudience, independent spirit messages and pictures, in both black and white and colors, independent spirit pictures on silk, skotographs, spirit photography, trumpet and independent spirit voices, universal thought, and lectures from master teachers and guides. I have also experienced materializations in red light and white light, trances, trance control, and the control of my vocal cords for spirit voices without trance."

Donnelly stated that his spirit teachers were of many races and of various religious faiths when they were in their physical bodies. "I have never been a professional public medium," he said.

Brad Steiger: Could you teach me to be a psychic or a medium?

Joseph Donnelly: Everyone is a spirit encased, or imprisoned, in a material body. Therefore, to a degree, everyone is psychic. There does have to be a certain chemicalization of the human body for certain types of mediumship, particularly psychical phenomena. With patience and under the guidance and direction of a good sensitive, anyone can become a medium. However, every pianist cannot become a great artist. This also holds true for training the faculties to receive psychic impressions. The method of trial and error is always advisable.

Do you think there is a hereditary factor in psychic ability?

In my case, my father and my grandfather did have psychic power. But, my father was afraid of it – although his life was saved on a number of occasions because he received spirit warnings. He could also discern certain spirits at times. He told the family of several of these ghostly appearances.

Do you feel there is a drain of physical energy connected with psychicism?

Definitely, because many of the mediums I have known passed to spirit at an early age in their forties and fifties. There is always a constant drain on the professional, or public, medium. They are particularly susceptible to heart ailments and other malfunctions of the body.

Incidentally, very few mediums ever died rich from using their gifts as a sensitive. As you may have discovered, many mediums lose their powers from time to time and, then, their so-called friends quickly desert them. A. J. Davis died friendless and alone. Cheiro died as a pauper. You can read the biographies of others and discover the same patterns.

What advice do you have for someone who is developing psychic ability?

They should pay close attention to their spirit guides and instructors. Test the spirits to see if they are of God, advises the Bible. Incidentally, there are hundreds of references to psychic phenomena in the Bible. When a person passes over to the spirit world, they are not suddenly endowed with great knowledge.

Do you feel psychics are set apart from what we might call "normal," or non-talented, people?

I don't think so. Of course, I would never try to use my power for financial gain by trying to forecast a lottery number or by gambling. I prefer to help in any way I can, and most of the time, this is anonymously. I am principally interested in the art of healing. There is simply too much pain and suffering in the world, and I would like to contribute the little I have learned for the relief of those who seek my help.

Can you use your psychic power all of the time? Or do you have the ability to turn it on and off?

My gift is available only when help is requested and, even then, not as a steady diet. There is only one level of consciousness available for the medium and that is a working arrangement with one's own spirit guides or teachers. They are simply not at the beck and call of the medium for all hours of the day and night. They have their own interests to attend to, as you might guess.

What occurs if they are not available?

If they cannot appear or give the information, then they will send a suitable substitute.

Could you suggest a program for a beginning medium?

Silence and quiet surroundings are essential for meditation. You can be only in a dimly lighted room or in perfect darkness. Learn to concentrate on a single object. Mentally focus on a speck of light, or clear your mind of all extraneous thought.

Then, simply let the thoughts flow through. Try this for 15 minutes to one-half hour each day for a week. It must be at the same time and at regular intervals. This is your appointment with your spirit loved ones, your guides, and teachers. You should also get the names of your teachers for later verification through a medium.

THE "HOW" OF APPORTS

Nearly every medium whom I have met has a ring, bracelet, or some object which has great value to him because it had been "apported" to him as a gift from the spirits during a seance. The term apport comes from the French, *apporter* (to bring) and the spirit friends are often said to bring these objects from great distances to lay them before the mediums. Old coins, semi-precious stones and pieces of jewelry, are not uncommon gifts.

"I would hate to think that your spirit control is some kind of cosmic thief," I said to a medium who had just shown me a beautiful old crucifix which she claimed had been dropped into her lap during a seance.

"Oh, no," she hastened to assure me. "The spirits never steal these gifts. They get them from old treasure chests that have been buried beneath the land or sea for ages. Sometimes the objects may be items that have been lost by owners who are now dead."

Maurice Barbanell has related that going to a seance conducted by the medium Mrs. Kathleen Barkel was like going to a party. Her spirit control, White Hawk, delighted in giving gifts to all the sitters, and the generous guide never failed to provide something of considerable value to every one who attended the seance.

When Barbanell once asked White Hawk the "how" of the mystery of apporting objects, the spirit guide told him that "... I speed up the atomic vibrations until the stones are disintegrated. Then they are brought here and I slow down the vibrations until they become solid again."

Joseph W. Donnelly spoke of a most remarkable apport which was reported to him by one of his students. It seems that just before her mother's funeral, the girl had attached a certain keepsake pin to her shroud. The pin had been buried with her mother. Years later, after the daughter had begun attending instruction in Spiritualism, she was pressing clothes one day when a spirit guide dropped the pin onto her ironing board.

At one of Donnelly's seances, a spirit hand removed an earring from the ear of a woman named Anita. When the lights were turned up at the end of the seance, the earring was nowhere to be found. A week later, a spirit guide told the woman that the earring had been apported to Camp Chesterfield, Indiana, and would remain there until she went there on her vacation. When Anita ultimately traveled to Indiana, she had the earring returned to her while she sat in seance with another medium.

Donnelly stated that apports are not confined to the seance room. "Once on Long Island, about noontime, after a tax conference with one of my clients, I returned to my auto – I am in the habit of closing all the windows and locking the doors – and found a fairly new flashlight lying on the front seat.

"At another time, in my private office, during a daytime conference with a client, a candy bar flew at the client's head – and I kept no candy of any kind in the office. My client jokingly asked me if the place was haunted.

"On another occasion, upon coming back to my closed and locked up auto, I found on my seat a series of coins lined up like a parade of soldiers."

CHAPTER FIFTEEN

Spirit Photography

Reverend Marion Owens, a native New Yorker, was the Supreme Councilor of the Supreme Council of the Independent Associated Spiritualists. Reverend Owens' spiritual gifts have been chronicled in numerous publications, and she is perhaps most well known for her remarkable gift of psychic photography.

One of her psychic photographs shows a saucer-shaped object displacing the congregation in a San Juan church in Puerto Rico. The entire main floor of the church was filled with the materialization while the balcony remained in full view.

In another instance, her camera displaced a sea view at Sidi-Bow-Said, Tunisia, Africa, with a view of the ancient city of Carthage swathed in flames. In some manner yet unexplained by physical science, her film was able to capture the Akashic record of the city as it was being destroyed by the Romans more than 2,000 years ago. On other occasions, Rev. Owens has photographed healing rays, emanations and colors streaming from healers in the process of administering their curative arts.

"The first time I ever used a camera was when I was in the Campfire Girls," Rev. Owens related. When her pictures came back from the developers, they were full of strange, pole-like objects and wispy wires. "It wasn't until years later that I realized that the wires were ectoplasm and the poles were psychic rods," the Spiritualist minister remarked.

Rev. Owens does not feel that the camera is really necessary for such work, but that it merely serves as a prop; spirit "chemicalization" accomplishes the actual phenomenon. "Pictures may be precipitated on silk or photograph prints entirely without benefit of camera," she said.

The talented medium admitted that, in the beginning, only about five out of every 100 shots she would take had a psychic quality. "Now I average about ten in every 100," she commented. "I have the most success at healing sessions and in churches. By experimenting, I have discovered that noon seems to be the best time to take psychic pictures."

It will surprise some readers, who have a certain stereotype of psychics as mystic dreamers and abstractionists, that Marion Owens attended the New York University School of Journalism and took nine years of postgraduate work in business administration. She also attended Hunter College and Columbia University and worked as a newspaper reporter, an editorial assistant, and a magazine editor in New York City. Upon leaving the field of journalism, Marion Owens became a court reporter. She freelanced in every municipal, state, and federal court in New York City's five boroughs. Somewhere along this very pragmatic and business-like route, she became interested in developing her latent psychic abilities. She joined the Temple of Light in New York City, and eventually became the pastor of this Spiritualist Church of the Independent Associated Spiritualists.

PHOTOGRAPHING ECTOPLASM

Ectoplasm is the name given the substance which is so often noted streaming from mediums. French researcher Dr. Charles Richet christened it, but Baron A. von Schrenck Notzing, a German investigator, gained a medium's permission to "amputate" some of the stuff and analyze it. He found it to be colorless, odorless, slightly alkaline, fluid, with traces of skin discs, minute particles of flesh, sputum, and granulates of the mucous membrane.

In *This Is Spiritualism* Maurice Barbanell wrote that ectoplasm is ideoplastic by nature and may be molded by the psychic "womb" of the medium into the equivalent of the human body. Barbanell gives "spirit chemists" the credit for compounding ectoplasm until it becomes "...a form that breathes, walks and talks and is apparently complete even to fingernails."

Numerous researchers, as well as Spiritualists, have noticed the nearly invisible cord which links the materialized spirit figure to the medium and have all made the obvious comparison to an umbilical cord. "The 'miracle' of materialization," Barbanell tells us, "is that in a few minutes there is reproduced in the seance room the birth which normally takes nine months in the mother's womb."

From time to time, Rev. Marion Owens would send me photographs of ectoplasm which she had taken.

She would often express her dissatisfaction with certain parapsychologists who insist that ectoplasm does not exist. According to Rev. Owens, she once photographed ectoplasm on a young man, who then informed her that he worked for the American Society for Psychical Research and that the Society had a sample of ectoplasm which it kept bottled. The young man insisted that he had seen the bottle and had smelled the contents of the specimen that had been taken at a seance.

Surely one of the most powerful mediums of recent times, Deon Frey also gained a well-deserved reputation as an extremely effective teacher of spiritual truths.

"It is a far simpler world in which to live if one refuses to recognize the substance of ectoplasm in its many ramifications as existing," Rev. Owens observed. "And it is far less simple for the parapsychologist in pursuit of his livelihood!"

Spirit photography is one phenomenon of the seance room which seems to function as effectively in a spontaneous situation as in the familiar trappings of the sitting room. Psychic photography is nearly as old as photography itself. Since the earliest daguerreotypes, people have been taking pictures which have shown unexplainable objects and figures in the background. Until recently, however, the idea that these figures and objects could have originated in the same paranormal manner has been rejected by almost all reputable scientists. Hazy figures have been credited to faulty processing of film. Clearly discernible and even recognizable features have been attributed to deliberate fakery.

Such skepticism was understandable because of the large amounts of processing which a photograph had to go through before it could be examined. With loading and unloading of the film, and the dark-room operations which sometimes took hours, so great were the opportunities for switching the plates that even the most open-minded person could not help becoming suspicious if he were shown a picture of a spirit form in his sitting room or the hazy Golden Gate Bridge photographed from Des Moines, Iowa. Technological advances in photography have managed to deal with all of these objections. With modern ten-second processing of film and the use of the observer's own camera, the opportunity for trickery to be employed approaches the zero level.

Ted Serios, a psychic from Chicago, time and again managed to produce weird, unexplainable images on film which was delivered fresh from the factory and sealed inside a camera Serios had never seen prior to the moment he picked it up and pointed it as his head. Even though some of the images of people and places were blurred, the fact that they appeared at all cannot be explained in terms of physical science.

CHAPTER SIXTEEN

We Need the Spirits and They Need Us

Al Manning, a Magna Cum Laude graduate from U.C.L.A. with a degree in Business Administration, is certainly one of the last people one would visualize in the role of a spiritualistic medium. Manning has served in an executive capacity at two aerospace manufacturing and research firms, as well as at a metalworking and electronics firm.

Although he is a practicing psychic of repute, Manning prefers to de-emphasize his own abilities and encourage others to develop theirs. He propagates the gospel that each individual has psychic abilities lying dormant within him and that conscious awareness of them can bring these powers to the fore.

How can one man make the seemingly impossible transition from business executive to practitioner and teacher of psychic science?

Manning's interest in the paranormal began with persistent stomach ulcers, migraines, and eye trouble. Medical science was unable to relieve the suffering businessman. Manning is convinced that he succeeded where doctors failed, with "prayer, spirit guidance, and manipulation of energy I call 'Living Light.'" His ulcers and migraines have disappeared. His eyes now test a perfect 20/20 vision.

Al prefers to do his healing with the recipient present, though he has learned that long-distance healings appear to be equally successful. He does not consider the malady cured until a medical doctor has confirmed it, for he regards the medical profession as filled with "students of the healing arts and sciences just as we are."

Al would be the last to claim that he alone accomplishes the healing in an afflicted person. At his ESP Lab the individual helps to cure himself by learning to direct the "Living Light" towards the source of trouble. The Lights are designated by different colors, each having its own special properties. When a patient taps these Lights or energy sources, he is, in essence, helping Spirit heal himself.

THE REALITY OF SPIRIT CONTACT

Al Manning has stated that help from our "Older Brothers" in spirit is always available to us if we but respond properly to their promptings:

Either you are growing in empathy and awareness, or you are inevitably slipping deeper into a personal prison of prejudice and narrow mindedness. Like most people, I spent years rejecting the small promptings that come as the first overtures of help from our Older Brothers of the "next dimension." For my own good, they finally backed me into such a corner that I had little choice but to pay attention. Most of our personal suffering is entirely unnecessary! It's simply the result of our refusal to turn on the faucet of help by that small act of paying attention.

Spirit contact is as real as the couch or chair you're sitting on. But my saying so doesn't make it true for you. And since science has yet to isolate a discarnate entity in a test tube, you are the only one who can prove it to your own complete satisfaction.

WHAT GOOD IS IT?

Let's take a moment to look at the "What good is it?" before we ask, "How?" First, why should a being from the next dimension want to help you? The answer comes simply from the basic concept of *one* totally integrated universe. The lives of those "in Spirit" are related to yours just as much as the dairyman whose cows furnish the milk for your breakfast cereal finds himself tied to you by "invisible threads." The plain truth is *we need each other*. We "humans" think our modern society is highly complex and "superior," but it's really just a speck on an obscure page of the great book we call the universe. The complexities of interrelationships between ourselves is as nothing in the vastness of the total scheme of things. Yet we live here – and we must grow here if we would fulfill our destiny. The *spirit people* need us because they need opportunities to serve, and thus earn their own growth.

On our earthly level, fortunes in money are amassed by innovation and invention – by finding better ways to *serve* our fellow beings. The old business about building a "better mousetrap" still connotes the earthly rewards of ingenuity applied as service. By serving mankind, through you or me, our spirit friends amass *their fortune* in spiritual good, growth, and advancement. So helping *you* helps them! And it's just such a mutuality of good that makes for profitable international trade, or in this case interdimensional help.

Al G. Manning believes in a no-nonsense approach to the question of whether or not we should make spirit contact.

NOW HOW DO YOU DO IT?

We've looked at "why" and "what good is it!" Now let's have a little go at the HOW. Since your spirit helpers no longer inhabit physical bodies, they don't often tap you on the shoulder or yell at you. Normally their guidance (and plain old sociability) comes to you through an increased awareness that is most often called extra-sensory perception or ESP. You have some degree of ESP already, and you can develop more. There are many good books that give basic exercises for the development of your ESP. Naturally I'd recommend my own book, *Helping Yourself With ESP*, but with or without a book, you will find it advantageous to seek a bit of Spirit

Contact now! And so prove it to yourself!

Find a quiet place where you will not be disturbed, and promise yourself that you will devote fifteen minutes each day for the next two weeks to unfolding your relationship with the tremendously helpful people "on the other side." Choose a time that you can keep regularly, and go to your quiet place armed with a pencil and paper for taking notes, and a serene mental attitude. Get comfortable and visualize yourself seated under a huge searchlight that is shining a shaft of soft white light directly down upon you. Then say aloud in a normal voice something like: "From the perfect protection of the pure white Light, I seek friendship and contact with the Spirit world, and guidance from my own spirit teachers. Please communicate with me now."

Then relax, and *pay attention*! It would be quite normal to feel a gentle touch on some part of your body, or a cool breath on your cheek. You might see a symbol in your mind's eye, a ball of mist before you, or one or more lights of almost any size or shape. There could be a voice whispering in your ear, or a wave of "electrical" energy may seem to pass through you. There might be the traditional knocks and raps, or your pencil could want to write without your pushing it – or you may simply be impressed with a new thought or some bit of inspiration or upliftment. Through its form may vary widely, *there will be a response*! If you fail to notice it the first time, you will certainly be somewhat in tune by the end of the first week. The more relaxed and yet alert you can be, the quicker you will be able to sense the presence of a spirit teacher or helper.

When you recognize a spirit response, answer immediately. Don't choke up or panic! This is a perfectly natural circumstance, and your answer will help the spirit being to reach you more readily – if not at once, then at your next sitting. You can talk to them in your normal voice, just as you would to a "living" friend who was sitting in the room with you. And that's an excellent key to your relationship with your spirit helpers. Think of them as people, too. They sincerely want to help you. And because they're no longer encumbered with the physical needs and drives of the earth, their vision is clearer, and their ability to foresee coming events is sharper than ours. They also have the ability to manifest directly on the material plane when necessary to bring you effective help.

There in your own quiet place with your teachers and friends from the next dimension is the perfect opportunity to talk over your important problems, and seek advice and/or tangible help. They're not apt to do something for you that you could just as easily do for yourself, but when you really need help, or when they find a way to speed your spiritual growth, they are always there, and always effective.

A whole new world and a completely new and richer understanding of life itself awaits you. Your ticket of admission is merely your striving for ever-increasing awareness and your willingness to pay attention to spirit help. It's senseless to keep ignoring or rejecting the tangible help that longs to minister to you from the "other side of life" – tune in on your own spirit helpers today. The life you improve will be your own!

RAPPING WITH AL MANNING ABOUT MEDIUMSHIP AND PROPHECY

Brad Steiger: Is there a regular method to obtaining your psychic impressions?

Al Manning: My psychic impressions come to me in two forms. The first form is a vision when I go to sleep. Once I am in a slumber, a revelation will be revealed to me. This method is accurate on a statistical basis approximately ninety percent of the time

The other method that I use is called "psychic insight." That is, I place myself in what is known as a transic state. That is to say, I am hypnotized into deep and continuous concentration by focusing upon a particular problem. Consequently, I am able to predict with accuracy that has been perhaps ninety-nine percent effective in the past.

At times there will be events that are emerging in the world. Plans may be made or plots developed. As a result of the vibrations these future events cast, I receive a certain almost indescribable feeling, and realize that very shortly I will be receiving a psychic impression that is to reveal something to me.

Do you always have to enter a trance to obtain a prediction?

Yes.

Do one or more impressions flood in and occur at the same time?

No. I am very fortunate in that only one impression, or scene, is revealed to me at a time.

Do you receive a time-frame of reference for your predictions?

With reference to my psychic insight, I do see a date and time revealed to me. This is, as if I was in the waking state and sitting before my television set, or scanning the screen in a movie theater. I consider this to be direct revelation.

This is the reason that throughout my entire life I have been able to accurately predict the day, date, and time of my prophecies. Unfortunately, not everyone in the psychic field has been able to do this. But I have been doing it all of my life.

Do you have any physical pain during or after a trance?

Yes, definitely. When I emerge from the transic state, I am extremely weak, as if I had just completed a grueling cross-country foot race. I am also very thirsty. On many of my appearances here in Los Angeles – although I have not done as many of these as I would like because I need attendants – I have come out of a trance feeling extremely weak.

I must have a nurse or a doctor attend me, in order that my vital life signs can be monitored. That is to say, my temperature, pulse, and respiration must be carefully watched or my body will go into a state of shock. As you can imagine, this is a very frightening thing. I must be very cautious.

This is a state of deep psychic insight. From a preliminary viewpoint, I can gauge my entrance into this state fairly well. I have learned this over a period of forty years. I know approximately how far to go into the state and still have a certain amount of accuracy and fore-vision. The basic difference between going into the state unattended, and with trained medical personnel in attendance, is one of deepness and time duration. I simply cannot remain in the state for a long interval without having my body's vital signs checked. In either case, attended or unattended, I am very thirsty when I come out of the trance state, but not hungry at all. On many occasions I have an overwhelming urge to fast, and I often forego food for several days.

If your vital signs start to plunge downward to a dangerous point, what can a physician do to awaken you?

It is actually very easy. The method I've found that works best after all of these years of experimentation is to put my feet into a container of cold water.

The cold water actually causes some type of stimulation to hit my brain. I am immediately brought out of the trance state. This is the best method I have devised thus far, although it may sound a bit unusual.

Once you have a psychic impression, can that insight be changed? Can the future be changed?

This is a rather interesting question and I have had several television interviewers ask it. Yes, the future can definitely be changed by an individual being warned of a future tragedy, or knowing something that seems destined to happen.

Let's take the case of a man who's going to be assassinated, or someone who may have an automobile accident, or anything that may happen in the individual's life. If the individual can be warned, as I tried to warn the victims in the Sharon Tate murders, then they can take appropriate steps to prevent the occurrence.

On many occasions, something happens to someone because he or she is ignorant of the fact that this could happen.

Yes, the future can definitely be changed. Now, a phenomenon like an earthquake, or any other disaster, is very difficult because there is no individual free will involved. All that can be done by the psychic receiving the impression is to give the warning.

But, so far as I am concerned, I do not have any power to change what the master, God, who has given me this gift, tells me. I do believe seriously that humankind cannot drastically change destiny. What we have is the power to change what may happen to each of us, as individuals. An individual can move from California and this will affect his personal life. The quake can occur, but the individual can use free will to decide if he will be in this vicinity when it happens.

CHAPTER SEVENTEEN

Capturing Spirit
Voices on Audio Tape

What would it mean to you to know absolutely and without doubt that you can survive physical death? Would you change and reorganize your life on the basis of this information? Beyond the personal considerations, what effect would verified truth of our immortality have on our earthly societies, institutions, governments and sciences? Would the present establishment accept the fact of an existent dimension which is completely uncharted by scientists and, in fact, has been ridiculed as being too "far out" to receive any serious consideration?

One of the main reasons neither science nor society at large has considered the immortality question seriously is the lack of tangible physical evidence disproving that there is anything but a void waiting for us when we die. Another reason is the reluctance of organized science to get into the abstract and esoteric elements of religion for fear of tarnishing their "objectivity shields" in the arenas of unverifiable phenomena, myth and superstition.

All this may soon be changing, thanks to the recent breakthrough into the hidden reaches of immortality made by modern technological instrumentation – in this case the audio tape recorder. Scientists have recently been recording spirit voices on tape and even communicating with these strange vocal manifestations. Perhaps for the first time in history, scientists have something tangible with which to work.

Although the most important work done thus far dealing with voice phenomenon has been carried out in Europe by Dr. Konstantin Raudive, a Latvian psychologist living and researching in German, Professor Walter Uphoff, an American psychical researcher, is on the trail of the phenomenon in this country.

Working independently and, on occasion, under the auspices of the late Harold Sherman and the ESP Research Associates Foundation of Little Rock, Arkansas, Uphoff investigated the validity of spirit voices recorded on tape by the Lamoreaux family in White Salmon, Washington.

The Lamoreaux tapes and transcripts are a significant addition to the growing documentation of voices from beyond, because they suggest the phenomenon is fast becoming worldwide and that the voices are able to communicate in all known languages. These tapes also reveal the successful techniques of interrogation being used by the Lamoreauxs.

Dr. Walter Uphoff has spent many years in a serious research of the electronic voice phenomena – the appearance of alleged spirit voices on tape.

What exactly are spirit voices? The voice phenomenon is the unexplained manifestation of voice-like sounds on recording tape. These sounds are in fact vocal sounds and human language is employed. You can understand what these voices are saying once you learn how to screen out the interference. The voices are genuine and have been conclusively verified by respected scientists. Where they are coming from and how they get on the recording tape is another question, however.

CAPTURING VOICES

Mike Lamoreaux was a former teacher who had been doing graduate work at a college in the Northwest. He became interested in the paranormal voice phenomenon after reading Dr. Raudive's book, *Breakthrough*. He tried for two months to capture voices on tape and followed the procedures set up by Dr. Raudive without success.

Then, during a visit to his brothers he told them about the experiments and his efforts to duplicate Raudive's results. The three brothers decided to try to obtain voices on their own inexpensive tape recorder. That very night they received paranormal voices. Following that success, Mike Lamoreaux determined to continue with his experiments.

By June 1973, the Lamoreaux brothers had accumulated hundreds of pages of transcribed paranormal voices which they had captured on tape. It takes great diligence and determination to work with the voice phenomenon because it is, quite frankly, hard on the ears. The voices are usually faint and the sentences and phrases are brief, rapid and barely audible, even with maximum amplification. The background noise and interference is enormously difficult to penetrate.

When someone is first exposed to the voice phenomena, the thought which comes immediately to mind is that the words and phrases might be random voices from a radio station or some other type of sound transmission. That objection leads to the most mystifying characteristic of paranormal voices on tape. The operator of the tape recorder is actually in communication with the voice. These voices not only answer questions, but they volunteer information. In some cases this information is precognitive and the intelligence seems to be aware of what is happening at the site of the recording. Moreover, these voices all claim to be the voices of the dead!

Mike Lamoreaux and his brothers carried on these alleged conversations with a number of deceased personalities. They filed and catalogued the tapes and transcriptions of all these recorded conversations. The process was as follows:

Mike Lamoreaux turns on his recorder and asks whoever (or whatever) may be listening some specific questions. He then lets the recorder run on the record setting for 15 seconds, rewinds it and plays it back. The voices cannot be heard during the recording period. They can only be heard on the playback. Atmospheric weather conditions often affect the recording adversely. When conditions are superior, the loudest voices become audible. Voices vary and appear to originate from different sending intelligences.

The Lamoreauxs identified many of the voices coming through on their tapes. Among them was Betty White, a name well-known in metaphysical circles (*The Betty Book, Unobstructed Universe*, etc). There have also been the inevitable famous personalities appearing in voice-form, just as they do in seances and automatic writing, such as Martin Luther King and Albert Einstein.

It has been taught by many spiritualist groups that it is imperative that certain protocol be observed when seeking an audience with spirits from beyond the physical plane. Even Dr. Raudive, a devout Catholic, always formally welcomes any spirit friends who may be present.

Not so, the Lamoreaux brothers. There was no fancy verbal foot work when they interrogated their voices. They were demanding, informal, critical and often challenging. As a result of this technique, Professor Uphoff reports that they have received information of a nature different from that obtained through more orthodox procedures. The Lamoreaux brothers pushed hard for details and pursued a matter until they were satisfied.

The paranormal voices which came through the tape recorder provided the Lamoreauxs with descriptions of life on the other side. Walter Uphoff describes this place or state from which the voices appear to emulate (at least according to the voices themselves) as "a frequency or vibration level, or as a dimension – rather than a geographic location."

THE WORLD BEYOND

The voices gave a description of the different planes of existence in the world beyond as follows (all unfamiliar words are phonetically spelled):

Pareenah: This is the name given to our plane of existence on earth. We are in, or on, Pareenah. The voices intimate life begins here.

Deenah: This is the main place or state a person goes to after death. It appears to be a subjective reality with some rather stringent rules. Most of the voices coming through say they are now in Deenah and refer to themselves as the Moozla.

Nilow: Nilow has been described by the voices as being a prison. Those who disobey the laws of Deenah go to Nilow. A conditioning seems to take place in Nilow. Once one is ready and perhaps made more fit because of conditioning, he or she may then return to Deenah. Some, however, seem to remain on Nilow and are called Nilowins.

Ree: The inhabitants of Ree, according to the Lamoreaux tapes, are in a type of hospital environment and are allowed only limited movement. It appears to be a matter of choice whether the inhabitants stay in Ree or return to Deenah. Deenah and Ree appear to be somehow associated with each other. Residents of Ree are called Moolit.

Montayloo: Montayloo is where one can go after death if he wants to and is ready. There is more movement there and it is more structured than Deenah, having 12 sections of planned progression. Those who reside in Montayloo are called Montaylooins.

Piloncentric: Piloncentric appears to be one of the places to which Montaylooins can advance. Three different levels have been revealed so far called *Sentra*. It has been suggested that the Sentra may influence us on Earth with what we know as inspiration.

UPHOFF'S JUDGMENT

Walter Uphoff is an authority on voice phenomena as it has manifested itself on both sides of the Atlantic. He has heard the Raudive voices and the voices of other successful trackers from around the world. He knows what legitimate paranormal voices sound like and, as a professional teacher and successful author, he is also a good judge of human nature. Professor Uphoff's judgement of the Lamoreaux tapes? "Something paranormal is occurring." On the Lamoreauxs themselves: "I am convinced they are sincere, intelligent and committed to learning all they can about this audio taped voice phenomenon."

Apparently there are surface voices which are reasonably loud and softer voices intermingled with the static, tape noise and other interference. According to Michael Lamoreaux, the most interesting voices lie under all the noise. It takes considerable practice to hear these voices and even the Lamoreauxs (after thousands of hours of monitoring tapes) estimate they only comprehend 60 to 70 percent of the voices which are recorded on the tapes. Here are several exchanges between Michael Lamoreaux and the paranormal voices.

Michael: Can you give me some advice on how to live my life?
Female voice: Difficult.
Michael: Are you there, Mark Flanders?
Male voice: I am here (or I am ready).
(Michael using the AM radio at a position where no station was broadcasting. The radio had just been turned on.)
Male voice: You better tune us in right.
Michael: Are you ready to give me loud voices?
Male voice: Ready.
Michael (on December 25): Merry Christmas, Moozlah!
Female voice: Merry Christmas.
Michael: I would very much like to talk to Agnes Stebbins.
Male voice: Always with me.
Michael: Tell me how healing works. How can I do it?

Male voice: I cannot help you out.

These are merely fragments from several taping sessions. The coordination of the taped responses to various questions put forth by the Lamoreauxs will be an arduous task.

When listening to tapes of the paranormal voices, one is immediately aware of the eerie, non-human nature of them. Some voices are mechanical sounding; others are whispered and echoing. They are strange and almost incomprehensible at times. Yet there can be no mistake that they are voices. The voices recorded in America were speaking English.

However, not all the voices are in English. The ones captured on tape by Dr. Raudive are polyglot. Voices come over the speaker in German, Russian, English, French, Latvian. Not only are there different languages in one sentence, but there are different languages in a phrase and even in a single word! One of Dr. Raudive's advisors, who is an expert in linguistics, opined that the ability to fashion words and phrases in such a manner is non-human.

Professor Uphoff travels to Europe frequently, combining research with pleasure. He speaks German and is at home in Holland, Austria, Switzerland and other nations where German is widely used. As a result of his travels, Professor Uphoff is in contact with parapsychologists and psychical researchers from all over Europe.

It was through these contacts that Uphoff first became involved in the voice phenomenon. He was skeptical at first as is everyone else when they are exposed to this extraordinary phenomenon. He was invited to Dr. Raudive's laboratory at Bad Kronzingen to hear the voices and to work with Raudive himself.

This initial exposure to the research being conducted by this eminent scientist has motivated Uphoff to explore the paranormal voice enigma as thoroughly as it is possible for any part-time psychical researcher. The role Uphoff has adopted is that of communications.

Credit for introducing the paranormal voice phenomenon to the world should go to the Swedish singer and artist, Friedrich Jurgenson, who first discovered the voices when he was out in the woods trying to capture bird songs on his tape recorder. His subsequent investigations and the publication of his findings were the lead for which Dr. Raudive had been looking. Raudive had been investigating post-mortem phenomena for 25 years before he stumbled onto the voices of Jurgenson.

This discovery changed Dr. Raudive's life, and he developed the professional standards of his research with such firm documentation that his material is not easy to attack from a scientific point of view, although his conclusions have been disputed. Science will have to accept, however, that paranormal voices are being captured on tape – voices which appear to be perfectly able to communicate with living human beings.

ANYONE CAN TRY

Tracking down the spirit voice phenomenon is an avocation in which anyone with a tape recorder can take part. In fact, there is a need for as much documentation of this phenomenon as can be collected. There may be an element of ESP or mediumistic ability involved but this has not been determined as a necessary ingredient for successful voice recording. Dr. Raudive is believed to have some abilities as a medium, although there are no published reports of his being aware of this ability before he began to seriously record paranormal voices. Similarly, Michael Lamoreaux slipped into a trance during one taping session. He had never experienced this state before and did not realize his "nap" of three or four minutes had turned into a deep mediumistic trance which had actually lasted for well over a half hour.

Professor Uphoff has prepared some guidelines for people who wish to conduct experiments with their own tape recorders. There is no guarantee that anyone can duplicate the successful experiments being carried out around the world. Neither is there any evidence that there is anything required except a tape recorder and a person who is willing to devote the time and effort to what may at first appear to be a silly and unrewarding pastime.

If a person is serious about recording the voice phenomenon, he should resolve not to become discouraged if his early attempts are unsuccessful. Mary Sharpe, former chairman of the research committee of the Spiritual Frontiers Fellowship, used up miles of tape before she got her first voice. Before her death, she was able to record 147 voice fragments.

Uphoff says he knows of 100 persons who have successfully captured voices on tape. In answer to how long it takes for the experimenter to get voices, Uphoff cites the following figures received from a survey done by a German researcher: Eleven out of 41 were successful immediately; six more got results during the first month; the rest said they finally recorded voices after a period of from one month to a year and a half. The average was two months.

Many of these experimenters have found it necessary to go back over their early tapes. They have discovered that as their ability to hear and understand paranormal voices improves, they are able to hear voices which they had initially missed.

BEST CONDITIONS

There is no absolute rule as to when and where a recording should be attempted. Professor Uphoff advises experimenters to select a place which is as free as possible from extraneous noises. The best time appears to be in the evening, especially at midnight. Since the weather is always a factor in radio transmissions, it would be advisable to avoid times when there is a large amount of static electricity in the air. Often, voices are heard in the pauses between words and sentences. Therefore, it is advisable to speak slowly and clearly.

Professor Uphoff is a realist. He is a man of science and education. He is also a man used to the tough infighting of labor and management negotiations. His book, *Kohler on Strike* (Beacon Press), was described by the late Robert F. Kennedy as being extremely important in the field of labor relations. It is this quality of objectivity that he brings to his investigation of paranormal voices, and which was demonstrated in his closing remarks at a lecture:

"What must be guarded against is becoming an uncritical believer. It is at the point when one becomes a complete believer or non-believer that the hearing aid is turned off and no more evidence is considered. Everyone I know who has devoted time to listening to the audio spirit tapes of Raudive, Schmid, Vanseelay, Lamoreaux, and others, grants that something paranormal is happening. Some feel more comfortable, or less comfortable, if they can somehow credit the voices to the work of the experimenter's subconscious. But no one has come forward with an explanation of the dynamics or forms of energy involved in producing the phenomenon.

"It is important that the investigator consider all possible hypotheses and explanations, and put them in some rank and order – from the most likely, to the least likely – and be willing at all times to change that rank and order as new evidence appears to strengthen or weaken a particular hypothesis.

"Tape recorders have become one more instrument to push the frontiers of the unknown back and to bring us closer to the awareness that man is more than a mere combination of chemicals and electrical energy – and that what we know as human personality may not cease at death."

The paranormal voices on tape say they are the surviving personalities of human beings who have lived on earth. Whether they did or not has still to be determined. The fact remains that the voices, at least, exist and have been captured on tape. It may no longer be necessary for those individuals who have an overpowering desire to communicate with their departed loved ones to seek out a medium to establish communications. Anyone who wants to, and has the patience, can now work with his own tape recorder and perhaps establish the truth of personal survival in a way that will answer the question of survival after death – that age-old riddle – satisfactorily for the first time in our history.

CHAPTER EIGHTEEN

Deon Frey—
A Channel for
Higher Intelligences

In December 1974 I underwent a visionary experience of an intensely personal, but extremely revelatory, nature. Within a few days of my multi-dimensional contact, I received a telephone call from Deon Frey in Chicago. It was typical of the strong bond my family and I have with this remarkable woman that she had "tuned in" on the entire experience and called to discuss what she interpreted as my "higher-plane initiation."

Our first meeting had not begun very harmoniously, however; and I have often mused about the comedy-of-errors circumstances under which we met.

It was in April 1969. I was in Chicago promoting one of my books and a friend of mine, Rosemarie "Bud" Stewart, was raving about this fantastic Tarot-card reader she had met. She insisted that I find time to go over to the Occult Book Store, on North State Street, where she was working, and arrange for a personal reading.

I at last succumbed to Bud's sales pitch and told her to call Deon and arrange a sitting.

What I did not learn until several years later was that in her excitement and her eagerness to bring two friends together, Bud came on a bit too strong to Deon, who at that time was working a full day as a telephone operator at a Chicago hotel, then filling in at the bookstore to help vacationing friends. To confuse matters even further, Deon was moving apartments that day and was in the midst of domestic upheaval. The one bright spot was that same chaotic day happened to be her birthday, and a friend had promised to take her to dinner if she could get off work early enough to mesh with his busy schedule.

And that was the night Bud Stewart chose to call to *tell* Deon that she simply *must* give Brad Steiger a reading.

Unaware of Deon's pique at being prevailed upon at closing time in the bookstore, moving day at her apartment, and the postponing of her birthday dinner, I walked into the Occult Book Store to meet a tall, redheaded woman with rather unfriendly fire in her eyes.

By that time in my investigative career, I was used to encountering all kinds of mediums and psychics, so I merely assumed that a rather stern demeanor was simply part of Deon's image – sort of a "sit before me humble client and hear the direct words from the Oracle" approach, which certain mediums seem fond of employing to establish what they consider to be the proper distance between them and their clientele.

We walked back to a small room literally swathed in beaded curtains. I almost chuckled at the stereotypical decor, but I solemnly seated myself opposite Deon at a small, round table.

She pushed back a strand of red hair, began shuffling the deck, then looked up at me and permitted a smile to break her former gruff facade. She tipped her head back and laughed softly at some private joke.

I smiled nervously, wondering if the cards were about to reveal me as the principal character in some vast, cosmic comedy.

I suppose I sensed then, on one level, what I would not know consciously for several years. Deon had established a *rapport* with a deeper level of my essential self, and she knew that before her sat a new friend, not a demanding boor. The mental barrier between us had been shattered, and Deon set about giving me one of the most evidential readings that I have ever received from a professional psychic-sensitive.

As her fingers deftly turned the cards of her small Tarot deck and her psyche tuned in on multidimensional wavelengths, Deon correctly told me that I would travel to New England within two weeks to visit a friend named Bill. She gave the month of my birth and stated that I was Aquarian-Piscean (February 19) married to a Gemini. She described each of my children with his or her peculiar identifying characteristic. She told of my father's recent heart attack. She very accurately described my wife and correctly said that Marilyn [who made her transition in December of 1982] had not accompanied me on the Chicago trip because she had elected to stay home to paint the basement.

And she went on and on, becoming more intimate in her revelations, casting farther into the future, suddenly delving deep into my childhood.

The reading terminated with my joining Deon's birthday celebration at her favorite Greek restaurant. In a matter of hours we had become fast friends.

REACHING UPWARD FOR SPIRITUAL TRUTHS

Deon was baptized in the Christian church and reared a Baptist. She took her faith very seriously. Although she has since left that church affiliation, Deon has always tried to emphasize the spiritual in her work.

"I've never wanted to be just a fortuneteller, someone who just sits and reads the cards for people," Deon often told me. "To me, being a psychic has to be more than simply picking up things on the earth plane. I must try to reach upward for more-meaningful, spiritual truths."

REMARKABLE HEALING ABILITIES

I know from firsthand experience that one of the higher-level manifestations that interests Deon is healing.

In August 1969, a cyst suddenly appeared on Marilyn's throat after a period of rather severe inflammation. Although the doctors said that it was nothing serious, they recommended minor surgery to remove the unsightly lump, which was about the size of a small egg and protruded from Marilyn's throat as if she had an Adam's apple.

A few days before Marilyn was to report to her doctor's office, Deon and a friend stopped by our home in Highland Park. At this point in our married life, Marilyn believed more in me than in my beliefs, and she was rather closed toward the whole concept of unconventional healing.

In spite of her protests, Deon placed Marilyn in an upright chair, and she and her friend began to work on her.

Marilyn squirmed uneasily. "This really can't help," she said, protesting what she must have regarded as some primitive bit of superstitious atavism. "I appreciate what you want to do for me, but seriously, it doesn't hurt all that much. The doctor will soon . . ."

Marilyn became quiet. Something was happening.

The healers had been placing their hands on Marilyn, praying. Now Deon stepped in front of Marilyn and began to make light stroking motions on her throat. Deon raised her fingers above Marilyn's flesh, but continued the stroking movements as she moved her hands higher.

Amazingly, the lump began to move, following the beckoning fingers. The out-of-place Adam's apple kept traveling until it reached the tip of Marilyn's chin – then it vanished!

Marilyn felt her throat in complete bewilderment. "It . . . it's gone," she managed. "The lump is completely gone!"

The demonstration was most impressive. Healing is among the most beautiful acts of human sharing on our troubled planet. All sincere practitioners, from medical doctors to chiropractors, from nutritionists to neurosurgeons, from medicine men to faith healers, have their part to play in alleviating human suffering.

One must be cautious. Once must not be gullible, but there is a place for the unconventional, as well as the conventional, in healing. Healing is a channeling of the love energy, an art of the soul as much as a science of the body.

PROOF OF ETERNAL LIFE

"I experienced my first conscious trance when I was fifteen years old," Deon once told us. "I was a student librarian at Wayne City High. I walked out the door in a trance state, across the street to our home, and into the room where my father lay dead. My cousin entered the school by a side door and told my teacher to send me home because my father had just passed away. She was amazed when she learned that I already had left the building.

"Eternal life was proved to me that very night," Deon recalled. "I was awakened by my father scratching on a screen beside my bed. My father had not been a churchgoer and had not been a believing man. 'You were right, Deon,' he told me. 'If I live, all these people live.'

"Father said he was sorry he had had to leave me so abruptly, especially since because of his death I would never again be able to attend public school. But he did say he would see that I received a different kind of education.

"A year later I moved to Chicago, and my sister Vivian introduced me to Eleanor Dunne, a spiritual medium. During the meeting, an image of my father appeared to me and I understood at once what he had meant by a 'different kind of education.'"

Deon became a member of the National Spiritualist Association and minister of the First Roseland Spiritualist Church.

One of the more interesting experiments in which Deon has participated concerned the identification of objects within a nest of boxes.

"This was March 1961," Deon said. "Wilbur Smart, who was a member of the Spiritual Frontiers Fellowship, first came to me for a consultation. He was impressed with my abilities and asked me to participate in an experiment with a psychical research study group in London.

"They sent him a large box containing five or six smaller boxes, each wrapped individually. He scheduled this experiment by London time so that the group over there could be sitting at the same time in order to send me vibratory impulses.

"After I was in trance, Wilbur broke the seal on the large box and handed the smaller boxes to me one by one. Wilbur taped my impressions of each box, allowed me to come out of trance, then took his tape recorder and the boxes home with him. He returned the boxes to London unopened.

"I personally never heard the tape, but after London replied I did receive confirmation from Wilbur as to what each of the boxes had contained. If I remember correctly, the boxes were filled with things like locks of hair, pictures, coins. Over all, they gave me a grade of 90 per cent accuracy."

Two weeks later, Wilbur Smart asked Deon if she would participate in another experiment with the British group. Once again Deon went into trance in her room at First Roseland Spiritualist Church while the Londoners sat in their own seance circle. The purpose of this particular experiment was to see if Deon could move an object in the London seance room through long-distance psychokinesis or – depending on one's point of view – the projection of her spirit guide. The experiment was judged successful when either Dr. Richard Speidel, her guide, or Deon's psychokinetic energy moved a large mirror that was hanging over a fireplace just above the heads of the London seance circle.

"The sitters in London attested to the moving of the mirror, which was quite a surprise to me," Deon said. "Wilbur was very secretive about things I did in trance to see if I would mention them in my conscious state."

DEON MEETS HER GUIDE

According to Deon, Dr. Richard Speidel appeared for the first time at her bedside one night in 1942. He was of sober mien, dressed formally in a black coat with a black bow tie.

"Will I do?" he asked the startled young woman.

"Will you do for what?" Deon asked with her customary directness and attempted to hide her fear.

"I have been sent to be your guide, your teacher," the entity told her.

Deon has been a part of the psychic world since the age of five. "Lily of the Valley was one of my earlier guides," Deon told me. "And from 1950 to about 1953, Dr. Thomas was my principal guide. He used to whistle for attention. Several people heard his whistle come from a source independent of me, the medium.

"My sister Vivian was an excellent independent voice medium, and the voices of those on the other side would sound from a corner of the ceiling and from distances greatly removed from either her physical body or my own."

COMMUNICATING WITH SPIRIT ENTITIES

Although Deon accepts the reality of Dr. Richard Speidel as an entity independent of her own psyche, she has been able to retain a certain objectivity in regard to her mediumship.

"I wonder sometimes if I really am picking up thought forms from sitters in the seance circle rather than seeing the actual etheric images of those who have passed over," she once admitted. "Or could it be that in

trance I somehow travel to another plane of existence and there communicate with entities, rather than that they come back to the earth plane? Can
it be that I am only a glorified relay station for vibratory forces?"

It is typical of Deon that she is always asking questions of her preternatural abilities. This is good, for when we are dealing with seances, spirit
manifestations, and physical materializations, there is no dogma yet realized that can provide all the answers.

During one seance I attended with Deon serving as the medium, a large,
slightly illuminated blob with a rather bright nucleus appeared near the
ceiling directly over the reclining medium. A young man, in a voice warped
by gasps and sobs, greeted his deceased father. One sitter beheld a
grandmother; another a departed friend. I could discern only what appeared to me to be a strange, glowing, jellyfish-shaped thing.

A SEANCE – STEP-BY-STEP

Once during a seance in our home, Deon went into trance, and at the
same time, described the process step by step for the information of those
in attendance.

"Okay, I'll face east. . . . I just lie down in the center [of the couch], place
my hands at my side. My mind goes in about a thousand different
directions. I just lie flat, see?

[In a hoarse voice] "See, they've already started taking my voice and I'm
not even in it yet." [Addressing the group] "Be sure you're relaxed, too. They
might want to use you. Now remember, even though I'm here in trance, it
is possible for me to walk, move, or whatever they want to do with me.

"If they move me around, I'll go anywhere without touching anything.
You don't call me Deon from now on. You can either call me 'one' or 'the
medium.' Call me that throughout the seance. Whoever you talk to
[referring to entities from the other side] will probably give you their names.
However, if they don't, you just talk anyway and try to find out who they
are and give them the same courtesy you would if anyone entered your
home and wanted to talk to you.

"My body usually gets cold. Last night I got so cold, people thought I
was dying. I might act out the part of a spirit, too. So I never know what
they're going to do, and I can't promise anything. All I do is lie here and see
what happens. . . . I can feel my chest getting heavy. . . . At this point I can
feel a terrific vibration in my hands and body.

"It is important to me that you do not keep silent. You must talk among
yourselves and create the voice. It is important to him [her spirit guide]. .
. . If you are able to see something or feel something or are aware of
something that is happening in the room, please talk about it. The louder
your voices are, the better the vibrations will be.

[After a few moments, Dr. Richard Speidel, Deon's principal guide, came through.] "Good evening, friends. I am very happy to greet you tonight and work with you in this manner.... Always be looking to see what may take place around the medium's face, even though you may become engrossed in conversation. Also keep working with me. Do not let the medium's voice go back to low tone. As you keep talking to it, it will keep talking to you. Do you understand? This is Dr. Richard Speidel, and I work with her in this manner in order to open up the seance and to talk with you."

Deon often uses ancient Tarot cards as a physical stimulus for her psychic abilities.

WORKING WITH THE CREATIVE GOD FORCE

"I know what I know," Deon once answered when I questioned her regarding the source of a bit of paranormally acquired information she had passed along to me. "I believe that the creative God force works through us at all times. This God force is not always tapped, but it may be used by us. As we use it, we enable it to grow within ourselves and around us."

Another time, Deon described for me a revelatory experience she had undergone:

"The light seemed to be emanating from one corner of the room, and I could almost make out a form. The color was indescribable. It had edges of violet hue, but it was crystal white, or mother-of-pearl, and so bright that it could almost blind me.

"I had a feeling of oneness with it, a unity. It was like being one with everything all at once. The only way I could describe it to myself afterward when I thought of it was like I was water in a sponge. I just became suddenly drawn into it. It was like a love that one really can't understand from the earth plane, because it's such a spiritual envelopment. You want to stay. You don't want to return. You don't want to come back to the conscious state, although you are in a conscious awareness.

"Although I heard no voice, I was filled with a knowing quality. I just knew things. It wasn't as if the light were speaking to me, but it seemed to give me direct answers to a lot of questions on my mind.

"For a moment I thought that the light was going to form into the Ancient of Ancients. I seemed to have an awareness that it could be a man, it could be a woman, or it could be both. But I knew that whatever it was, it was not anything that I should fear. I think this is what is meant by becoming one with the light and letting your light shine forth.

"If the revelatory experience comes, you become one with it. You must grow into it, become a part of it, let the light become a part of you.

"But learning to grow into the light is a process that cannot be rushed. You must learn to experience the light, let it flow through you, giving it force so that others may feel a portion of it through you. Become a channel for the light, and you will leave a portion of it with whomever you meet. I think that everyone should seek illumination, the process of becoming one with the spiritual principle."

THE SPIRITUAL PRINCIPLE

I asked Deon how she would define the spiritual principle.

"I look at it as an energy, a source, something that works within and without and all around us. Something that we can tune ourselves into by constant meditation, by wanting to help others, by desiring to become one with the universe. By becoming one with spiritual principle, you, in one sense, give up your life; but you balance your life because you still must live on the earth plane and do the things that other people do. But you must work more and more for others; you must always be ready to help; you must be ready to do whatever is needed of you. You must remember that you are only a channel for God, the spiritual principle; and you must help others become fully aware so that if they should receive this illumination, this spiritual unfoldment, they will know how to handle it correctly."

"Is it possible to subvert this force?"

"Any force that can be used for good can be used for evil. There is a positive and negative aspect to everything. We must keep our own light strong. We must be constantly aware, working in the light, becoming light, because that is why we have been set on the earth path.

"I think that the young people today have come into life with less karma than we older people have. They are more ready to receive spiritual things and to become spiritual. They're not so wrapped up in materialism. I feel that with their knowledge and their expression of truth they're sending out a purer light to the people of today, because so many of them really seem to love each other and to be more truthful with each other than we as a group used to be. Even though their language may seem different, it is a pure language, because to them it is the language of love, and they express it in their voices and in their faces."

EVERYONE HAS ESP

One of Deon's favorite theories is that everyone has latent ESP ability. I witnessed an impressive demonstration of this thesis when Deon once noticed my children "testing" one another with the Zener ESP cards.

Deon called to my four-year-old, Julie, who had been playing with her doll while the older children guessed the cards. Once Julie was comfortably seated on a chair opposite her, Deon told the child she would help her guess the cards just as the older children were doing.

"Those symbols don't have much meaning for a four-year-old," I protested, "and I don't believe her attention span . . ."

Deon waved me to silence. "You just look into Deon's eyes, Julie, and call out the card that you see there."

Amazingly, with Deon's psychic assistance little Julie scored thirteen out of a possible twenty-five. Julie's misses seemed to occur when she shouted her guess before she concentrated on Deon's eyes and the ostensible subconsciously transmitted impression.

TEACHING OTHER PSYCHICS

Seer Daniel Logan, author of *The Reluctant Prophet*, credits the lessons acquired under Deon's tutelage and her repeated words of inspiration and guidance as being responsible for his becoming a career psychic. It was at a seance conducted by Deon that Logan first went into trance. The evening had been devoted to psychometry. Logan was holding some keys in his palm, attempting to psychometrize them, when he began to feel drowsy. His eyes were fixed on a wavering candle flame, and he felt himself drifting away. He was fully conscious of what he was experiencing; yet he seemed to be floating farther and farther away from the seance circle.

Deon told Logan not to be afraid. "Nothing bad or harmful will happen to you," she said soothingly. "I'll be here to guide you out of it. Now, open your senses. Allow the higher forces to take over. Let go, Daniel"

Logan recalls that Deon's words gave him confidence.

"I relaxed and stopped fighting," he writes; "I felt now as though my real self were no longer in my body but that I was floating above the group, looking down on them and on my body below."

Logan heard low mumblings coming from his own throat. Then a querulous old voice shrieked through his mouth: "Bill! Bill! Where are you?"

One man in the circle spoke up and was told in obscene words that he was not the right "Bill."

Deon recognized the voice and manner of her fiancés deceased mother. She spoke to the entity, telling her she must release her hold on her son.

"I won't let him go, and I don't have to!" the voice shrilled. "You want him for yourself, but I'll be damned if you're going to have him. I'm going to take him, and I'll do it tonight!"

Deon continued to speak in a calm voice. She explained that Bill was happy on the earth plane, that she would lose his love if she continued to act in this manner. Deon told "Mother" she must accept the light. "You'll be alone forever if you don't turn toward the light," Deon added sternly.

Logan says that during the trance his body seemed to shrink, his hands became clawlike. The entity complained through his vocal cords, "The damned pain; my arms and hands hurt, and I can't walk."

Other members of the circle joined Deon in telling the entity that they wished her to turn away from darkness. Eventually a less harsh voice whispered its thanks and promised it would try to release itself from the earth plane and turn toward the light. Gradually the voice became unintelligible, then inaudible, and Logan was aware of Deon carefully guiding him out of the trance state.

Deon explained to the circle and the now-conscious medium that her fiancé's mother had been bedridden with a painful arthritic condition for a year before she died. The once devoutly religious woman had grown bitter. It seemed that the only thing that kept her alive was her intense desire not to leave her son. But at last she had died, a hating, resentful woman. Since his mother's death, Bill had been disturbed by terrible dreams and appearances of the bitter woman.

The day after the seance, Deon spoke to Bill by long-distance telephone and learned that he had had a particularly vivid and horrible nightmare during the time they were conducting the seance.

When Deon's circle met again a week later and Logan slipped once more into trance, Bill's mother returned. But this time the voice was tranquil. After thanking the group for their efforts on its behalf it said, "I am trying to turn toward the light. I will leave Bill alone. I will release him."

Logan later learned that Deon's fiancé was no longer plagued by grim dreams of his dead mother. At that time, when Logan's psychic abilities were still in an early stage of development, he was not completely convinced that he actually had served as a mediumistic channel for the spirit of a deceased personality. But he writes: "I could not argue, however, with the fact that the vocal, mental and even physical characteristics that I had manifested during the trance were (as Deon assured me) incontrovertibly those of Bill's mother."

In *The Anatomy of Prophecy*, Daniel Logan reveals that it was through trance sessions with Deon that he learned the identity of his own spirit guide, Dr. Stanley Podulsky, who, on the earth plane, had been a Polish chemist and pharmacist. Logan explains that he did not mention Dr. Stanley in his previous writings because he wanted to protect him from put-downs and to wait until the times were less critical toward psychic practitioners.

It was Richard Speidel who provided Logan with information concerning Dr. Stanley, then requesting that Logan prepare himself for trance work, as this would be his spiritual development in the future. Logan recalls that Richard Speidel told him that Dr. Stanley would work through him.

"He will utilize your body and vocal apparatus to accomplish this. There will be many souls that will be guided by Dr. Stanley. You will learn much from your association with him yourself. You are to be the channel through which Dr. Stanley will work, a vessel for his being."

Deon Frey has often served as a vessel for intelligences who claim to be spirit entities, and she has touched many lives in her role as High Priestess of the Tarot, as Spiritualist minister, and as a teacher in the most arcane tradition of Real Magick. Privileged, indeed, are those who have received private tutelage in the esoteric arts from this most gifted woman.

CHAPTER NINETEEN

We Are all Multi-Dimensional Beings

"No," the man whom many regard as the greatest physical medium of our time replied to my question, "you know that I do not believe in death. Oh, of course, there is the physical death, but the spiritual essence survives."

Olof Jonsson had told me before that he saw the life of the soul as inter-dimensional, dwelling within a fleshy domicile in our material dimension, graduating to a higher plane upon the physical death of its bone, blood and tissue.

"I feel more alive when I am in the right condition to *en clairvoyance* than I do when I am just eating my breakfast toast or working at my drawing board. Why is that? Because I know that my soul-self is more in the higher dimension than it is in the lower dimension with my physical body. When we hold seances, I am able to see the soul-bodies of other people from other dimensions sitting there around us. I cannot talk to them, but I can pick up psychic impressions from them."

I reminded Olof that once he had told me that even before death, our souls exist in more than one dimension.

"Yes, of course. We live in one dimension, but our souls really belong to another. In meditation and in dreams this fact becomes very apparent. It is quite simple for the transcendental element within us to rise to the higher plane of existence. It is really a matter of a rate of personal vibration. If you look at a fan, and it is going very slow, you will be able to see the blades. If the fan is going very fast, then you cannot see the blades. They have become invisible, and you can see through them. So it is with our souls as they begin to "vibrate' faster and faster. In time they require little effort to pass from one dimension to another."

But how do our souls pass through the "fan" – the barrier between material and spiritual dimensions – without getting chopped to pieces?

"For most souls, this passing through the barrier will be accomplished at the moment of physical death," Olof answered. "The vibrations will be so fast in the next life that we will be able to pass through walls, through concrete, through any physical barrier – like sunlight passes through glass, like heat passes through a steel pipe.

"But as I keep emphasizing, life, existence, is inter-dimensional, and through proper techniques of meditation, man may achieve full consciousness of his true potential before the transition of physical death. When one meditates properly, he learns to flow with the dimensional frequencies and to enter the higher planes of being while his soul still retains residence in the body," Olof continued.

"Of course, if one has allowed his psyche to become crystallized by an excessive interest in material possessions, proper meditation becomes all but impossible to achieve," the psychic went on. "Material objects belong to the lower dimension, and if one cannot release his hold on them, he will find the liberation of his psyche, both before and after physical death, very difficult."

MOVING THROUGH THE HIGHER DIMENSIONS

In his discussions with me, Olof Jonsson has repeatedly stressed the importance of meaningful and effective sessions of meditation in which the transcendent level of mind is allowed free reign to move through the higher dimensions freed from bodily concerns. According to Olof, such a meditative state is so valuable because "....it will help people to understand that this life really means almost nothing compared to what we can expect in the next life."

It is Olof Jonsson's firm conviction that once one has gained insight into the next state of existence, he has received a valuable perspective that will aid him in living his present life on the material plane much more significantly.

"I believe in everyone living the good life," Olof has said, "but I think we can do so honestly. We don't have to be cruel to one another. When man sees what awaits him in the afterlife, he will regard all the worries of this life to be but petty considerations."

What can man expect in the afterlife?

He can expect to know more about the universe, because he will have more senses than he has now, and he will be able to travel anywhere he desires in an instant.

Will the surroundings in the next world be similar to our earthly environment?

They will be similar, but much more wonderful, more colorful, and richer in texture.

But we ourselves will be mind-soul, rather than physical body.

Yes. Now we see our material world with five senses, and only occasionally do we utilize the transcendent level of consciousness which we call "psi," the sixth sense. In the next world, all souls will have full control of this unknown faculty and their existence will be fuller, richer.

In the next life, we will not have the temptations that we have in this life. There will be no need to steal, for example, because everyone will create with his own mind whatever he desires. Whoever wishes a large castle will build it with his mind. Whatever you want, you will have but to think it and it will be there.

The phenomenon of the seance room can be very impressive. Here under laboratory conditions, the Swedish psychic Olof Jonsson has caused a member of the circle to be levitated by unseen energies.

A WORLD OF PURE MIND

Olof Jonsson's vision of the afterlife is one of pure mind in which the techniques of existence seem very much like the mechanics of a dream. One dreams of an adventure on the open sea, and the marvelous dream machinery supplies full-masted sailing vessels, a complete crew, sea gulls, white-capped waves, and an exotic South Sea island. Can it be that one's life after death may be as personalized as his dream life on the material plane?

"Then," I asked Olof, "if the afterlife is a world of pure mind, or pure soul, one's yearnings and repressed desires might be realized and fulfilled after physical death."

Jonsson: Yes, but we will not long be interested in such things. We will know many more of the secrets of life, the real meanings of existence, so that we will not long be satisfied with building dream castles. We will become more concerned with learning more of the great spiritual lessons of the Universe. It is my impression that in the afterlife there will be another kind of "death," that is, a "transition," which will graduate the soul to an even higher plane of being. We will continue to evolve from plane to plane, on each level vibrating faster and faster, until we have become pure light, cosmic energy. At that time, we shall have achieved the highest of harmonious states.

"Even then, we will still have personality and intelligence?"

Jonsson: I believe that we belong to a system of universal intelligence. One can splinter off and become an individual any time he likes, even after harmonizing with the Supermind.

"Is there also a system of punishment in the afterlife?"

Jonsson: No. In this life we must have a police force to protect the so-called normal people from those who were born with flaws. It is my philosophy that we have no bad people, only those who are born with abilities or disabilities that differ from others. I believe that we all belong to a Supermind which we may call God, a Supermind that must obey the same universal laws which it has established for the most minute and flawed atom of its whole. In the afterlife, there is no punishment, no suffering, no good or bad; there is only perfect Harmony.

CHAPTER TWENTY

Questions and Answers on Life After Death

During the past thirty years, I have interviewed and corresponded with scores of mediums, ministers of Spiritual Science, psychic investigators, spokesman for Spiritualist publications, professional seers and clairvoyants, and ordinary men and women who have had extraordinary experiences that defy the tenets of our orthodox science. In this chapter, I have selected excerpts from discussions which were centered around the survival question. I have decided against giving attribution to source in order that I might set the bits and pieces down in a manner approximating a single freewheeling interview.

Scientist friends of mine have chided me by saying that psychical research can never become a science because the phenomena which it claims exists cannot be repeated at will. How could you react to such a statement?

"Many so-called psychic phenomena are able to satisfy the 'scientific' requirement of repeated performance, as note the statistical experiments in telepathy and clairvoyance.

"One should also point out that there are several phenomena under the aegis of orthodox science which do not lend themselves to this much-touted replication requirement. There is the whole area of natural phenomena, for example, which must be observed at the moment of occurrence and cannot be controlled by man. What about meteors, eclipses, lightning flashes, and the Northern lights? Because they are transitory, sporadic phenomena incapable of being repeated at the will of an investigator should someone declare that they not be recognized by scientific orthodoxy?"

But can you say that the reality of psychical phenomena has ever been proved?

"If you demand such proof as that offered by a mathematical formula or a chemical distillation, the answer would have to be that it has not. But let us remember that there are many areas in conventional branches of science where such certitude cannot be attained. There is the entire area of theoretical physics and our conjectures about space. How much of astronomy can provide this kind of tangible proof? And what of psychology, biology, and sociology? Who can ever really accurately predict anything with certainty when living creatures are involved?"

I have noticed that Spiritualists and psychical researchers have one thing in common and that is an inordinate amount of criticism from those outside the field. How do you account for this?

"The man in the street would not think to correct the computations of a higher mathematician, but he has no compunctions whatsoever about heaping ridicule and scorn upon those who seek to demonstrate the reality of nonphysical man. These critics, both lay and professional are generally little read in the field and have never attended a seance with a reputable medium. Many of the world's most prestigious scientists have invested a considerable amount of time in the research of spiritistic phenomena. Although these scientists may have had divergent opinions as to the origin of such manifestations, all of them who took the time to examine the raw data or to attend demonstrations of psychic phenomena later published positive opinions on the reality of the force at work."

For some time now it has been observed that perhaps the largest percentage of psychic phenomena center, in some way, around physical death. What is the possible significance of this observation?

"Statistical inquiries have demonstrated the correlation between death and the exercise of spontaneous psychic phenomena to be far more than an 'observation.' What such occurrences may be telling us is that something very potent may be freed from the limitations of the physical body at the moment of death."

Could you clarify just how Spiritualists and psychical researchers differ and how they may or may not be working for the same goal from opposite directions?

"Spiritualism is a religion with an entire religio-philosophical system which is built upon the 'fact' of survival beyond death.

"Psychical research is a systematic investigation which examines these `facts' (the phenomena of spiritism and spontaneous 'psi' phenomena) in an impartial manner in an attempt to establish their reality and their laws of operation."

Is it possible to explain away a great deal of mediumship through abnormal psychology?

"But how then would one account for the paranormal knowledge which these mediums often divulge during the trance state? A schizoid personalty, for example, cannot make accurate predictions of the future, or summon up information which is only known to a deceased personality."

But do such talents as telepathy and clairvoyance have their origin in spiritistic contact? Are not these phenomena natural manifestations of the living human psyche?

"Psychical researchers have advanced many hypotheses to explain paranormal phenomena. Spiritualists will, in their bias, interpret these manifestations to be direct actions of surviving personalities. More objective researchers admit the reality of the phenomena and their paranormal nature, but they remain skeptical about the spiritistic origin."

Do you, as a psychical researcher, believe that the essence of human personality may lie in an invisible spirit or entity?

"I cannot speak for all psychical researchers any more than one doctor can speak for all medical men, but I feel that the reality of the invisible human spirit is demonstrated to us every day. For example, and perhaps this is a simple analogy, when we speak with a person, we are looking at the individual's exterior – his clothing, his skin, his hair – but the actual 'person' to whom we are speaking remains invisible to us.

"Whether or not that invisible, essential stuff of personality can survive without a physical brain, is a question which can only be solved by the demonstrable facts which we are accumulating in psychical research."

Could mediumship be an inherited trait?

"Yes. My mother was a medium; my grandfather was one of the most powerful physical mediums of his time. Now, my second daughter seems to be displaying pronounced mediumistic ability." (*A medium*)

"It is highly probable that mediumship is to some extent hereditary." (*A psychical researcher*)

If mediumship is heredity, why hasn't such a trait been passed on to more people?

"During the Middle Ages, the Inquisition burned witches by the thousands. It seems highly likely that the witches of the medieval period were those people who displayed the talents of mediumship. You cannot have descendants if you have done away with the ancestors." (*A Medium*)

"The gifted medium is as rare as genius is rare in all fields of human endeavor. The brilliant and extraordinary mediums are as hard to find in each generation as the great musicians and painters." (*A psychical researcher*)

When I first became interested in the paranormal, I was warned about the dangers of psychic research. Do you feel such research to be dangerous?

"The dangers exist within the individual researcher, not within the subject under investigation. If an individual is an extremely nervous sort, he would do well to leave the field alone. There would also be no place for the emotional or the overly credulous investigator. If one maintains his common sense, his objectivity, and his sense of humor, there is no reason why this field should be any more fraught with dangers than any other."

How are the cases of spontaneous communications with those who have passed away regarded by the investigators of the survival question?

"Those cases in which an apparition of friend or loved one appears at the moment of death or in which an individual feels that he has in some way communicated with the spirit of a deceased personality, are extremely convincing and valuable to the recipient of such an experience. It is unfortunate, however, that such dramatic episodes are extremely difficult to relay in a manner that is convincing to a third person. Interior and subjective experiences always suffer when one attempts to communicate them to others.

"In the East such subjective experience of mystic phenomena is accepted at face value and is avidly sought after by others. Here in the West, we demand objective proof; and in cases where veridical information was not passed on, it is impossible to prove the reality of subjective experience – regardless of how meaningful it may have been to the individual recipient."

The power and adaptability of the subconscious mind has not yet been fathomed. Cannot all alleged spirits, which appear to communicate through the agent of the medium, be attributed to some creative facet of the subconscious interpreting a role, dramatically breathing personality in numerous characterizations with the facility of an accomplished actor?

"We have learned that the subconscious is, indeed, quite capable of fabricating personalities and of imitating the personal characteristics of actual people.

"Critics of the spiritistic hypothesis usually get around to drawing parallels between the spirit guide appearing during mediumistic trance and the various impersonations to which a hypnotized subject might give expression in an hypnotic trance. The great difference between these two 'beings' – the spirit guide and the charade of the subconscious during hypnotism – is that the creations of the subconscious are unable to provide us with information that has been gained through supra-normal means.

"It is one thing to tell a hypnotized subject to 'be' an old man and to imitate the actions of this hypothetical character, but it is something very much different to ask the spirit control to summon the personality of a specific elderly gentleman whose idiosyncracies would be well known to you.

"If you were to tell an entranced subject of hypnosis to play the part of your Uncle Edward, he would be at a loss to imitate the actions and speech of your uncle unless he had prior knowledge of the man.

"Now the hypnotized subject might very well put on an extremely good act, and his friends might swear that the personality which he is portraying is completely different from his own. As convincing as this performance might be to those who do not know Uncle Ed, you would find the imitation to be completely ineffectual and far from the mark.

"In mediumistic trance, the spirit control personality is able to provide the sitter with accurate descriptions of those who have passed on who were completely unknown to the medium when he lived. In direct voice control, the surviving entities may speak and act in a manner which is quite familiar to the sitters. In addition, they may supply them with knowledge which can be supported by investigation. Simple telepathy cannot explain such experiences."

But what if certain facts about a deceased personality might be present in the subconscious of the sitter? Isn't it possible that certain facts of which he has no conscious awareness may be dredged up in the course of a seance and "revealed" to him? Apparently the communications of a discarnate entity, these would really be the result of telepathic rapport between the sitter and the medium.

"It cannot be denied that telepathy is difficult to rule out in some cases, but there are numerous instances wherein the medium has relayed information which could not have been present in the mind of the sitter because the knowledge was known only to the deceased.

"Of course the unyielding skeptic might insist that if any living mind were aware of the content or substance of the spirit communication, then the survival hypothesis is invalid and telepathy must receive credit for the information. This theory would suggest either a universal mind containing all thoughts and memories of all humankind, or an incredible telepathic omniscience on the part of the medium, which would allow him to reach any living brain anywhere in the world. The survival hypothesis seems easier to accept than either one of the alternatives offered by the skeptic."

What kind of proof does the parapsychologist hope to obtain in support of the survival hypothesis?

"The kind of proof which is obtained in such material sciences as chemistry and physics may never be achieved by the parapsychologist. The proof which the psychical researcher hopes to offer the world would more nearly resemble the legal proof acceptable in the courtroom. Evidence presented in such an open and objective manner that any reasonable person, upon examination of the evidence, will conclude that the *cons* balanced by the *pros* indicate the probability of the thesis."

CHAPTER TWENTY-ONE

The Mediums
Among Us

What kind of a person becomes a medium? Is it the "odd" or poorly adjusted members of society who most often demonstrate a tendency to psychic sensitivity? Is it true that the general level of intelligence among mediums is very low?

The first thing I learned when I began an investigation of mediumship is that mediums are people. They are nurses, accountants, journalists, real estate agents, advertising executives, ordained ministers, housewives, farmers – in short, one finds as wide a range of occupations among medium as he would find among people who are left-handed. Few mediums are fulltime professional psychics.

As far as social adjustment is concerned, psychic researchers have found that those who are well-adjusted socially and who are possessed of an extroverted rather than an introverted personality consistently score higher in ESP tests. The same may be said of medium. One consistently encounters the enthusiastic extrovert rather than the moody or misanthropic introvert.

There is no conclusive evidence to indicate that high or low intelligence contributes to either ESP abilities or mediumistic sensitivity. Again, one seems to find generally average to high-average intelligence among mediums. Certainly not the low I.Q. dullards that some people like to consider as being representative of "someone who talks to ghosts."

I have been interviewing mediums and other psychically gifted individuals for thirty years. Although my primary goal has been simply to accumulate as much information as possible about these "special" people, one of my main objectives is to attempt to determine certain patterns of personality development which might be consistent in the evolution of mediumistic abilities. If it is possible to find at least a few common denominators, then it may also be possible to understand why some people become mediumistic. Once a few such factors – if such factors exist – can be isolated, then we may find ourselves holding a key or two to what it is that enables certain people to unlock remarkable powers – although those powers may be in a latent state in everyone.

For example, one thing which I have noticed in my correlations is the fact that nearly every medium has undergone a series of personal crisis in his childhood or youth. Dr. Gardner Murphy, one of the United States' leading contemporary parapsychologists, has noted that "....severe illness, things that are biologically or in a broad sense personal crises – disrupting, alerting situations" may encourage psychic experiences.

John Pendragon, England's remarkable clairvoyant, and I discussed this aspect of psychic precipitation at great length. Pendragon suffered a number of childhood illnesses and traumas which were both physically and mentally taxing. A sickly childhood seems common to a good many mediums and psychics.

"Certainly I have had a great many personal crises," Pendragon told me, "but I do not hesitate to point out that it would be quite wrong to say that those who suffer are necessarily Occultists. (John Pendragon was a clairvoyant who did not doubt the survival of human personality after death, but he did not attribute his abilities to the interaction of discarnate entities.)

"The development of my psychism appears to have come about as the result of combined mental, emotional, and physical stress. Yet to be dogmatic about such a statement would indeed be unwise, for I have known persons of both sexes who had had stresses greater than mine and these crises have not caused psychic activation. I think that emotional, mental, and physical stresses, in certain rare instances, produce psychism. I was one of those instances."

As I cross-check the results of the questionnaires that mediums and psychics have voluntarily answered for me, I cannot help noting certain parallels between the creative personality and the psychic personality. It would seem that the divine spark which burns within each of us – brighter in some than in others, of course, but nonetheless, always there – must find its own level of expression; and whether it be in musical composition or clairvoyance, painting or precognition, scientific experimentation or spirit communication, may only be a condition of circumstances and environment.

My interviews have raised a good many points which some mediums may consider inconsequential, perhaps even ridiculous, but each has been included in the interest of adding some new clue to the enigma of mediumship. I offer the following, then, in the form of a survey rather than a thesis.

Question: What has been your formal education?

None of the mediums which I questioned were without a high school education. A large percentage had B.A. or B.S. degrees, and some had graduated from law schools, religious seminaries, or had obtained their master's degrees.

The powers of the legendary Kahunas of Hawaii are impressive even to a seasoned investigator such as Brad Steiger. Here, circa 1972, Steiger calls upon Morrnah Nalamaku Simeona, one of the most gifted of the remaining Kahunas, to share her knowledge with a conference audience.

Question: At what age did your mediumistic abilities begin to manifest themselves?

I had always been told that a "natural" medium gives evidence of his powers when he is but a child. I have found this old psychic maxim to be true, at least with regard to the sampling of mediums I have interviewed. The majority have indicated the age of five as the time of paranormal rebirth, although some claim to have given evidence of psychic gifts as early as three, and others state that they worked to achieve a psychic development which did not come until much later in life.

Question: From what source do you consider your mediumistic abilities to be derived (i.e., God, guiding spirits, the subconscious, etc.)? If your answer is "spirits," do you have a spirit guide? What is his name and background and what do you feel is his relationship to you?

The great majority of mediums credit God and a spirit control as a dual source of their abilities. Some recognize the role of the subconscious in some of their manifestations but hold such phenomena to be very much different from the higher phenomena inspired by the Deity and the spirit guide.

"God and spirit forces guide me," says one medium. "I do not reveal the names of my spirit guides or anything else about them."

Question: Do you feel that your mediumistic abilities are compatible with the main bodies of organized religion, that they transcend organized religion, that they complement organized religion, that they have little to do with organized religion?

Among mediums who have completed the questionnaire, not one considers the exercise of his mediumistic abilities to conflict in any way with the tenets of organized religion.

"These powers both complement and transcend organized religion," is a fairly typical answer.

Question: What "part" of man do you believe survives physical death?

All mediums questioned indicated that they believed man's soul to be immortal. Some phrased this sentiment in such expressions as:

"The seat of conscious individuality. Call it soul if you like."

"The Spirit of God never dies and I am part of him."

"The Psyche is immortal, eternal, and indestructible."

Others made mention of the "spirit body" which would be utilized in the Beyond.

"We will have a body nearly like the one we have now."

"An astral form will encase the spirit."

"A higher vehicle of finer vibration will persist."

Question: Are you aware of any sensory impressions or responses (perspiration, quickening of the pulse, dryness of mouth, etc.) while giving a reading, receiving an image, or in the performance of any mediumistic abilities?

A few mediums stated that the onset of their psychic gifts were "...as natural as it is to be talking to you."

Some said that they needed nothing to get in the mood. "My workers are from the spirit," says one medium, "and I have been trained to work when and where I am needed."

Other mediums blamed their inability to function properly on certain occasions to the attitude of the sitters. "Sometimes my guide simply refuses to work with certain people," stated one Spiritualist minister.

Several mediums admitted that there were times when it was difficult to summon the psychic energy necessary to establish spirit contact, and they suggested such remedies as prayer, psychic development exercises, and playing music of an inspirational nature.

Question: Does your "talent" makes you feel uneasy at time?"

All mediums questioned answered with a firm, "no."

Question: How do your friends or family react to your mediumistic abilities?

This query brought a number of interesting responses. Some families, it seems, are quite proud to have a medium in their numbers; others gradually accept the fact with the same resignation families come to accept one of their members to be an alcoholic; and still other families make outcasts of a mediumistic member and accuse him of being in league with the devil.

It was not surprising to learn that mediums tend to marry mediums in about the same ratio that members of any profession or occupation intermarry. A considerable percentage have received divorces from mates who were unsympathetic to their mediumship and later married fellow mediums or convinced Spiritualists. I also found it quite interesting to learn how many children had inherited the psychic abilities or tendencies of mediumistic parents.

Here are some of the responses to this question:

"My wife is 'one of us,' an excellent spiritual healer. My son has displayed good potential, but needs to develop. My mother is a firm skeptic.

"Some of my own blood think I am doing the work of the devil!"

"My family *believes* in psychic phenomena, but they feel it is something to be shunned."

Question: Do you follow any special diet?

Here there were rather sharp dissension among the mediums. Some were very strong for a vegetarian diet. Others stated that if one had to rely on a special diet to establish contact with the "other side" then his mediumship was terribly weak to begin with.

"A routine of special diet is essential. Fasting also proves beneficial, especially in healing phenomena."

"I lean toward vegetarianism, but my wife must have red meat."

"It is essential to eat a great deal of fresh fruits – especially grapes."

Question: Do you find that a small amount of alcohol may aid you in achieving impressions? What about drugs" Do you think that the psychedelic drugs, such LSD, may be helpful to a medium?

I have often heard enemies of Spiritualism accuse mediums of being problem drinkers or drug addicts. It would seem, judging from the preliminary tabulations of my survey and interviews, that another stereotype has been laid to rest. Virtually all of the mediums who have completed my questionnaire are total abstainers. Less than two percent would even admit to taking an occasional social drink. The suggestion that drugs may be used to implement psychic expression met with violent negative responses. It would seem that, with the exception of prescribed medications used in the treatment of specific illnesses, mediums have no use for any kind of drug.

Some typical comments:

"I never use drugs or liquor. I will not even use drugs when I am ill!"

"I believe in ESP, not LSD!"

"I think anything that dulls the normal senses will dull the 'extra' senses, too. We are careful not to mix alcohol with our work, and we are definitely opposed to drugs."

"The powers within do not need any stimulation from artificial powers without."

Question: What is the relationship, as you see it, between sexual expression, or frustration, and the functioning of your mediumistic abilities?

This was an area that would, of course, bring a wide range of responses, depending upon the sexual inhibitions of the respondent. Some mediums seemed shocked that the interviewer could suggest that the slightest correlation might exist between their sex lives and the functioning of their abilities. Others frankly stated that they had long noticed a definite interaction between sexual and mediumistic expression.

Representative comments would be:

"There is no question in my mind that mediumistic phenomena is related to sex, and I know a good many of my fellow mediums who have severe sexual problems."

"Good sex is necessary to psychological health. And anything that contributes to better psychological health will help one's mediumistic abilities."

"Good sexual expression is a great asset to the effective functioning of my mediumistic abilities."

"The development of the spiritual strengths reduces the desire for sex."

"There is absolutely no relationship between sex and mediumism. I consider the question in extremely poor taste."

Question: Have you ever had what you consider to have been an authentic out-of-body experience (astral projection)?

I have thus far encountered only one medium who says that he has not made at least one astral voyage. Researcher Frederic W. H. Meyers has written that cases of astral projection present   "...the most extraordinary achievement of the human will. What can lie further outside any known capacity than the power to cause a semblance of oneself to appear at a distance? What can be more a central action – more manifestly the outcome of whatever is deepest and most unitary in man's whole being? Of all vital phenomena, I say, that is the most significant; this self-projection is the one definite act which it seems as though a man might perform equally well before and after bodily death."

A number of leading psychologists have recently declared that certain specially gifted people are able to separate their minds from their bodies, so it hardly came as a surprise to learn that nearly all mediums claim to have experienced at least one out-of-body projection.

"I have made about a dozen astral flights under test conditions. In one experiment, a tape recording of my voice was made from my astral body while my physical body lay a great distance away."

"I have had many out-of-body experiences. I have traveled to distant places, people, and scenes while in my astral body."

"For nine months, while my physical body lay ill with sleeping sickness, I travelled constantly in my astral body and saw things which I could later verify."

Question: Do you have vivid dreams? Are you able to exercise a certain amount of control in your dreams?

I was very curious to compare the dream-life of the medium with other studies of dreams and their possible relationship to certain personality types.

"I have never had what you would call a pretty dream. It seems most of my dreams are out of terrible frustration. I am usually lost and wandering. I don't often remember my dreams."

"I have vivid dreams. I have successfully experimented with dream control and analysis, but I feel that there are less cumbersome ways of accomplishing the same things."

"I have always had extremely vivid dreams since early childhood. I have never attempted to control these dreams, however."

The great majority of mediums interviewed admitted that they have vivid dream-lives, but I was surprised to find quite a number who claimed that they never dreamed at all. Research at the various "dream labs" around the country has told us a great deal more about sleep and dreaming that we formerly knew, and we have learned that the person who claims that he never dreams is only admitting that he does not remember his dreams. Each of us dreams every single night, probably in dream cycles. There is certainly no rule book which decrees that every medium must have extensive recall of his or her dreams, but somehow I have always felt that dreams would play a rather important role in the psychological life of every medium.

CHAPTER TWENTY-TWO

Seeking Evidence of Reincarnation

The young man sat slumped in his chair, speaking in a soft monotone that had begun to accelerate and take on more dramatic fluctuations in voice pattern. Then his eyes widened in fear and he gripped the arms of the large chair in which he sat: "They swarm over the ship!" he screamed. "Drive them back into the sea! Kill them!"

The great Swedish mystic Olof Jonsson moved forward. "You will relax," he told the young man. "You will be able to see things in a more detached manner. You will be able to tell us everything that is happening around you, but you will feel no fear, no pain."

The hypnotized subject was describing an ostensible past life that he had lived as a Dane in about the year 892. He had already told Jonsson and the assembled experimenters that he had lived in Jylland and had been a fisherman by trade. He had a wife, quite plump, and six children.

He was called Sten the Weakling, not because of a lack of physical strength, but because he was regarded as a bit mentally slow by his fellows. As a Viking warrior, however, he had distinguished himself in many rugged battles. Now, as his unseen audience listened in silence, "Sten" described the last battle of his life.

"Over the sides with the swine!" he shouted amidst wild battle cries. He and the Danish comrades were doing battle with a marauding Swedish longship, and it was a vicious encounter with members of one tribe of Vikings pitted against another. "By Odin! Feed the swine to the fish!"

In mid-shout, the young man gasped and clutched his side. He clenched his teeth so that he would not whimper his pain.

"Remember, you will feel no pain," Olof reminded him. "What has happened to you?"

"A spear," he cursed. "A spear from that coward. He came at me from behind, and I turned in time to catch the throw in my side."

"Is it bad?"

"Sten" nodded. "I can hear the sound of the Valkyrie. They came to take me to Valhalla. One of the Swedish dogs raises his sword and hacks at my throat, but I do not care. I feel no pain. I have died in battle as a true Viking warrior."

The young man "Sten" released a last breath, and one of the witnesses stepped forward to clutch Olof Jonsson's sleeve. "My God, man!" he whispered hoarsely, "don't let him die!"

Olof assured the witnesses that he retained control of the personality.

"Sten," Olof said to the dying man, "tell us what happens now – after the state known as physical death."

"I s-seem. . . ."

"Yes?" Olof prompted after several moments of silence from Sten.

"I seem to be floating," the entity answered. "Just floating in the sky."

"Can you see your body?"

"Yes," the entity answered. "It is right below me. I can see it on the deck of our longship. How strange it seems to see me down there and yet know that I am really up here. My head... its head... has nearly been chopped away from the neck. There is blood all around. It appears that my comrades are losing. The Swedes are too many for them."

"Can you see any Valkyrie around you?" Olof wanted to know. "Are they taking you to Valhalla?"

"I thought I heard them as I was dying," the entity known as Sten answered, "but I do not see them."

"Is there anyone there with you?"

"I seem to sense other presences," the Viking replied. "But I do not seem to know them. I cannot yet see them too clearly."

"Can you tell anything at all about them?" Olof pursued the matter.

"Now, Sten, I want you to move through time and space until it is July 15, 1950, ten fifteen p.m. You will be once more in the library of Dr. Petersen of Stockholm, and you will be once more the entity known as Lars Torkelsen." Olof commanded. "By the time I count to three, you will be back in the present. One, drifting through time and space; two, coming closer and closer; three...."

MOVING BACK IN TIME

Olof Jonsson: Before I left Sweden, I had placed nearly one thousand people into hypnotic trance and had led them back to relive what appeared to be their former lives. One young woman gave names which we were able to trace through old church records. She named many members of her family in her former life, and we located old records and deeds to support her apparent memory.

There were many other cases in which a great number of details of an alleged former life were given by the subject, and we were often able to substantiate a good many of these facts. I have also sent subjects back thousands of years; but even though observing historians and investigators may agree that the subject has the flavor of the time, there is no way to check a story that goes back so many years.

Brad Steiger: What have you been able to learn about the nature of reincarnation in your research?

One time when I had a subject in deep trance and had moved him from the death experience to a spiritual plateau between lives, I asked him to talk about how the soul progresses.

He said that around the soul is built a body that later develops until the point of physical death. At that time, the soul continues its wanderings in the world of spirit. A span of about 144 years passes before the soul again takes habitation in a new body, and each soul is reborn on an average of twelve times. After the last incarnation, we become wholly spiritual creatures.

When I asked what it was like to live in the world of spirits between incarnations, he answered that it was wonderful: he felt so in harmony with the Universe.

He also informed me that each soul is reunited with his soulmate, the mate he had in his first incarnation. The soulmate is like one's true "other half," and one will be whole and happy after his final incarnation.

Let us examine what awaits man in the afterlife from the viewpoint of reincarnation. Olof, what do you feel happens immediately after the soul leaves the body in physical death?

I feel that the soul is translated into a higher dimension, the soul will be born a spirit, not as body. On this plane we are used to seeing bodies in order to identify a person, but I don't believe that a body structures is necessary in a higher life condition. I feel that the material plane of existence on which we are living now is but a moment in our *real* lives.

Where does the soul go after physical death?

The soul leaving the plane of materialism is very much like a voyager leaving the Mainland and venturing out to sea. As time passes, he drifts farther and farther away from the old. After he had docked in a fascinating new world, he becomes less interested in what he has left behind him and becomes more concerned about developing the new opportunities before him. At first, the voyager may feel a bit insecure while he is getting to know new friends and so forth, but when he has established a new home, the old Mainland becomes only a part of his memory.

Then why reincarnation? Why do people come back to the Mainland?

Not everyone does. I do not believe that everyone reincarnates, or at least not so often.

I think it is like when the farmer puts a seed into the earth: sometimes the plant grows and sometimes it doesn't. I think it may be the same with souls. Not all of them grow properly.

And if they do not grow properly, they must be replanted.

Yes.

Do you believe in Karma?

Yes, if you mean the Divine Laws of Compensation and the Supreme Law of Spiritual Growth. If you mean Karma as some kind of punishment for the soul, then I do not accept it. I do not accept punishment in the afterlife or in a series of incarnations. I believe that we may have to endure certain kinds of sufferings to learn important lessons, to clear a situation. I do not believe that suffering is meant by Divine Intelligence to be a punishment for sins.

At what moment do you believe the soul enters the physical body?

I believe the soul enters the body when the infant takes its first breath of life upon achieving independence from the mother's womb.

What affect do you think birth control pills might have on the Wheel of Rebirth?

I don't think birth control pills have any effect at all on reincarnation. If one misses the train, he simply waits for another.

What about abortion? How might abortion affect reincarnation or Karma?

I don't think abortion will interfere with reincarnation in any way. If you do not buy one automobile, you may soon be interested in another. If you don't get into one body, you'll get into another.

What do you think is the ultimate goal of life in view of the spiritual progress of reincarnation?

I think what we are working for is not something materialistic. We are striving to achieve Harmony and a reuniting with the Great Mind and its complete knowledge of the Universe.

CHAPTER TWENTY-THREE
Other Lives

In 1966, I made the acquaintance of Loring G. Williams, a New Hampshire school teacher-hypnotist, who had begun researching cases suggestive of reincarnation through hypnotic regression techniques. "Bill," as he preferred to be called, had investigated the case of a new Hampshire schoolboy, who under hypnosis, recalled details of a life as a farmer in Jefferson, North Carolina, during the period of 1840 to 1863. The multitude of details were so precise and convincing that I suggested a collaboration with Bill, which resulted in *Other Lives* (Hawthorn, 1969).

Other Lives received very good reviews in even the "straight" press. In one instance a team of journalists followed our trail and double-checked our research. Although they might not have concluded their detective work by declaring themselves open advocates of reincarnation, they did state that we have not hoaxed or misrepresented our work and that they – and others – should keep an open mind toward such research as ours.

I became thoroughly fascinated by the concept of researching ostensible past lives through hypnotic regression, and I found that I wanted to continue such investigations.

Interestingly, one of the very first articles on the paranormal which I published when I was an Iowa high school teacher back in the 1950s was a piece on past lives entitled, "How Many People Are You?" Robert A. W. "Bob" Lowndes of *Exploring The Unknown* bought that work and a number of others, which encouraged this budding author, who was writing mystery stories on the side, to devote more effort toward his greater love, the unexplained.

From 1967 until his death in 1975, Bill and I investigated dozens of cases suggestive of reincarnation, and we taped hundreds of hours of men and women dramatically providing details of what seemed to be actual life experiences which they – or their spiritual essences – had lived in other times. Together with Bill, I became, for a short time, obsessed with *proving* reincarnation to a Western world populated primarily by skeptics or denominational dogmatists; and we did manage to unearth a great deal of supportive data for "other lives." In numerous instances we located birth certificates, land grants, property transfers, military papers, and death certificates of the actual personages whom our hypnotically regressed subjects claimed to have been.

BELIEF AND INTERPRETATION

But again and again I found that what a person believed prior to our exposing him to such data determined his interpretation of such evidence. If the data somehow violated his religious belief structure, he had to reject it for fear of losing his Soul (I could never understand why the evidence would not be evaluated as *proof* that he had one!) If the data offended his sense of the natural, materialistic order of the Twentieth Century, he had to reject it as a matter of loyalty to the mechanical gods of the Space Shuttle and I.B.M.

On the other hand, if one were receptive to our research, it was usually because he found it excitingly supportive of his metaphysical belief structure. If anything, such a person might criticize us for not going far enough in dealing with the Lords of Karma, the Akashic Records, and a host of colorful entities who comprise a rather rigid hierarchy for certain occultists.

And if we had expected to be warmly embraced by the academic parapsychologists, we were to be disappointed. Some spoke augustly from behind the walls of their tenure and their scholastic degrees and declared that Bill and I did not have the "right" to be conducting such research. According to them, one could only be rewarded such a "right" by being part of a noble line who passed the holy grail from one to another and who paid homage to certain solidly entrenched academicians.

Those parapsychologists who were friendly to us were the laboratory scientists who recognized that we who were in the field actually doing the research could make significant contributions to a body of knowledge that might be considered as growing, rather than as rigidly set. But in their cautious acceptance of our worth, they also made an undeniable point:

They reminded us that such data, as impressive and as convincing as it might be, still did not actually *prove* reincarnation or survival of the spirit essence after physical death. What our work did appear to prove was the enormous reach of humankind's non-material self through such faculties of mind as telepathy, clairvoyance, and psychometry. In other words, our subjects were somehow able to gather a great deal of accurate information about actual people who had once lived – people about whom they would have no way of knowing *anything* through normal, sensory, data-receiving mechanisms.

Again, in the final analysis, each individual must interpret the evidence of reincarnation research for himself or herself.

A LIFE IN COLONIAL AMERICA

A young woman named Mary Tobbin came to the Williams' home and asked if the hypnotist could help clear up a mild skin rash on her arm. Bill was intensely interested in the medical applications of hypnosis, especially in the diagnostic aspects. Of course, he never prescribed for any illness, and he did not pretend for one moment to accomplish miracle healings; but he found that the minor complaints which fall into the area of the psychosomatic can often be cleared up through the applications of hypnotic power of suggestion.

Mary Tobbin proved to be an excellent hypnotic subject. She went into light trance quickly and easily. After Bill had planted the suggestion that her skin rash would disappear, he brought Mary back to full consciousness and obtained her consent to place her into a deep trance so that he might attempt to regress her. Mary readily granted her permission, and the following remarkable transcription is a result of that initial session.

Oh, oh, I see some rats! Yeah, all sorts of rats.
Where are they?
They're on a ship.
What's your name?
Abigail. Abigail Daws.
And where is the ship going?
It's suppose' to go to America.
Oh, what year is this?
1692.
Where does this ship come from?
England.
How old are you?
I'm fourteen.
I see. Who is with you on this ship? Your mother and your father?
No, I'm by myself.
How come you're all alone?
I'm a servant.
Whose servant?
I don't know.

How do you know who to work for if you don't know them?
I'm going to find out.
Oh, I see. They're not with you. Well, were you sold to someone in America? (Abigail appears to have been an indentured servant.)
Yeah, I lost my money and they put me in jail.
I'm going to count to three and we'll go back two months when you were still in England. One, two, three! Now what are you doing, Abigail?
I'm in jail.
Why?
I stole some bread.
Do you have a mother and father?
No, they're dead.
How long have them been dead?
About five years.
And how old are you?
I'm (slight pause) fourteen.
So you stole some bread and they put you in jail. How long are they going to keep you there?
I don't know, maybe forever.
Well, I'll count to three, and we'll take you to the day that they're going to let you out of there. One, two, three! Now what's going on?
They tell me I'm going away, that I'm going to America. I don't want to go. I don't want to go there!
Who's telling you all this?
A man, a big man. I don't know who he is. He's nasty. He's a big man. He's got black hair and a black beard, and he smells dirty. Ugh, he smells awful!
We'll count to three and you will be on the other side of the water; you will be in America. One, two, three. Now what do you see?
Getting off the ship. It's coming to Virginia.
Virginia, what port in Virginia?
I don't know! I never heard of it.
Are there many people there?
(Abigail begins to cough violently.)
What's the matter? I'll count to three and your cough will stop. One, two, three. What was the matter?
I had a bad cough.
Where did you get that, on the ship?
No, I had it before.
How long have you had it?
About a month, I guess.
Does it get worse?
Yeah, I don't feel very well.
Does it make you spit up blood?
Yes, sometimes.

You say the ship is just coming into town Okay, it will be one week later so you can be settled. One, two, three. Now what do you see?

I'm working in the kitchen.

Whose kitchen?

The Jacksons.

What town is it in Virginia?

Richmond.

How did you get to Richmond from the boat?

In a cart.

How do you feel now?

Not very well. They don't make me work very hard, those people.

They're pretty good to you?

Yes.

What kind of a place do they have?

A big place, real nice. They have lots of land. (Another fit of coughing)

We'll count to three and the coughing will stop. One, two, three. What do they raise on this farm?

Oh, some vegetables and some chickens, and they have some cotton.

Do they have a lot of help?

Yes, they have a lot of help.

Do they have slaves or what?

They have nigras, they're called. (Black slaves were first brought to Virginia – and the Colonies – in 1619. After 1690, large numbers of slaves were brought to the plantations to fill the demand for cheap labor).

What do you do – cook, wash dishes, or what?

I bake bread.

Oh, I see. Who does the cooking?

The black mammy.

Do you get good food?

Yes, pretty good.

Do you get lots of it?

No, there's too many of us.

What do you get to eat?

Onions, carrots, a lot of beans.

What do you have for meat?

Salt pork, Ech! I hate that!

How do you make bread?

Well, you take some flour, the flour they grind down. . .and you knead it....Then you let it set overnight. Then you knead it...and...put it into little things.

How many loaves do you have to make a day?

Oh, maybe fourteen or maybe thirteen, lots and lots of them. Then you put in into the oven.

What do you have for an oven?

It's a great big thing.

How do you heat it?
With wood.
We'll count to three, and it will be five years later, and you will tell me what's going on. One, two, three. Now what do you see?
Nothing. (The death experience has taken place).
What are you doing?
Floating.
All right, I'll count to three again, and we'll go back to your last day as Abigail. One, two, three. Now what do you see?
(Violent spasms of coughing)
Abigail, you don't have to cough. I'll count to three and your coughing will stop. One, two, three. All right, you don't have to cough; you can tell us what is going on.
I'm sick.
Where are you?
The work house.
Where are the Jacksons?
They're going away. They're always gone away.
How old are you now?
I must be about seventeen. Yeah, I'm seventeen.
How long have you been here?
It must be three years.
Do you like it here?
Yes, it's nice and peaceful here, and the sun shines.
Do you like it better than England?
Yes.
So you're glad you came over?
Yes, I'm glad I came over here.
How do you feel? How has this cough of yours been?
Awful, it gets worse.
Do you still spit up blood now and then?
Oh, yes, all the time. Yes.
They don't do anything for it There's nothing you can do?
No.
We'll go along and you an tell us what happens now? One, two, three. Tell me what's happening now.
I'm awful sick. I keep coughing and coughing, and I keep spitting up blood. I'm dying and people tell me I'm dying.
Are you glad you're dying?
No, I don't want to die! I don't want to die! (Becoming hysterical) *No, I'm too young to die! I don't want to die, no! I can't die! I'm too young! I don't want to die. I'm too young to die!*
I'll count to three and it will be all over with. One, two, three. Now what do you see?

Nothing. (The tone of the voice is now relaxed, almost to the point of total indifference.)
Where are you?
Floating.
Can you see your body there?
Yep.
What's happened to it?
Nothing. It's lying there.
Is anybody attending to it?
Yes. The black mammy.
What's she doing?
She's cleaning me up. Oh, yeah.
Oh, now what's she doing?
She's lifting me into a pretty dress.
She's quite nice to you.
Yes, she is; she's good. Yes.
Now what's going on?
People are walking by.
Do they have you in a box or anything?
Yeah.
What kind of a box?
A pine one.
Are the Jacksons there?
No.
Who is coming by?
All the nigras.
Are they all good friends of yours?
Yeah, I'm friendly.
Do they have a preacher or anyone for you?
Yeah.
What's he have to say?
He just says I'm nice. Yeah, I was a good girl.
Is that all he says?
Yeah.
What do they say at the grave?
They just say from ashes to ashes, from dust to dust. Then they throw me in the grave. They cover me over.
What are you doing, just floating and watching all this?
Yeah.
It doesn't bother you to watch?
Naw.
Are you glad now that you died?
Yes!
It's a lot better, isn't it?

Yeah, I like it! I like to float!
You're just floating?
Yep.
I'm going to count to three, and you will wake up in the present time. You're going to feel very relaxed and very, very rested. Better than you have in a long time. One, you're starting to wake up. Two, your eyes are beginning to open now. Three, you're wide awake and feeling fine.

THE ULTIMATE DESTINATION

In his *The Destiny of Man* , J. G. Fichte argued that since man is not a product of the world of sense, his existence can never be attained in that world. Man's ultimate destination, it would seem, lies beyond time and space and all things connected with the world of sense.

Pierre Leroux points out that if we learn to regard the world as a series of successive lives, we may be able to perceive, at least partially, how God, for whom neither time nor space exists, can permit suffering as being a necessary phase men must pass in order to reach a state of true happiness which we cannot conceive from our mortal viewpoint.

"A lifetime may be needed merely to gain the virtues which annul the errors of man's preceding life," said the novelist Honore' de Balzac. "The virtues we acquire, which develop slowly within us, are the invisible links which bind each one of our existences to the other – existences which the spirit alone remembers...."

A HERMIT IN THE WOODS

In another session of hypnotic regression, Mary Tobbin recalled a life in which she was born a boy in the United States about 1840. She describes in great detail her life as a farm boy who lives with an abandoned mother and a younger sister. When he is in his early teens, the boy leaves home and goes in search of the father who deserted them. Although he spends a good deal of time wandering about the countryside, he never finds his father.

When the Civil War breaks out, the young man, who has become something of a misanthrope, refuses to bear arms, but he does serve as a drummer for the Union forces. After the war he completely withdraws from the society of men and becomes a hermit. He lives along in the woods for the rest of his long life, surrounded by Jolly, his pet bear, a raccoon that sleeps on his bed at night; and other animal friends. It should be noted that the hermit's speech patterns are markedly different from those of either Mary Tobbin or Abigail Daws.

This tape is most remarkable as it records the encroaching old age of the hermit and his death scene. The voice of the narrator becomes weary and enfeebled. Associations become slow and confused.

At one point on the tape, when Williams asks the hermit if he would like to live another eighty years, the old man replies, "Oh, I couldn't stand it."

An acceptance of death is clearly seen as the hermit observes that "it's about that time. I'm gettin' ready to go."

A friend, who had died several years before the hermit's own reported demise, circa 1910, stops by for a visit in his ethereal form. (This was one of the many cases which Williams had on tape in which a deathbed visitation is reported by the dying subject.)

When the hermit passes on, he, too, reports his essential self floating above the body. He is resentful of two trappers who stop by the cabin and bury him. "I don't know those men, and I don't like them!" he complains.

He watches the men putting his body in a crude coffin and covering it with dirt. He reports this without emotions, because, "It isn't me in there."

At this point, Bill asked the entity to "float" on for another ten years. "Who are you now?" the hypnotist asked the embodied soul.

The entity gives the name which it possessed as the hermit, then pauses as if uncertain. "I think that's who I am."

Another ten years and the entity must struggle to remember the hermit's name. At Bill's next count the entity states that it has no name.

FLOATING THROUGH TIME

Throughout his research, Williams found an average of approximately eighty years between lives. He was by no means dogmatic about this finding, and, obviously, this case was to prove an exception, because, according to the hermit, he died in 1910, and the young woman sitting before Williams had been born in 1943. Bill was determined to lead the entity up to the birth experience in its present incarnation.

Are you floating?

Yeah, I'm just floating.

You're going to float on a little more, a little, more, nearer today now. What do you see?

I don't know. I don't know, just things.

What things?

Just things. I don't know. People. There's a field near a beach. There's lots of people.

What's your name?

I don't know. I don't have a name.

Are you still floating?

No, I'm there! I'm watching!

What are the people doing?

I don't know! (Becoming excited) *I don't know what they're doing, but they're awful. They're hurting him! It's awful! They're awful* (beginning to cry). *They're hurting him!*

We'll go on to three years later. One, two, three! Now what do you see?
I see a house.
Where?
I don't know. It's just a little house. It's cute.
What's your name?
Mar-r-y. (Drawing out the name in little girl fashion)
How old are you?
Two!
We're going back to your first day as Mary. You can tell me all about that. One, two, three. Now what do you see?
Black.
I see. What are you doing?
Nothing.
Where are you?
I don't know.
All you see is black?
Yep.
In just a few minutes now you will have to see something. One, two, three. Now what do you see?
White.
Where are you now?
I don't know. Oh, look at the people! Oh!
What are they doing?
I don't know. Oh, a lady there!
What's she doing?
I don't know!
What's she got on?
White.
What do you have on?
Nothing.
How big are you?
I'm little. Yeah, real little! Awful little!
What's your name?
Mar-r-y.
How old are you?
I'm about two minutes old!
Do you remember being born?
Nope. All those people are happy. Ha-ha! Ha-ha!
(Begins to laugh wildly.)
I'll count to three now, and it will be the next day. One, two, three. It's the next day. What do you have on today?
A pink nightie.
Do you like that Is it comfortable?
Yeah, I like it. (Then, changing her mind) My hands are tied in, though; I

don't like that, I don't like my hands tied. It's awful.

I'm going to count to three, and it will be six months later. One, two, three. Now what do you see?

I'm with my daddy. I've never seen him before. He's my daddy, though. (Mary Tobbin's father had been in military service at the time of her birth and was unable to see his child until she was six months old.)

In the autumn of 1969, during what was quite likely the first live televised regression into an ostensible past life, Loring G. Williams sent New Hampshire schoolboy George Field back to a lifetime as a poor Southern farmer during the Civil War. (Left to right) Brad Steiger; Field; the producer of ABC's *Chicago*; Williams; host Paul Benzaquin.

CHAPTER TWENTY-FOUR

The Rebirth of a Civil War Victim

George Field, a fifteen-year-old neighbor of Loring G. Williams, decided one evening to sit in on the weekly sessions which the teacher-hypnotist had been holding in his home. During these meetings, Williams would regress volunteers in the hope that he might find a subject whose story could be checked.

Such a search is not an easy one. As Williams put it, many subjects when regressed are hazy about details. They cannot remember their full names or their parents' names, are not sure where they lived, and are unable to give other details that would be needed to check a story. Others, though they may go into vivid detail, describe an existence so long ago, or in so remote a place, that investigation is out of the question. Then along came George.

George Field proved to be an ideal subject for hypnosis. He went easily into trance and was amenable to hypnotic suggestion. Within a short time, George was describing a past existence which had taken place in North Carolina at a point in history which would be near enough to check out.

THE RETURN OF JOHATHAN POWELL

While in deep hypnotic trance, the New Hampshire teenager "remembered" a life as "Jonathan Powell." He recalled that his father's name had been Willard and that his paternal grandmother was named Mary. He could not remember the name of his mother.

According to "Jonathan," his father worked a small farm and labored in a nearby tin mine. The family were Quakers, ministered to by a traveling parson named Brown. Mr. Brown lived in the "villie" of Jefferson in Ashe County.

Williams continued to move George-Jonathan forward and backward in the time sequence of his lifetime. As the boy spoke, a tape recorder caught every word so that, if possible, Williams could substantiate the physical existence of Jonathan Powell.

MURDERED FOR A SACK OF POTATOES

Finally, the hypnotist took Jonathan up to his last day in that incarnation. When Williams asked the personality what he was doing, Jonathan replied that he was busy loading potatoes for those "damn Yankee soldiers."

According to Jonathan, the soldiers were willing to pay only a few cents a bushel for the crop which he had worked so hard to harvest. He cursed the men in their gray uniforms.

Williams queried Jonathan at this point. If the soldiers were wearing gray, they must have been Southerners, not Yankees.

"They ain't Southerners," Jonathan said firmly. But the farmer was more concerned about the men who were surrounding him that the color of their uniforms. They wanted five sacks of potatoes, but they weren't getting them for ten cents a bushel! The stubborn farmer told the soldiers to keep their money.

Then George-Jonathan made terrible sounds of pain and began to cough.

Williams spoke softly to him, tried to reassure him that all was well, and let him speak again.

When the hypnotist had taken away the awful hurt, Jonathan told him that he had been shot in the stomach by the plundering soldiers because he would not take their "damn money." The personality complained that it still "hurt a little."

Williams progressed the farmer another five minutes in the time of his last day of that incarnation. When he asked the personality what he felt at that point, Jonathan answered that he could feel nothing.

At the count of three, Williams brought the boy back to the present.

AN EXPEDITION TO JEFFERSON

Williams was most eager to travel to Jefferson, North Carolina, to substantiate Jonathan's story and to attempt to confirm the physical existence of the personality from whom he had learned the apparent details of a previous earth life.

Due to the limitations of a close budget, Williams, his son Jack, and George Field decided to make a camping trip to Jefferson just as soon as school was out for the summer.

"Camping was a new experience for me," Williams wrote to me, "although both boys had had considerable experience with camporees in the Boy Scouts and had quite a bit of equipment. George had a tent that would sleep three, and between us we had plenty of sleeping bags. A friend provided camping stoves. Finally, much to my wife's dismay, a pile of equipment began to form on the dining room table, ready to be packed. Since we were traveling by Volkswagen, a careful list had to be made and every unnecessary item eliminated. We did consider it very necessary that we take my two tape recorders – the large one on which to play the tapes made in Keene (at the home of the president of the New Hampshire Psychic Research Society) and, if needed, to tape any conversations which we might have there where A.C. power was available, and a small portable for use in the car in and around Jefferson."

Williams was fortunate in that he had an old army buddy, who was now a minister serving a congregation in Watuga, Tennessee, living in Johnson City, just a short distance from Jefferson, North Carolina. The clergyman's backyard provided the expedition from New Hampshire with a base of operations from which to conduct its research in Jefferson.

Williams' enthusiasm and his hopes were high. He had visions of Jonathan-George running about recognizing familiar landmarks, leading them to his mother's grave, falling weeping upon his own burial place. Then it would be simple matter to proceed to the courthouse and find all the records which would substantiate the previous existence of George Field in the physical person of Jonathan Powell.

"Things did not work out that way," Williams said.

BACK TO 1860

Upon approaching the village, George claimed to have had strong feelings that he had been there before. Williams placed the teenager into a deep trance and regressed him to 1860. As he brought the boy's personality back to become Jonathan once again, he cautioned the lad to pay no attention to automobiles or other modern contrivances. Williams wished to take no chances on frightening Jonathan or to distract him with the puzzling artifacts of the twentieth century.

When Jonathan opened his eyes to Jefferson for the first time in over a hundred years, he was completely dismayed.

"Picture yourself, if you can," Williams wrote, "going back to your old neighborhood after a hundred years. There are all new houses and streets, and you are trying to find your own backyard."

When the investigators visited the Ashe County courthouse in Jefferson, they were disappointed to learn that the county had not recorded births and deaths before 1921! There had, however, been a registry of deeds.

On Page 430, Volume A, Williams and the boys found the copy of a deed in which a Stephen Reed had conveyed to a Mary Powell a parcel of land in 1803. This discovery excited the group very much. Jonathan had named a Mary Powell as his paternal grandmother. In 1803, Mary Powell would have been about the right age to be buying farmland. The investigators became even more sure of their research when they were told that Powell was a very uncommon name in that area.

The register of deeds referred Williams to a local historian who might be able to tell them the genealogy of the old families of Ashe County. Williams called the historian and made an appointment with her for that afternoon.

"I DON'T BELIEVE IN THIS KIND OF THING'"'

When the historian learned the purpose of Williams' expedition into North Carolina, she went firmly on record as saying that she did not believe in "this sort of thing,"

She did, however, agree to offer what help she could. And, after listening to the tape recording of George-Jonathan's session at the Keene Psychical Research Society, she had to confess that she was most impressed with "Jonathan's" knowledge of Ashe County.

After the historian had heard the tape, Williams regressed George to Jonathan so that the woman might question the personality concerning the Ashe County of 1860.

"Remember to keep your questions in the present tense," Williams cautioned the historian. "To Jonathan it still is 1860!"

The historian queried Jonathan about a total of twenty-five persons and events in the history of Jefferson. Jonathan knew nothing about some of them. He did, however, claim to know about fifteen of them, many in detail. He mentioned such things as these people's financial status, their children's names, and when they built their houses. These details proved to be substantially correct. In Williams' opinion, he gave enough detailed answers to make any possibility of chance very remote.

In addition to the historian's confirming Jonathan's knowledge of the people and events of Jefferson circa 1860, she substantiated his claim that there had been a Mr. Brown who had served as a circuit-riding preacher. She could find no records of a Quaker church, but she rapidly conceded that a group might have met in private homes.

They replayed the tape which they had made when the historian questioned Jonathan about his life in Jefferson. They wanted to once again get her reaction to his answers. To Williams, it seemed amazing and very significant that one who had never had any connection with Jefferson could know so much about it.

A PINCH OF SNUFF

Williams recalled a humorous incident which occurred while he was riding about Jefferson with George and Jack. The boys asked him what the "snuff" was that they had seen for sale in numerous places in the village. In New Hampshire and in New England in general, the taking of snuff is practically a lost "art." Later that day, while shopping at a supermarket, Williams bought a can of snuff as a souvenir for each of the boys.

Williams had worked in the South and had seen the chewing tobacco used on many occasions. He explained to the boys what little he knew about the "taking" of snuff.

"About all I could really remember," Williams said, "is that the old-timers used to pack a wad behind the lip to get the flavor from it."

As the three of them were riding around the countryside a bit later, Williams regressed George to Jonathan. He hoped that Jonathan might recognize some landmarks and locate his farm, but then, suddenly, another idea occurred to the hypnotist.

"How do you like snuff, Jonathan?" he asked. "Do you want some?"

"I shore do!"

Jonathan had trouble getting the snuff out of "that kind of a box," but once had the tobacco tin open, he set about "blowing" it in a skilled and expert manner.

Williams was startled. He had never seen anyone "sniff" the tobacco up the nose before. It took him a few puzzled moments before he remembered an article he had read which described this manner of using snuff as being the most popular method years ago. But it was still amazing to watch someone actually "sniffing" tobacco. It was an accomplishment which obviously took considerable practice and experience, not to mention a strong nose! Williams knew that George had never seen this done.

MEMORIES OF AN OBSCURE VILLAGE

In his evaluation of the tape as compared with the uncovered evidence, Williams pointed out the difficulty of substantiating such a nondescript life as Jonathan Powell's one hundred years after his death. At the same time, the hypnotist stressed the fact that Jonathan-George spoke of an obscure village in a small North Carolina county, a place of which George Field would hardly be aware. "Jonathan" was able to identify and provide details of the lives of several old families of Ashe County. He was able to identify much of the county's typography which no maps of the area name. Then, too, there was a Mary Powell – a woman with an uncommon surname for the county – who bought farmland and who would have been the right age to be Jonathan's grandmother, just as the personality claimed.

Williams felt that one of the most significant parts of the tape is Jonathan's description of his death. Jonathan claimed that he was shot to death by Yankee soldiers in gray uniforms because he refused to sell them potatoes. Even the most casual student of American history knows that the Yankees wore blue uniforms. Furthermore, Williams' research established the fact that there were no Northern troops in North Carolina in 1863.

"Once again, though," Williams said, "Jonathan was right. The local historian told me that at that time there were bands of renegades who came down from the north, using the war as an excuse to raid and plunder. They could well have dressed in gray because they would have stolen their uniforms."

A GREAT-NIECE MAKES CONTACT

Later, Williams and George Field received further substantiation of Jonathan's existence in a letter from a woman who claimed to be the great-niece of Jonathan Powell. The woman went on to clear up a number of items which were unclearly stated by the personality of Jonathan.

"He [Jonathan] was killed by the Yankees, so my father said; but he didn't know any details at all about the case on how he was killed. Willard Powell was Jonathan's brother. Jim Powell was Jonathan's father [Jonathan stated that his father's name was Willard and that he could not remember having a brother] – and he was red-headed, or sandy haired; and all the family had blue eyes. We never knew what became of Willard or his family.

"...My mother often talked about the Quakers and they would spend the night with her family over there. There was no Quaker church....

"...I haven't done any research on history, but a lot of those eastern Tennessee men fought for the South. That could have been some of them in the gray uniforms that killed Jonathan or it could have been the renegades."

In subsequent sessions of hypnotic regression, Williams led George Field back into three lives prior to his incarnation as Jonathan Powell.

"These were short lives in England in the fifteen- and sixteen-hundreds, so they are impossible to check," Williams told me. "They do, however, paint a vivid and seemingly accurate picture of life during those periods. In two cases, he was a girl, once a boy. In no case did he or she know his parents. It is a historic fact that during those years there were thousands of orphaned or deserted children living in the streets."

CHAPTER TWENTY-FIVE

Proving
Jonathan Powell

"Unfortunately the written word cannot convey the feeling that is expressed in the voice and actions of the subjects as they recount their past lives," Loring G. Williams told me. "They sound old and weak as old age approaches; they register pain and distress when injured. If anything modern is brought to their attention, such as an electric light, a radio, or an automobile, they are amazed and usually frightened."

Williams pointed out that it is out of the question to check most of the cases. "In this sort of work, however, the fact that something cannot be proven does not make it false. In many cases the subject will recount accurate details of things that he could not possibly know.

"Under hypnosis and regressed to a previous life, many subjects possess skills that are normally quite foreign to them, and often are lost arts.

"If, in a former life, the subject was literate and could write, I will ask him to write something for me. When I compare the handwriting of the previous personality with the script of the present personality, I am able to see that the two styles are completely different. While regressed, the hypnotized subject is reliving another life in every detail.

"One argument that is often raised is that there exists a blood relationship between the person today and the prior incarnation. It is then claimed that the subject is just recounting old family stories that he has heard long ago but forgotten.

"I have never found any blood relationship from life to life.

"There is also the argument that the subject may be telling about someone or something that he has read.

"In the case of 'Jonathan,' the previous personality was from a small town, unlikely ever to have been heard of by George Field. Jonathan Powell was an obscure, poor, uneducated farmer, who would never make the history books.

"Another argument which is often raised against the reincarnation thesis is that the subject is only picking up the psychic record or image of one who has lived in the past and is not reliving his own past life.

"This can be accomplished through hypnosis, and I have done it. However, when this is done, the subject see the people and events only as an observer, as if he were watching a movie. This is quite different from a regression to a subject's own previous life. When a subject is regressed, he relives the experiences which he describes.

"A phenomenon which can happen, and apparently does in some cases of spontaneous recall where the person has died recently and nearby, is the partial possession of a subject by a discarnate spirit. This, of course, is considered to be nonsense by the materialists, but this belief was accepted by the early Christians. This is the reason cited for Jesus casting the demons into the herd of swine and then sending them on to drown."

HITS AND MISSES

When Williams returned with "Jonathan" to Jefferson village, their encounter with the historian yielded a great many veridical facts. For example, when the historian asked if Jonathan, placed in the time context of 1860, could remember Joshua Baker, the high sheriff of Ashe County, Jonathan gently corrected her by stating that Baker had been high sheriff ten years before, in 1850. Later, after brushing up on her knowledge of the old county records, the historian learned that this was true.

The historian asked about the drowning of Colonel George Bower, and she expressed some surprise when Jonathan seemed astonished to learn of the colonel's death. Again, after she checked her records, she found that Colonel Bower had drowned in 1864, four years later than the time sequence in which the regressed entity was transiently dwelling.

The guileless historian often phrased her questions in a manner that could easily have encouraged either conscious or unconscious lying or guessing on the part of the interviewee; but Jonathan answered the queries in a straightforward manner, regardless of the historian's promptings. When she insisted that he must have known the "rich old merchant Wall," Jonathan said that he did not, but that he knew Samuel Wall and gave the correct location of his home.

The historian, who was at first reluctant to participate in such an experiment, eventually entered wholeheartedly into the spirit of things, and she chuckled and nodded enthusiastically throughout Jonathan's vivid characterization of one of the wealthy members of Jefferson village society circa 1860. Later, when Jonathan indicated extensive familiarity with the historian's own ancestors, she seemed to be satisfied that she had not really embarked on a foolish chore.

MORE THAN ESP

In certain instances, Jonathan gave details of the ages, home locations, occupations, and marital status of Jefferson citizens. For those who would seize upon this assertion and attempt to convert it to proof of Jonathan's reincarnation being but a manifestation of "psi" ability (i.e., that he "picked the knowledge of Jefferson's forebears from the historian's subconscious), one must immediately ask why Jonathan should apparently miss totally on the identification of other residents of that era.

If George Field were but a brilliant clairvoyant and actor, why should he miss at all simply to make his performance seem more convincing? If one were out to hoax knowledge of a past life, the more perfect the score the better one would be able to deceive the gullible into accepting "proof" of reincarnation.

HOW WELL DID JONATHAN "KNOW" JEFFERSON?

In going over transcripts of the sessions with the historian, Williams and I asked ourselves why it was that Jonathan seemed to know more of the obscure members of the village than he did the prominent, the wealthy, and the clergy. Part of the problem may have lain in semantics. When the historian asked if Jonathan "knew" such and such a prominent person, the poor dirt farmer may have taken the question literally. A hand-to-mouth farmer does not really "know" the town banker, the attorney, or other wealthy professionals, even in a village as small as antebellum Jefferson.

In a number of instances, Jonathan did, in fact, state that he "knew of" a certain individual. Perhaps this should have been picked up and clarified during the actual interrogation, and Jonathan should have been told that identification, rather than profession of intimate knowledge, was all that was being asked.

Then, too, Williams and I did not lose sight of the fact that the person of Jonathan Powell, as depicted through hypnotic regression, was basically a loner, who cared not at all for the society of women, little for the company of men, and who had abandoned churchgoing early in his life. Jonathan would have been the sort to have withdrawn from the leading citizens of Jefferson with whom the historian admonished him to get better acquainted.

BEYOND CHANCE

Since the historian's interview of Jonathan Powell was much more than a yes-or-no quiz, it is impossible to provide the odds on his hits and misses. The historian asked Jonathan about a total of twenty-five persons or events in Jefferson circa 1860. The entity claiming to be Jonathan Powell readily admitted having no knowledge of some of them, but he did know something about fifteen of the individuals and items on which he was queried. Over fifty percent of his "hits" mentioned such correct details as financial status, physical descriptions, children's names, locations of residences, and the construction of homes.

On one hand, it would be correct to say that George Field should have know *no* details about Jefferson "villie," North Carolina, in 1860. At the same time, he could have answered yes to every question. The fact that he offered correct details in his answers would seem to rule out the possibility of guessing. His misses only prove that Jonathan, the reclusive young farmer, did not know everyone in Jefferson. In our opinion, Jonathan gave enough detailed and correct responses to make the possibility of chance very remote.

CHAPTER TWENTY-SIX

If it isn't Reincarnation What Else Could it Be?

A rather successful technique in the therapy of some kinds of mental illness is psychodrama, those spontaneous impersonations of the patient's problem in which he is given an opportunity to enact the conflicts which have inflamed his psyche. I have wondered if some of the cases suggestive of reincarnation might not be a kind of psychic psychodrama in which some segment of the subconscious seizes control of the subject during his regression and impersonates a fictitious personality for the purpose of providing insight into the darker recesses of the subject's character.

In cases in which an individual has made an accurate prediction of his contracting a particular disease, I have often felt that perhaps some transcendent level of his mind might have been subconsciously aware of the inroads of the disease upon the body quite sometime before the overt symptoms of the illness began to manifest themselves. Perhaps during the individual's sleeping hours, when the conscious relaxes its control, the image of the disease may have been reproduced in the subject's dreams, thereby allowing him to "predict" the approaches of the disease.

THE TRANSCENDENT LEVEL OF MIND

Could we have something of this sort in certain cases in which our regressed subjects recount what appear to have been other lives? Hypnosis frees the subconscious by simulating a sleep-like state which virtually anesthetizes the conscious mind. Perhaps regression permits a transcendent level of the mind to dramatize some conflict of character, some weakness of moral fiber, or some approaching crisis by personifying itself as a previous physical embodiment of the present entity.

The fact that the regression personality is so often of a sex different from that of the entranced subject brings to mind Dr. C. G. Jung's theory of the *anima*, the female element in the male unconscious, and the *animus*, the male element in the female unconscious. In *Man and His Symbols*, M.L. Von Franz, a pupil of Jung, writes: ". . . whenever one of these personifications of the unconscious that takes possession of our mind, it seems as if we ourselves are having such thoughts and feelings. The ego identifies with them and see them for what they are. One is really 'possessed' by a figure from the unconscious."

POSSESSION BY DISCARNATE ENTITIES

If it is not some element of the subject's own unconscious playing the role of a previous incarnation, then perhaps in certain cases suggestive of reincarnation a discarnate entity has invaded the psyche of the living, eager to tell its story to the hypnotist. Dr. Carl A. Wickland's *Thirty Years Among the Dead* recounts many such possessions and has, since its publication in 1924, become one of the classics in the literature of the paranormal.

There are many documented cases of apparent spirit possession, including many which have occurred in contemporary times. Whenever I would propose possession as an alternative to reincarnation, Bill Williams would only shrug, admit the possibility, then add that he would have to discount it as a factor in any cases which he had personally investigated. "I have yet to see evidence of spirit possession," he would tell me.

INVADED BY THE SPIRIT OF A BROTHER

All that changed when a young sergeant, who had just been invalided home from Vietnam with several wounds, came to Bill with a story that he was being possessed by the spirit of a younger brother. Just a few months before, the sergeant, Ed, had been called home to attend the funeral of his fourteen-year-old brother, Marty, who was killed in a gun accident. Marty, who had stood six feet tall at the age of thirteen, was noted for his phenomenal physical strength. At the funeral, Ed said that he had felt the presence of Marty and had seemed to hear a whispered promise that Marty would "look after him."

After Marty's funeral, Ed returned to Vietnam where he was immediately involved in a serious battle. He was wounded, and blacked out. The young soldier may have been separated from his buddies and left for dead, but at this point Marty entered the body of the unconscious Ed and took control. With a speed and strength that Ed had never possessed, and despite having been wounded in three places, he got himself to a hospital. Doctors were amazed when the severely wounded sergeant walked into the base. Ed remembers nothing after he blacked out from sustaining the wounds.

Now, the sergeant told Williams, it was apparent that Marty had saved his life, but it was also alarmingly apparent that Marty had liked the feel of a physical body once again. Ed had been conscious of Marty's constant presence and his repeated efforts to get into his body. Even as he sat talking to the hypnotist, the sergeant said, he could feel Marty's approach, which always was evidenced by a feeling of chill, prickly sensations, and goose pimples on his skin.

Bill brought Ed to the home of Professor Charles Hapgood, a man of varied experience who had dealt with cases of a similar nature in the past. In the Hapgood home, Bill placed Ed into trance. As soon as the young man was in deep trance, Marty took advantage of the situation to speak through his brother's vocal equipment.

The entity insisted that he only wished to protect Ed. Hapgood asked him if he did not realize how much his possessing Ed's body upset his brother. Marty said that he was unaware of making Ed feel uncomfortable and that he would continue to possess his body whenever he felt like it.

When Ed heard the tapes of Marty speaking through his mouth, he told Williams and Hapgood that he felt Marty wanted a test of strength. Marty had always been able to best his older brother in any contest of physical strength, but Ed felt that he now had the muscle power to win. He asked that Marty be allowed to take full possession for the contest. Williams and Hapgood counseled against such a test. Marty might not be so easy to pry out once he had taken full possession of a physical body. Ed continued to argue that Marty could only be bested in a physical contest.

"No sooner had Bill and I agreed to the experiment than Marty took over Ed's body right before our eyes," Professor Hapgood said. "There was a complete change in the control of the body's action and in the facial expressions. The body now acted physically like the body of a fourteen-year-old boy. The features were contorted into the expressions of a rather petulant, frustrated child. The body stood up and tried to grasp and raise the heavy chair in front of it by one leg. It did a very poor job. It seated itself again and there was evidence of great agitation. . . . Marty said the test had been unfair, because Ed had been trying to push him out. He wanted another try. Reluctantly, Bill and I assented to this. First, however, we had Ed try to lift the chair, which he did without any trouble, holding it steadily above his head with one hand. (He was then not in trance, and he explained that Marty had previously been able to beat him in such a contest of strength.)

"We assented to the second test. . . . Marty took over Ed's body with grimacing and contortions that reminded Bill of nothing less than Dr. Jekyll and Mr. Hyde. He then arose from his chair and bent to pick up the other chair, but could scarcely get it off the ground. After violent efforts, he tried his other hand, but he couldn't do it."

Marty admitted to Bill that he had been bested in a fair test.

"What are you going to do now?" Bill asked the entity.

"I'm leaving," Marty said quietly. "I won't try to enter Ed's body again. But I'll come back again if ever he should need me."

Certain readers who have had a smattering of psychology in their academic careers will at once begin to theorize and conclude that the Marty-Ed case was just a rather dramatic case study in psychopathological phenomena. If one should study the literature of alleged "demon" and "spirit" possession, however, I think he would come to consider that there is something, perhaps as yet undefinable, but *something* more to such cases than neuroses running rampant.

In May of 1987, Brad Steiger was inducted into the International Hypnosis Hall of Fame. (Left to right) Penny Dutton Raffa, presenter of the award plaque; Sherry Hansen Steiger; Brad Steiger.

DELUSIONS OF MEMORY

We are all well aware that our recollections of certain facts and experiences may become either dimmed or distorted through the passage of time. Such errors and illusions of memory are quite familiar to all of us and nearly all of us have lost bets and arguments when our memory of a particular happening has been demonstrated to be incorrect. We shrug off such minor embarrassments. After all, no one has a perfect memory

When, however, some people recall what would seem to be a memory of a previous existence, they compound their error by adding interpretation to their faulty reproduction of a pseudo-memory. Let us illustrate by a hypothetical situation. We'll say that we are sitting around the fireplace some wintry evening discussing the fierce blizzard of '53. Suddenly our young friend, a schoolteacher in his mid-thirties, speaks up.

Yes, he says, he recalls the blizzard well. He remembers how the drifts were piled across the highways and how stranded motorists met grim deaths in the snow. His recollection of nights without electricity because of downed power lines is vivid. He even sings a few lines from the songs that were popular that winter. We are puzzled for a few moments, then express our amazement that our friend is so old. Of course, he was quite young, he assures us, but he remembers it all very well. We ask precisely when he was born. August 25, 1955. A strange look crosses his face, and we need say no more. How could he remember so clearly an incident which took place before he was born?

There is no mystery here. As a young boy, very often he must have heard his relatives discuss the big blizzard of '53. Perhaps every Christmas when his parents took him with them to visit his grandparents, there were whole evenings of reminiscences about the depth of the snow, how Uncle Mert, the salesman, got stranded and barely made it to the farmhouse, how the children made tunnels in the huge drifts. Our young friend may have been sitting on the floor playing with his new Christmas toys, but yet he was hearing it all; and the grim but exciting tales were making indelible impressions on his subconscious. It would be natural for the young man to make the transition from listener to participant and subconsciously claim the memories for his own.

James H. Hyslop dealt with such delusions of memory in 1906 in his *Borderlands of Psychical Research*. Hyslop observed that our conscious memories seldom extend back beyond the age of four. "When they do they usually represent some isolated or striking event that impressed itself on our minds. Usually, however, the life of that early period is forgotten. . . . Now if at any time some event should occur which recalled enough of the experience previously to that which represents our present consciousness of personality to make us feel that it belonged to a time previous, and yet we could not recall any sense of personality corresponding to it, we might be excused for describing the facts as representing a previous existence. It would be a perfectly natural illusion."

BEYOND THE CREATIVE POTENTIAL OF THE PSYCHE

Delusions of memory may certainly explain many of the common "I've been here before" sensations which nearly everyone experiences from time to time. Delusions of memory may even explain certain instances in which a subject claims to remember a life immediately preceding his present existence.

I am convinced that possession – mental, spirit, "demon" – does occur, but in no case of possession with which I am familiar does the entity claim to represent a former life of the subject whose physical frame it has inhabited. The possessing entity is an invader (and usually makes no bones about it), not a reactivated memory pattern.

Receiving an award for his contributions to a greater understanding of the philosophy of reincarnation at the same induction of the International Hypnosis Hall of Fame was John Harricharan.

Because of my many years investigating "psi" (ESP) abilities of the human mind, it is very hard for me to let go of clairvoyance, telepathy, and psychometry as being the principal contributors to many cases suggestive of reincarnation. And because I think the creative potential of the human psyche is virtually unlimited, I find that a good number of cases could also be left at the doorstep of psychic psychodrama.

But there are always those stubborn cases that resist any theory other than the heretical, unspeakable doctrine of reincarnation. If clairvoyance provided George Field, the New Hampshire schoolboy, with information about the life of Jonathan Powell, a man who had died more than one hundred years before in a faraway Southern village, then young George's "psi" abilities must be developed to a degree which would enable him to pick up messages from a distant locale and concerning a man long dead. In order for a telepathic percipient to receive impressions, some living agent has to be "broadcasting." This means that a great many villagers in Jefferson, North Carolina, must have had Jonathan Powell on their minds at all times and were constantly "transmitting" psychic impressions of his life and colorful times. As we know, Jonathan Powell lived and died in obscurity. When Williams investigated in Jefferson, there was no one who had ever heard of the young farmer who had been shot in the marketplace by the "Yankees."

Once George Field had been brought to Jefferson, one might make some kind of case for the "psi" hypothesis, but it would be a very weak one. Why should George have singled out the farmer Jonathan for the object of his clairvoyance? Could Jonathan's murder have so supercharged the psychic ether in Jefferson that the impressions of this single act of atrocity reached out and touched a psychically sensitive teenager over one hundred years later? But if this were true, the impressions must have reached all the way to New Hampshire, and we have endowed George Field with superhuman powers of mind.

Clearly, in the case of Jonathan Powell and a good many other cases which I have researched, there is more at work than ESP, genetic memory, spirit possession, psychic psychodrama, and delusions of memory. Can we, as products of twentieth-century Western culture, admit that reincarnation might well be that something more?

CHAPTER TWENTY-SEVEN

Reading the Akashic Records

Some metaphysicians believe that there exists what are called the Akashic Records, eternal accountings of individual life patterns which have been somehow impressed on ethereal mechanisms. These records detail each lifetime and are perpetuated like vast computer-like memory banks in the collective unconscious. Certain gifted individuals may, in altered states of consciousness, rise above the normal limitations of Time and Space and "read" these past lives. When they return to the mundane world, they may recount these memories in such a way as to aid men and women who seek their counsel to avoid certain errors which were committed in earlier lifetimes.

Brian Seabrook, a nationally recognized psychic, author of *The Power of Psychic Awareness* and *Cosmosis*, is said to have the ability to "tune in" on the Akashic Records. In July 1977, I had the opportunity to renew an old friendship with Brian at his Desert Shadows Church of Essential Science in Scottsdale, Arizona.

I began our conversation by teasing him a bit about the description of him in Alan Weisman's, *We, Immortals*: "Almost portly, bespectacled, looking about forty or so, his shirt cuffs a little too short, [Seabrook's] aura . . . was more that of someone's pleasant, candy-giving uncle than that of a spiritual medium."

Eventually our dialogue got around to survival of the spirit in general and reincarnation in particular. Here, edited for publication, are a number of the topics which we discussed that day:

Brad Steiger: How did you begin to realize that you were attuning to the Akashic Records while doing psychic counseling?

Brian Seabrook: Much of what I would "see" seemed to be symbolic, a different time and place, perhaps, as if I had attuned to a dream. Several clients suggested that this material might be of former lifetimes and relationships. Slowly I began to accept this explanation and tried to gain greater detail with this type of visual feeling. Later, in many cases, my psychic impression was verified by a hypnotic regression. In other cases a new love-person came into the life of my client, who had also a vague recollection of having been in a previous lifetime with that individual. Often these relationships blossomed to the point of forming a new marriage, a new permanence.

Do you have a general theory about how reincarnation seems to work?

I think we do exist in a cosmic scheme that is orderly, logical, and predictable. But the paranormal experience suggests to me that we do not know all there is to know about just how our universe is organized or why we are here to understand people whom we seem to attract to ourselves. In retrospect it appears that all experiences seem to be programmed, seem to fit into an overall scheme of which we are only partially aware.

I have often wondered if we do not all undergo similar experiences in one lifetime or another under the guise of new times and places. It seems that there may be a universal pathway that we follow. Maybe our experiences, reactions, and relationships are interchangeable, actually symbolic themselves, even though they seem to be firmly rooted in physical reality.

To say that all of this is designed to allow us to grow into our full potential, our divine-human combination, is not explanation enough. The process of the soul's growth and self-awareness of its presence and growth, of its influence over our present experience pattern, is complex indeed.

But, there are some strange repeating situations.

One conclusion that I would reach is that most evolving souls, those who are coming to an idea of self that is universal and not personal, rarely continue one basic marriage throughout a lifetime. Most often they seem to create new intimate relationships as they reach new stages of growth and greater levels of complex awareness.

The most common pattern here is a fundamental marriage, usually in the early twenties, that appears to have as its purpose the creation of new biological entities – children. Then, there is a time when these children approach early maturity, their own early-twenties time, that a "crisis" occurs in a marriage. Suddenly the duo finds that they are actually moving along separate pathways in life, have different needs, and may require new patterns. There is the need, at this point, to share new breakthroughs in consciousness with another soul who may be searching for a higher, more universal, less egocentric meaning. The very inner stress of this type of turning point brings into play Karmic memories, haunting ideas of the ideal mate, of a better time and place, of something slightly out of kilter about present reality, of Earth as it now is.

And, sure enough, without a lot of prompting in most cases, as if by an unseen plan, the new mate comes into view.

Are you saying, then, that one of the central meanings of reincarnation is for various souls to interact and exchange energies somehow?

If humankind is going to advance to the place where we can live on this planet in peace and harmony, with a sense of balance and inner poise, we must share our insights and feelings in most intimate circumstances. Otherwise we can look forward to a future, like the past, that is warlike, greedy, destructive.

Are people sometimes surprised by what may be revealed?

For some the idea that they have had past lifetimes as women and as men is shattering. Evidently for these people their identity is firmly fixed in what they see as male or female roles, as mother or father. Thus, when they come upon the concept that they have played many roles, it stops them cold. Then, upon reflection they find that, even now, they have both masculine and feminine characteristics.

I personally think that this androgynous nature of ourselves makes it easier for men and women to relate successfully. They see something familiar, yet different, in each other. If our purpose were simply to create new biological persons, we would probably get together just to mate and then depart until "next year's" mating season, as many other life-forms do.

As it is, there is an intrinsic purpose, an overwhelming quality to more meaningful relationships that takes the simple biological union, sex, into a transcendental experience, a feeling of totality, or union with the divine. In these rare instances, the male and female energies of each party are co-joined and euphoria results.

As we come into the Aquarian Age, of course, this means we have many types of intimate relationships available, many different life-styles, more room for difference and diversity. That automatically breeds a tolerance for the other fellow, for his needs, at his particular stage of growth.

Are these stages of personal growth and evolution as pre-programmed as you claim? Or are there alternative explanations?

I don't think they come in one, two, three order. We seem to move three steps forward and two back. The blending is beautifully random and not as controlled as one might think at first glance.

I also have a feeling for "soul groups." That is, there seem to be people who have a marvelous affinity for each other. Their background of experiences appears to be similar, and they have arrived at similar points of conclusion.

It is amazing to me that so *many people* who feel that reincarnation is a good explanation for our cause-and-effect experiences have lived in ancient times. *Very few* to whom reincarnation is valid were around on this planet during the time between about 700 A.D.-1500 A.D.

Maybe the idea of reincarnation is only acceptable to those who intuitively feel that they have lived before. To others the NOW is the principal reality.

I'd sum up Karma as: "What we need is what we get!"

What about the idea that we live in an Eternal Now, and that we simply tend to view it as happening in a literal time-space way when it is really a gigantic three-dimensional chessboard, filled with parallel selves, multiple selves, and so on.

The concept of the Akashic Records is that they are available now, that everything that has happened, maybe everything that is going to happen, does exist in another reality, in a different dimension of reality.

But I personally find the idea of multiple selves coming in all over the place a little confusing. I don't see the practicality of this concept for me. But, of course, it might be very helpful to others.

My world, however, is peopled with spiritual entities, souls, who, I think, are available for the spirit side of life. I have investigated the whole question of life after death, and I do not have any problem communicating with souls that are in the afterlife. Perhaps for some people the idea of multiple selves serves the same purpose as Guides and Teachers for the spiritualist. If an idea works for you, use it. If it doesn't, forget it for now.

Frankly, it is a little frightening to me to think that I've got some multiple parts of me still hanging around. I've got enough to do just figuring me out as I seem right this minute. To each his own.

Why do people come to you to check into their past lifetimes?

The overwhelming question is, what is my purpose in the present lifetime and am I fulfilling it?

People are interested in reincarnation to gain some glimpse of their sense of unease, of causes to a lack of fulfillment and harmony. Also, many people that I meet feel that there is a mission to which they should respond. They are literally overcoming more rigid views of self-hood; they want to dedicate themselves to something meaningful, purposeful, and transcendent. This is not confined to any one age group, or any single social category. It is a common thread throughout America.

Second to personal relationship questions is this curiosity about life purpose, mission, and direction.

Can you reach any conclusion about life directions? Is there something that many people see in common as their purpose?

The most striking common characteristic is the surprise that many people evidence as they approach a major turning point in life. A death of a loved one, a divorce, or change of occupation are obvious ones. But evidently there are other, more subtle, inner changes of values, priorities, life-styles, and psychological needs that prompt an investigation of past-life influences.

In other words, many people reach a point in their self-awareness when they ask, "Is this all there is?"

Or, to put it another way, many have set their lives into molds, assuming that they have everything "figured out," only to find that their assumptions are outmoded, that they are in a different state of self-sensitivity; the personal world has changed and they must adapt. As they adjust to new circumstances, new levels of awareness, there are discoveries of one's inner world.

I think what we are seeing is a discovery of a higher self-hood, a more

Brad Steiger and John Harricharan, brothers from lifetimes past, pose for the camera during a break at one of the seminars that they have conducted throughout the United States.

universal, less restricted, personal identity. This causes uncertainty and doubt, at first, of course. But, a tolerance for ambiguity is evidently one of the signs of personal growth and evidence that a more fulfilling life is coming into being.

This stage requires an inquiring mind, a non-judgmental, open attitude and faith that there is something to be gained, a new potential to be realized, lived, enjoyed.

Reincarnation answers the quandary for many people; it erases the unease, the lack of purpose. It replaces these feeling with new adventure, hope, and, above all, places the individual in touch with aspects of his own personality and being that may have been hidden.

There is the understanding, too, that all humankind is alike in many ways; we all sense the same joys, fears, hopes, and aspirations through many lifetimes.

Since reincarnation deals with the history of the soul, what do you find in the attitude of traditional religions on this subject?

Strangely enough, most people do not see an investigation of reincarnation as having anything to do with their traditional religious affiliation. This might surprise most clergymen. I think this is because once a person has grown into a feeling of universal truth, he or she may view traditional church concepts as nearly useless, simply a form of truth, a window on some aspect of life, not rigid, dogmatic, or doctrine-clad.

A seeker after truth will simply ignore those theological constructs that are not relevant to his discovery. A student of reincarnation may not be anti-religious, but he is probably willing to overlook the incongruities of organized religion in favor of an ever-changing spirituality.

Some are able to maintain an active religious affiliation that they see in a more symbolic light. Religion may be more like an art form than like a specific science.

Students of reincarnation are open to new ideas, are willing to sacrifice self-concepts for a higher, more satisfying diversity of experience. While a crisis may have prompted the original inquiry into the subject, a steady balance soon emerges and often paranormal insights dawn.

We are still faced with how previous life influences draw individuals, particularly those in love relationships, together. Many feel there are times of release when previous soul ties are fulfilled and new freedom of relationship choice comes forward.

We find that marriage partners, for instance, often find themselves moving in different directions. A new relationship with another partner presents itself as a strong possibility. This new partner may have a "feel" for the *subject* of previous lifetimes, may "sense" an inward draw to the soul to be released from a marriage. Hence, a new bond is born out of the distant past and is less explained by traditional psychology, or present life facts. Two people are magnetized to one another for reasons which are not easily articulated out of the present, but which have their origins in a past association, sometimes dimly recollected.

Many people whom I have counseled about their own past lives have felt that the Earth plane is not where reality is. They have felt uncomfortable with the entire game of Earth life. And they talk about another plane in the universe that seems more like home. We may not be outcasts sent to Earth. We may be "missionaries" placed here to seed a new consciousness for humankind.

Many people sense lives, then, on other planets, at other places in the universe. They have no difficulty feeling an extra-dimensional life, of communicating with "unseen" forces and entities.

CHAPTER TWENTY-EIGHT

The Woman Who Has Done Over 45,000 Past Life Readings

It was February 9, 1924. Under the pallor of gloom that attends a stillborn child, the obstetrical team at Harper Hospital, Detroit, Michigan was working with trained efficiency. The doctor had pronounced the baby dead as he pulled it from the birth canal. A nurse set the silent little bundle aside while the team concentrated all efforts on saving the unfortunate mother.

An unshakable and quite insistent feeling began to work on one of the nurses present. She went over to the body of the infant, feeling that there was something she could yet do to save it. Acting on this impulse, the nurse fetched a pulmotor and used it on the dead child, pulling the blood from its lungs. She was startled and overjoyed to see the tiny chest lift with its first breath. It had been thirty minutes from the moment of actual birth to the first breath, but the infant was definitely living and subsequent medical examination revealed no brain damage.

Patricia-Rochelle Diegel, a psychic of growing repute who specializes in past-life readings, has relived her traumatic birth under hypnosis, and she can add even more fascination to this unusual vignette.

"Under hypnosis I could remember seeing the delivery room, and I described it in detail, which my mother later verified as correct. I was also able to observe the activity, and it seemed as though the baby had been dead a long time, compared to any normal situation," Patricia recalls.

FROM DEATH TO LIFE – AT BIRTH

"I remember observing the original soul leaving this body and deciding not to stay there. I apparently was an entity looking for a body, and by the time the pulmotor was brought in, I, having ascertained the situation and knowing what my future destiny was, decided to inhabit this body and live the life planned for it."

Under these seemingly unorthodox conditions, Patricia-Rochelle Diegel was born. It is possible that during those thirty minutes of official death, the body resorted to supernormal means of survival, as it is rather astonishing for an infant to be without oxygen so long and yet suffer no brain damage. Regardless, Patricia feels she received a jolt of psychism at birth which never left her – and which has continued to grow with her throughout her life.

From her home in Sedona, Arizona, she and her husband, Jon-Terrance Diegel, have traveled extensively throughout the United States, lecturing on the nature of reincarnation and offering readings for those who desire them. Patricia has now given over 45,000 past life readings for a very satisfied clientele.

Her psychic consultations are of inestimable value to persons seeking to understand their true talents, their relationships with those around them, and the way to spiritual growth. Her organizational and business abilities are rendering much-needed service to the vast and scattered psychic community of this country.

Patricia feels that her many experiences throughout life have prepared her for this varied role she now fills so enthusiastically. She began expressing her psychism in her childhood, and throughout her early years and young adulthood she demonstrated a remarkable business and organizational sense. Her stints in many jobs and professions throughout adulthood broadened her compassion for humanity, and Patricia feels that she cleared much of her Karmic slate through a series of marriages, which culminated in her very happy union with Jon Diegel.

Shortly after her birth, Patricia was taken, together with her three-year-old brother to the tiny town of Ebner, in the southwestern corner of Colorado, a mining camp near where her father was a mining engineer and geologist. The road into the camp was known as Slick Rock Hill, and comprised nine-miles blasted out of the side of a sandstone cliff.

The little mining camp was hardly a center of learning, but Patricia's parents made up for the educational lack by supplying their own extensive knowledge to their children. Her mother was a graduate of a nursing school and of a business school as well. Her father was a former teacher of classical languages at Rochester University in New York before he went to the Colorado School of Mining and inherited the radium mine.

A very special part of Patricia's education was one not planned by her parents. It was their habit to read to each other nearly every night, sometimes for stretches as long as four hours. Patricia supposedly asleep, would actually lie awake in bed, absorbing very word.

When it was time for the children to begin receiving a more formal education, her parents moved the family to Cortez, Colorado, where they stayed until she completed the sixth grade. It was during those years that Patricia became more fully aware of the abilities she possessed, and the possible stigma attached to them.

EAVESDROPPING ON THE "PSYCHIC PARTY-LINE"

Many times the little girl would *know* someone was coming to visit, and inform her mother of the impending guest. The only explanation Patricia's mother could come up with was that her daughter was listening in on the party line. Even though the guest would neither call nor write in advance, he or she would always show up, according to Patricia's predictions. No matter how hard the young psychic protested her innocence, her mother would accept no other solution than eavesdropping on the party line.

Shortly after moving, Patricia had another experience, the memory of which has stayed with her for these many years.

Her mother had received a telephone call that Patricia's grandmother in Michigan had died. Before going to bed, the children had been told the news, and that they would be traveling east for the funeral.

That night, Patricia's grandmother appeared before her in the child's room. Grandmother admonished her to be sure and bring a warm coat, for it was snowing in Michigan. Later, Patricia's aunt confirmed that it had, indeed, been snowing in Michigan the night Grandmother died. In fact, there has been a severe blizzard.

One day, while in the sixth grade, Patricia glanced over at two boys in the classroom, and they disappeared before her eyes. She immediately had a strong premonition of tragedy.

The next day the two boys found some live dynamite caps at an old blasting site. Hours later, forgetting the caps in his back pocket, one of the boys slid down a natural rock slide and blew himself up. The other boy, realizing what had happened, tried to get down the slide another way and suffered injuries which later proved to be fatal.

Other incidents such as these filled Patricia's childhood, but she was too sensitive to ignore the unsettling effect they had on people around her. She halted her psychic impressions as surely as if she could turn them off by flicking a switch. For the rest of her schooling she concentrated on the many adjustments and awakenings of adolescence, and she began to realize her potential in the business and organizational fields.

This internal shift of attention corresponded to a physical change in surroundings, for after the sixth grade Patricia moved with her family to Washington, D.C., where she attended the seventh grade. Thereafter, the family moved to California, settling first in Oakland, and finally settling in Santa Monica.

Dr. Patricia Rochelle Diegel has conducted more than 45,000 past life readings.

A STUDY OF GROWTH OF PSYCHIC TALENTS

In the ninth grade Patricia shook loose from her introverted ways, largely under the guidance of a teacher who recognized in her the ability to get things done. She feels that this year was particularly important, for she began to feel like a real "someone" rather than just a face in the crowd. Furthermore, the realization came at the height of adolescent introversion, and the inspirational jolt to her psyche packed double the emotional punch.

In high school, Patricia discovered another psychic talent which she had not known she possessed. She could receive psychically the answer to an algebra question without working out the problem. She could answer the questions on quizzes and exams without having to study. Schoolwork took less and less of her time; and by graduation she could say that she had been a leader of many school clubs and extracurricular activities.

"Over the period of the next several years," Patricia explained, "I received my education at UCLA. Then I dropped out, got married, bore children, was divorced, and went back to school again. Finally, many years later, I was able to complete my education with a Ph.D. in psychology. However, I feel that my other lessons in life, and being away from counselling work for periods of time, were also very important to my development."

Over the years Dr. Diegel entered into more than one marriage. She feels strongly that each of these marriages has been "...a clearing up of past life Karma. It has been a thing of importance to clear up these Karmas; and therefore, I have had more than one marriage in this lifetime."

Patricia is the mother of three children by her first husband, and one child, a son, Michael, by her second husband. "I firmly believe," she has stated, "that Michael, on the other side of life, drew myself and his father together for the purpose of bringing him into this world. His father died of leukemia three weeks after he was born. I believe this was brought on because he, my second husband, had fulfilled his mission here, that of helping to create this extremely psychic young man, our son."

After Patricia's second husband died, she went through a very traumatic change – and a dramatic one. She refused to experience her grief, and fled from it into the social world of parties, gatherings, and headlong circumstances. Many times she has felt that the strong metaphysical base of her childhood saved her from more unhappiness at this time. Finally, she went back to school, and was able to "...be doing what I should do."

In succeeding years, Dr. Diegel became an accomplished jack of all trades. "I worked as a private detective," she notes, listing her diverse employment background. "I worked as an advertising executive. I sold real estate. I was an office manager. I even worked in Hollywood as an associate producer and casting director."

HELPING PEOPLE THROUGH PAST LIFE AWARENESS

It was during this extremely busy part of her life that she was invited by friends to attend a meeting in Las Vegas, Nevada of the A.R.E., the Association for Research and Enlightenment, the organization formed around the readings and philosophies of the late Edgar Cayce. This meeting, Patricia feels, was the beginning of a new life for her. She reclaimed the psychism of her childhood and allowed it to mature within her. Her wanderings in and out of jobs, marriages, and residences ceased.

"Something began to click inside my head," she remembers. "I had come home."

Patricia underwent hypnotic regression and remembered more and more of her past lives. The fascination of her new life and the commitment it fired in her caused her to spend less and less time on her businesses. She started to give away her concerns, by setting other people up in managerial positions, then turning the business over to them.

"Finally, I was able to completely extricate myself from all businesses," she recalls. "I then moved into this work of scanning past lives – helping people."

Brad Steiger: Patricia, you have had an extremely varied background. In what way, do you think, has this affected your present psychic work?

Patricia Rochelle Diegel: Well, I would say that ninety percent of the people I see come from some type of work or profession with which I have already had some experience. I have owned total, or parts of, restaurants and other businesses, and because of this I have a very broad knowledge of how business is run. It is quite exciting to have somebody sit across from me at a reading, and for me to tune in and discover he is doing something I have already done. Therefore, I can talk his language.

You received some chiropractic training, didn't you?

Yes, I had three years in chiropractic college, which I feel is invaluable to me now. As a psychic, I can sense in my body the places where another person hurts. I know the place that is out of alignment, or the place where something is wrong. By giving clients this information and then having them check with a doctor, many of them have been able to get immediate help. Others have had help right during the counselling session by accepting what I have said and by releasing old Karmas.

For instance, a certain color in the aura indicates heartbreak, which means that at sometime in a person's lifetime his heart has been broken – or in one of his past lives. Quite frequently there is a pattern of a person sticking his neck out to get his heart broken because of an original cause. Now, in getting to the past life with the original cause and then getting him to release the first heartbreak, I have helped to release the chain of heartbreaks down through time, right up to the present incarnation.

Does your degree in clinical psychology assist you in your psychic work?

Well, I did spend some time doing clinical psychology. I worked with people on dream analysis primarily, and also did a lot of counselling for people who were my friends and relatives, or just acquaintances, over the years. This gave me a lot of practice before coming into the psychic field. I

Dr. Diegel has taught classes on the Trinity Process, which she developed with her husband Jon, to thousands of students throughout the U.S. She also channels an entity from the future that identifies himself as "Orion."

had a lot of techniques that were very valuable to me that I am still using.

Can you tell us your method for giving a reading or what it would be like for someone to come to you for consultation?

I have evolved a system of doing past-life readings while wide awake, but I am in an altered state. Using this system, I have now trained over 1000 people to do their own past-life readings and to read for others. Most of them are not doing it professionally.

Primarily, I am a past-life reader, or a reincarnationist, as I prefer to be called. I have called the consultation that I do an "Immortality Consultation," so that I'm able to handle the person as an immortal being, using his entire time track.

You can picture a figure eight lying on its side as a continuous strip. It is called the mobius strip, and it is the symbol that I use to show people that they have had more than one incarnation, meaning that they have had many lifetimes, that they have worn many suits of clothes, and that this body they are now using is just one of several suits which they have worn. By being aware of these other lives, they can bring the talents, the knowledge, and the abilities they had before into this body and this mind and have the benefit of all those past lives.

As for the actual consultation, I have evolved a system whereby in two hours of time, sitting across the table from someone, I am able to give them the information that they need at this time. I usually identify the potentials with which they brought into this lifetime—that is, the creative, psychic, and other types of knowledge they need to fulfill the mission for which they came into this life. In other words, I tell them the types of careers they are supposed to do, and I tell them what they have already accomplished, materially and spiritually, so that they know what is left for them to do.

I also give them the aura colors pertinent to their present life, and then answer five questions on current problems.

I then proceed to the second part of the reading, which includes six of the most important past lives, and the connection of people currently around them to those previous lives. I usually limit the reading to ten names, so that we can cover all of those people. If they appear in the past six lives, fine; if not, I still tell them something about those people and where they have been together before.

There was a period of time when I felt it was necessary to give physical descriptions of these past lives, but I have found out that it does not serve too great a purpose. When they come into my past-life and Trinity-Power workshops, then they themselves are able to get into other of their past lives. I feel that by my offering them various techniques, including my own Trinity Process, they will find the one that suits them best.

I believe the day has come when all people who are above a certain level of evolvement are supposed to start knowing about who they were in past lives. They should also be able to reach into those lives and pull out the talent, the knowledge, and the abilities they had before, so they can utilize them in this life. This is the main reason I give Immortality Consultations.

What is involved in your role as a teacher?

I feel that my main role is as a teacher's teacher, because I have the unique ability of synthesizing knowledge. By reading half a dozen books I can boil down the really pertinent information from those books to an evening's class or lecture. I am led to the correct books to read by intuition. I will at times buy books without knowing why I have bought them, but months later I will reach for that book just before I need to give a class or lecture based on information given in its pages.

Can you impart some case histories from your files?

Yes. One young man who came for a reading was a seminary student, studying to be a priest. He came for the reading dressed in a white T-shirt and dark pants, with his ten relatives on his list. I was able to tune in on him in my regular manner, but during the reading I picked up additional names of people, not on his list, and gave physical and emotional descriptions of them. Later I found out that these additional names were those of the seminary students who had chipped in to pay for his reading.

Another young man who came in was skeptical about the subject of reincarnation. He left a believer, because when I got to his brother's name I felt some kind of blockage and a tremendous pressure on the chest. I felt something shutting off at the neck. After I gave him this description, the young man told me his brother was in a hospital paralyzed from the neck down. I picked up that this brother need not be paralyzed anymore. He had been repaired physically from the accident, but psychologically he was "pretending" to be still paralyzed in order to keep control over his mother and his wife. This condition stemmed from a past-life incident. The young man who received this information was so grateful that he sat at the table and cried.

I have also run into many fascinating cases of people who have been their own ancestor, some as recent as a grandparent. Primarily, people following their own family line are not only working on their own personal Karma, but are working out family Karmas as well. People with a family name used as a middle or first name normally will have very strong Karmic ties to that side of the family where the name appears.

In the course of your work you see many students from a variety of back-grounds. Is there any advice that you could give, in general, to the student of metaphysics, or the budding psychic?

Well, first of all, I feel that everyone has, to some degree, psychic ability. Our belief is that you must practice, but you must practice with care so that you don't hurt anyone. Always move slowly. Study all you can, find the right teachers, but remember that it doesn't happen overnight.

CHAPTER TWENTY-NINE

How to Explore
Your Own Past Life

My position is that knowledge of past lives is a form of awareness that can aid one to create a more complete present-life existence, which, in turn, will help to shape a more positive, productive, peaceful future.

It is not important to me to argue whether past-life recall is pure fantasy or the actual memory of a prior existence. What is important is that, time and time again, I have witnessed men and women obtaining a definite and profound release from a present pain or phobia by reliving the origin of their problems in some real or alleged former existence.

If you should be troubled by a phobic response to any aspect of your life, it is important that you determine the cause of your phobia. You must make your channel as pure as possible. If you have spent several contemplative – but unsuccessful – moments seeking the cause of your problem in your present life experience, you might now decide to turn back the pages of your past-life soul memories. When you relive what may be a past life, you become capable of accepting responsibility for a past action that may have been performed in another lifetime. Once you have made the transfer of responsibility to the present life and you have recognized that the fault lies in a time far removed from current concerns, you will be able to deal with the matter without embarrassment or shame.

Knowledge of past lives is but another form of extended awareness that can bring you much more than past-life memories – even more than the resolution of specific current problems. By exploring prior-life experiences, you may truly come to know yourself and to recall physical and mental skills that you may have mastered in other lifetimes. You may rediscover talents that can bring greater creativity to your present life. You may relearn how to become more efficient in the performance of daily tasks.

Interestingly, the extended awareness which you receive from past life memories will serve to enhance all the pleasures that you derive through your senses in your present life. Your sight, your hearing, your touch, your smell, your taste will all become keener. You will be capable of detecting subtleties that you've never before noticed. You will achieve a deeper insight into the actions of others, and you will gain a greater control of your life and yourself.

Along with such increased self-mastery, you will begin to notice an increase in your ESP abilities. You will observe an enrichment in those spiritual capacities which will enable you to transform your entire life.

Brad Steiger has conducted seminars and workshops from Israel and Egypt to Hawaii, from New York to California, from Florida to Washington state. The powers of mind belong to everyone, he informs his audiences. If one practices spiritual discipline, awareness can bring meaningful rewards

PUTTING THE "GREATER PAST" TO WORK FOR YOU!

You may have already determined your own personal philosophy regarding reincarnation. There are many schools of thought detailing aspects of belief constructs, and they may each contain valid observations of the cycle of rebirth. Explore them all. You will certainly find the philosophy that feels most comfortable to you. But when you know *your* way, be certain to avoid dogmatism.

It is only essential that you believe that each man and woman has the ability to get in touch with some aspect of the past – our own, as well as that "Greater Past" which exists in the common, collective unconscious – and that this ability can be extremely useful to us if we are troubled with deep problems and phobias – or if we simply want to become more aware of who we really are.

The past – or an idea of the past – can become a very useful tool which we can utilize to our great benefit.

Just be cautious that you do not use your tool simply to build a large ego for yourself. Don't waste precious moments "remembering" your lifetimes as great and illustrious historical personages. Put the past to work in order to construct a brighter, more fulfilling future.

It is easier to face the future once you have come to terms with the past. If for reasons of face-saving and self-preservation, whether real or imagined, you have been falsifying your memories of a certain past event, it is important that you face the truth about the matter and recognize just how things really were. By remaining truthful with yourself about the actual reality of your past, you will have a much better chance of building a more positive tomorrow. And the more positive your future appears, the more deeply you can freely delve into the past.

A PROCESS WHEREBY YOU MAY EXPLORE
AN IMPORTANT PAST-LIFE EXPERIENCE

Here is a process to be utilized in exploring a past life, so that an effective dialogue may be established between the prior self and your present self.

Use *any* of the relaxation techniques that may have been successful for you in previous altered-states-of-consciousness exercises. You may wish to play appropriate background music and to pre-record the process.

Once the body has been relaxed as deeply and completely as possible, permit the real *you* within the physical flesh body to become aware of a beautiful figure robed in violet standing near you.

This beautiful figure is surrounded by an aura, a halo of golden light, and you know at once that you are beholding a guide who has come to take the *real* you out of your physical shell and to travel with you to a higher dimension where you will be able to receive knowledge of a past life that you need to know about, a past life that has greatly influenced your present-life experience.

This will be a past life in which you will probably see a good many men and women who have come with you in your present life – to complete a task left unfinished, to learn a lesson left unaccomplished.

Whatever you see, it will be for your good and your gaining; and your guide will be ever near, allowing nothing to harm you. Your guide will be ever ready to protect you.

YOUR GUIDE AND THE REAL YOU

Now you will permit your guide to take your hand and to lift the *real* you out of your body.

Don't worry. Your spirit – the *real* you – will always return to your body, but for now you are free to soar, totally liberated of time and space.

The swirling purple mist is moving all around you; and hand in hand with your guide, you begin to move higher and higher, higher and higher.

You seem to be floating through space, moving gently through space, moving through all of time.

INTO THE SPIRAL OF TIME

Time itself seems to be like a spiral moving around you, a spiral never ending, never beginning, never ending, never beginning.

You know that you have the ability to move through time and to see a past life that you need to know about for your good and your gaining. A past life that will tell you very much about your present life.

This past life is the lifetime that sowed what you are now reaping. This past life is primarily responsible for your present lot in life, for you are the counterbalance for your soul's previous expression.

Ahead of you, suspended in space, is a great golden door. And you know that when you step through that door you will be able to explore the past life or lives of your Karmic Counterpart.

WHY YOU CHOSE YOUR LIFE PATH

You will be able to see the reasons why your soul chose the parents, the brothers or sisters, the friends, the mate, the nationality, the race, the sex, the talents, the occupation you have.

You will see the soul-chosen purpose for the agonies, troubles, pains, and griefs that have entered your life.

You will see what you presently need to accomplish to complete a work left unfinished, a lesson left unmastered.

Now your guide is ushering you to the great golden door. The door is opening, and you step inside....

You see yourself as you were when you were a child in that life.

If it is for your good and your gaining, you are able to know what country you are living in – as you would understand it today – and what period of time you are living in – as you would understand it today.

You see the color of your eyes, your hair, your skin. You see clearly what sex you are.

Now see your body unclothed. See if you have any scars, birthmarks, or other peculiar characteristics that are visible on your naked body...and which may have come with you today.

Now you are clothed. See yourself in characteristic clothing for that time. See clearly what is on your feet.

MEETING YOUR PARENTS FROM A PAST LIFE

A man and a woman are now approaching you. Look at their eyes. It is the man and woman who were your *father and mother* in *that* life.

Understand what kind of relationship you had with them. Did they love you? Understand you? Reject you?

If they did love you and understand you, did you always wish that they might have loved and understood you more?

And now, for your good and your gaining look at their eyes and see if either of them came with you in your present-life experience...to complete work left unfinished...to master a lesson left unlearned.

YOUR BROTHERS...OR SISTERS

Someone else is approaching you, and you see that it is a brother or a sister with whom you were very close. Look at this person's eyes.

This is a brother or sister who *loved* you and *supported* you.

This is the person who was always there whenever you needed help.

And now, looking into these eyes, for your good and your gaining see if that beloved brother or sister came with you in your present life – to complete work left undone, to finish a lesson left unlearned.

Now, from *that* same life someone else is approaching you in the home that you shared with your parents in that lifetime.

It is a brother or a sister with whom you had *rivalry* and *conflict*. Look at the *eyes*.

This is one who seemed to be undermining you in your relationship with your parents and with others.

Look into the eyes and see if you ever resolved your conflict with this person.

Look into the eyes and see if this brother or sister came with you in your present life in any way.

See if that brother or sister came with you to complete work left undone, a lesson left unrealized.

Now, back in that same lifetime, scan the vibration of any other relative or family member—an uncle, a grandparent, a cousin—and see if any relative or family member from that time has come with you in your present life...to complete a lesson left unlearned, work left undone.

YOUR ACTIVITIES

In that same lifetime you are growing older, moving into young adulthood, and you see yourself performing some *favorite* activity, a game, a sport, a hobby, that became so much a part of your life *then* that is has, on one level of consciousness, affected your life today.

You see yourself performing that activity, and you understand how is has been impressed on the life pattern you exercise today.

YOUR WORK SITUATION

You are now beginning to see clearly and to understand what *work* you did in that life...how you spent your days.

Someone is approaching you from that work situation. Look into the eyes.

This may have been someone who was your employer, your boss, your overseer.

This may be someone who was your employee, your servant, your slave.

But this is someone with whom you interacted closely at your work.

For your good and your gaining look at the eyes, see if this person came with you in your present-life experience, to complete a work left undone, to learn a lesson left unaccomplished.

ENCOUNTERING YOUR SOULMATE

As you move away from your work situation, you are beginning to feel the *vibrations of love* moving all around you. You are aware of someone standing there, to your left, standing there in the shadows.

You are feeling love – warm, peaceful sensations of love – moving all around you, as you realize that standing there in the shadows is the person whom you loved most in that lifetime.

Look at the eyes. Feel the love flowing toward you from those beautiful eyes of your beloved.

Look at the smile of recognition on those lips as the beloved one sees you and begins to move toward you.

This is the one with whom you shared your most intimate moments – your hopes, your dreams, your hurts, your moments of deepest pain.

This is the one who always cared, who always loved and supported you.

Go to those arms again. Feel those beloved arms around you. Feel those lips on your again.

Now, for your good and your gaining, look at the eyes. See if this beloved one came with you in your present-life experience.

See if your love, like a golden cord, has stretched across time, space, generations, years, to entwine you again in the same beautiful love vibrations. See if you were born again to be together.

See if you have come together again to work out a task left incomplete, a lesson left unlearned.

YOUR MARRIAGE PARTNER

You are growing older in that life. See now the one whom you *married* in that life. Was it the one you loved most? Or was that beloved one taken from you by death...or by circumstances?

If the one you see before you now was not the one you loved most, then looking at the eyes, see for your good and your gaining the person you *did* marry. And see for your good and your gaining if that person came with you in your present life...to complete work left undone, a lesson left unlearned. If you had *children* in that life, see them now. See their eyes looking at you. Feel their little hands on your fingers. Feel the love flowing from them.

YOUR CHILDREN

Did they grow older with you? Or were they taken from you by death or by circumstances?

Look at their eyes and for your good and your gaining see if any of those children came with you in your present-life experience to complete a lesson left unlearned, to be with you again in your love vibration.

THE SOUL'S EVOLUTION

Now see scenes from that life that you need to remember for your proper soul evolution.

See scenes that will trigger memories that will help you in your present-life experience.

See scenes that will show you clearly how certain patterns were formed then that have intruded, both positively and negatively, into your present-life experience.

These are scenes you need to remember, but you will see them in a detached manner. You will feel neither guilt or shame. You will feel neither pride nor ego pleasure.

You will understand them – *why* they happened. You will understand these acts so that your soul may grow and gain.

The first scene you are viewing is a *negative* one. It is a scene in which you did something that has negatively influenced your present-life experience.

It may be a scene of violence, greed, lust, theft, brutality – murder; but you are observing it now and you are understanding *why* you did this act.

The second scene you are viewing is a *positive* one. It is a scene in which you did something that has positively influenced your present-life experience.

It may be a scene of charity, kindness, love, self-sacrifice, martyrdom; but you are observing it now and you are understanding *why* you did this act.

THE TRANSITION OF DEATH

And now, for your good and your gaining, witness the moment of your *death* in *that* life.

Perhaps you weren't ready for death...perhaps you fought against it...cursed it. But understand *why* your soul withdrew its energy at that time.

See who was with you at that last moment. Was the one you loved most there? Your family? Your children? Or...were you all alone? Did you face that last moment all alone?

See your spirit rising from its physical shell. See yourself being met by your very own angel guide, the same guide who is with you from lifetime to lifetime.

With a flash of insight your angel guide is showing you *why* you lived that life and why you lived it with those with whom you did.

YOUR TRUE MISSION OF LIFE

You see clearly *why* you had to come again to put on the fleshly clothes of Earth.

You see *why* you had to come in your present life as the person you are now.

You see *why* certain people from that life have come with you again...to complete work left undone, to master a lesson left unlearned.

In another flash of insight you are seeing and understanding *why* you came to Earth for the very first time.

You are remembering *why* you chose to put on the Karmic vibrations of Earth and come to this planet for the very first time.

You are remembering clearly *why* you came here. You are remembering your true mission in life.

You see and understand clearly what you are to do in your present life that will most aid you to accomplish your mission.

You are filled with a wonderful sense of well-being for now you know what you must do. You see clearly what you *must* do to fulfill totally your true mission in life. You no longer feel sensations of frustration and anxiety.

Now you *know*. You know why you came to Earth, why you chose to put on the clothes of Earth, why you chose to assume the Karmic vibrations of this planet.

You are beginning to awaken, feeling very, very good...very, very positive.

You are filled with a beautiful, glowing sense of your mission.

You are filled with the positive knowledge that you will be able to accomplish so much more good and gaining toward your true mission now that you are filled with awareness of your Karmic Counterpart.

Now you understand how that lifetime has been affecting your present life.

Now you understand so very much more of the great pattern of your life.

And you know that your guide will aid you, will assist you in completing your mission, in accomplishing what you truly came here to do.

Awaken filled with positive feelings of love, wisdom, and knowledge. Awaken feeling very, very good in the body, mind, and spirit. Awaken feeling better than you have felt in weeks, in months, in years. Awaken filled with love, filled with knowledge.

John Harricharan wishes to serve as a bridge between East and West, in a manner similar to his idol, Paramahansa Yogananda.

CHAPTER THIRTY

Making Intuition Practical

John Harricharan is a most unique blend of East and West. Bright, well-educated, professional in demeanor, he brings a welcome practical approach to metaphysics.

Born to East Indian parents in a remote area of Guyana, South America, Harricharan was reared by his Hindu father to be tolerant of all religious expressions and metaphysical philosophies. Formally educated in British schools, he became a Christian, married the charming daughter of a Lutheran pastor, and went on to complete his education with honors in the United States.

With degrees in both science and business, Harricharan became a problem-solving professional in a number of Fortune 500 and smaller corporations. He has traveled widely in the Far East, Africa, Europe, South America, the Caribbean, Mexico, and he studied extensively under the spiritually gifted Swami Purnananda and Sri Dayanand Mishra.

Because of his ability to incorporate eastern wisdom with western pragmatism, he is as effective as a metaphysical teacher as he is a business consultant. A dynamic and magnetic speaker, Harricharan also reveals himself to be a compelling writer.

In his book *When You Can Walk On Water, Take The Boat*, he chooses the literary device of an extended allegory, and he presents the reader with a fascinating mixture of personal experience and spiritual pilgrimage. He blends the world of physical reality with the in-between universes and provides us with a glimpse of the Greater Reality.

Harricharan's essential message seems to be to encourage us all to continue to learn and to grow and to keep pushing through personal crises and chaos. We all have the ability to make choices and to seize upon life's trials as opportunities for growth and gaining.

HARRICHARAN ON HARRICHARAN

John Harricharan: My origin is neither of East nor West but of eternity. People, no matter where they were born, have more similarities than differences. I seek to synthesize rather than to separate. In spite of artificial walls and barriers, we all learn from one another and sooner or later we rediscover that we are simply but one.

All great truths are simple. We are the ones who complicate things by our method of thinking. The best solutions to problems are usually the simplest ones. If we were to return to a child-like faith, we would behold the true simplicity and joy of our being instead of the complexities of our existence.

One may succeed in spite of one's education. I know of many who have gone to college without ever having obtained an education, and I know of others who have obtained an education without ever having gone very far in school.

My education serves as a means to an end and never as an end in itself. As you know, many individuals in the executive business community seek my metaphysical consultations. Here, my education assists me in relating to them in a business-like manner and in comprehending the language of business. However, my metaphysical awareness makes it possible for me to understand and assist them on another level.

Concerning degrees, I place mine in the bathroom under glass with the inscription, "Break in case of emergency."

THE POWER WITHIN LIES WAITING

Knowledge is obtained through "tuition" and/or "intuition". We come into this world with the ability to access all the knowledge of the universe. However, most of us have forgotten this. I have but remembered that which was always there.

Actually, we are all "masters," but some are more aware of their "mastership" than others are. For those who are more aware (notice I did not say "more advanced"), it is their duty to assist the others who are not. We are all shipmates on the common voyage of life, and we cannot sink our shipmates without sinking ourselves.

Within each and every one of us is an inherent guidance system. We are not thrown helplessly into a seemingly cold and cruel world without the necessary tools for taking care of ourselves. Yet most people go through an entire lifetime never realizing the power they have at their command. This power is not the exclusive province of gurus, avatars, saints or the high and the mighty, but is available to all people as their cosmic birthright.

The power within lies waiting to be tapped by anyone who is willing to use its guidance. It is always there and it is always providing us direction for our lives. But because we are surrounded by the noise and activities of everyday, outside existence, we tend not to hear the gentle proddings from within. We become blind and deaf to the sights and sounds of our higher selves. To begin using this guidance, one must first be aware of its existence and then follow its directions. The following true life story is an excellent example of this principle.

A BABY GIRL FROM INDIA

My wife and I had been married for several years, and we felt it was time to start raising a family. "Why not start with an adopted child?" she asked.

It didn't matter to me whether our first child was adopted or biological, so we contacted the necessary agencies. Our decision was to adopt a baby girl from India, and as a result we waded through an ocean of bureaucratic and political red tape. The entire aura around us was one of excitement and anticipation. Only one more document remained to be processed by the Immigration Department.

Then something went wrong and there was a delay. We were informed that it would be another week or two before the necessary visa for our "soon to be" daughter would be issued.

Having waited for seven months, a delay of a week or two seemed inconsequential – except for one thing. On the very day we were notified of the delay a telegram arrived from India. It stated that a baby girl, a few weeks old, was available for adoption and that we should travel to Bombay as soon as possible to complete the formalities of the adoption process. This was the notice for which we had been waiting. Everything was in order except for that one visa document from the Immigration Department. Only one week to go and we would be on a plane to India. Both my wife and I were of Indian descent and this would be our first visit to our ancestral land, and this added to our excitement.

A PREMONITION OF DISASTER

At first, logic dictated that all was well and that in a short while, we would be the parents of a fine baby girl. But all was not well.

That night I could hardly sleep. My sleeplessness could have been attributed to excitement and anticipation, but that was not so. Instead, there was an uneasy feeling around me – a strange premonition of disaster. I was filled with overwhelming apprehension.

As the day progressed, the feelings of apprehension and anxiety increased. I examined the situation but could find no reason to justify such uneasiness. Try as I might, however, it was impossible to dismiss them. I felt that I must leave for India within 24 hours. I expressed this resolution to those closest to me.

Without exception, they all advised that I wait until the final papers were processed. It would only be another week, they reasoned. I had waited so long, surely a few more days would not make any difference.

I called my attorney and asked if he thought it was necessary to wait for the final papers. His response was a resounding "Yes." My business associates tried to talk some sense into me. "Why, John?" asked one of the wiser ones. "Why the rush? I have never seen you like this before."

I could not explain the strange urgency I felt. Finally, in desperation, I phoned the Immigration Department and asked for the office handling the case. "Please, could you speed up the process?" I asked.

"We are doing the best we can," was the reply.

"I really would like to leave for India tomorrow. When they are ready, would you air mail the papers to me in Bombay? I will leave you the address."

"We are sorry, but we cannot do that. You will have to wait until everything is in order."

"What would happen if I leave tomorrow?"

"There would be longer and more serious delays. We would suggest that you comply with our procedures and wait until the papers are ready. Thank you for calling. Good-bye."

TRUST IN INNER FEELINGS

Experience had taught me to trust my feelings even when I did not understand them. I, therefore, disregarded everyone's advice, called the airlines and made reservations for a flight leaving the following day. When I told my wife what I had done, she, too, thought that I must have lost my mind. "Why not wait for another week?" she asked. "Everyone seems to think it would be wiser."

"You wait if you want to," I replied. "I am going to India to get our daughter. I had never spoken to her in that tone before.

"But the papers and final approval?" she protested.

"Be that as it may," I replied, "The child first, papers later."

Reluctantly my wife agreed to humor me. The following day found us hurtling across the Atlantic on a 747 jet – the first leg of our journey to the mystical land of India. Exhaustion finally forced me into a deep sleep. When I awoke, we were somewhere over the continent of Africa. I was surprised and relieved to discover that the feelings of doom and despair had vanished.

I began to reflect on my behavior of the past 24 hours. I did not regret my actions. It was almost midnight when we touched down at the International Airport in Bombay. What a joy it would be to see our daughter the next day.

First thing in the morning, we were off to the agency. We introduced ourselves to the manager and waited while they went for the child. There are times when seconds seem like hours and this was one such time.

Finally a nurse arrived carrying a little bundle. As we looked at the baby wrapped in the blanket, a sense of shock overcame me. Our child, whom we had imagined to be a healthy baby weighing approximately six or seven pounds, was an emaciated little thing, perhaps slightly over three pounds. She seemed to be suffering from malnutrition and among other things was covered with sores. Only her eyes moved as they followed us around the room.

"This baby is very sick," said the nurse, "the doctor thinks that she may not live through the day. Would you like to consider taking another one?"

THE INFANT MUST NOT DIE

Anger, resentment and fear sprung up within me. After all the preparation and hopes to be faced finally with the possibility of losing the child.

No! We had not gone through everything for this. Something had guided me, against the dictates of reason, to be where I was at that moment. The infant must not die. Now I understood why I felt impelled to leave for India when I did. A day or two later and the child surely would have died. By being here, I was able to do whatever was possible to save her life.

"No!" I fairly shouted at the nurse, "we will take our baby. This way, she has at least one chance in a thousand. Leaving her here, she has none."

Without hesitation, we asked for the necessary documents and signed them. Quickly we left with the little bundle in my arms. We went directly to the office of a pediatrician whom friends back in the States had recommended.

While examining the child, the pediatrician asked, "Do you know what you have done? This child is deathly ill. I don't know if she'll make it."

The desperation in my heart was being replaced by a strong determination and a sense of purpose. I looked at the doctor and said, "Please do all that you can."

It was impossible to get the child into a hospital because of the local rules and customs. With the help of the good doctor we were able to obtain the services of an additional doctor and two nurses. One of the nurses was a woman who had once attended to Mahatma Gandhi. That night, in a hotel suite overlooking the Indian Ocean, the nurses and doctors worked feverishly to keep our child alive. We made it through the night.

Days ran into weeks and the child gradually improved, though she was far from being out of danger. Because I had left the United States without the proper visa papers, the red tape compounded itself. We were informed by the American Embassy in Bombay that a new application for a visa for the child had to be made and sent to Hong Kong for approval.

In the meantime, rumor had it that the Indian Government was about to declare emergency rule. There was unrest in the streets.

As if that were not enough, we were displaced from our hotel to make room for some wealthy, visiting Arabs. We found new lodging in a small rundown motel until we were able to return to our first one. Money was running short, the child's life was still in danger and the other problems seemed overwhelming.

Back in the United States, some friends and influential business associates had heard of our plight and had petitioned our government leaders to do something about it. However, we could not wait. We had to take the baby back to the States for proper medical care. Without a visa for the child it was impossible for us to get her on board a plane, and even if we did, there would be problems from our Immigration Department when we arrived home.

Yet, where there's a will, there's a way. Somehow with the help of a few Indian friends and the guidance of my inner voice, we managed to pass through the various check points at the airport in Bombay and literally smuggle the child aboard a plane bound for the United States. Finally, we were on our way home.

Arriving in New York after a long and tiring flight, we were apprehensive that the Immigration Department would deport the child for a lack of a visa. Our friends had prevailed on our Government to make an exception, and we were welcomed by a delegation. A visa was issued on the spot.

We named our daughter Malika. With proper medical care she continued to make excellent progress.

Today, Malika is a happy, healthy young girl who recently celebrated her eleventh birthday. She seems to remember very little of her early years and is currently involved in the normal pre-teen activities of endless phone conversations with girlfriends, shopping for clothes and wistful dreaming of boys and TV video stars. But every once in a while when I look into her beautiful, dark eyes, I relive the steps that brought her to us. Had I not followed the strange feelings of urgency in me to leave for India on that day, many years ago, our daughter would not be with us today.

THE POWER OF THE "STILL, SMALL VOICE"

Many of the greatest minds of earth have testified to the "still, small voice" within them. It is an ancient saying and well worth repeating that before the demand is made, the supply is available.

To become aware that we have all we need to solve our problems and to make our lives work, we must follow certain simple guidelines. First, there must be quiet times – alone times. It is in the quietness of our beings that we can hear a whisper directing us to a path of greater fulfillment. Take time for yourself. A five minute period, once in the morning and then again in the evening, will prove very useful. Surely all of us could find ten minutes in a twenty-four hour day to become quiet and feel the life-force flow through us.

Next, use the gifts that are all around you. Music is one such gift. It has healing and calming properties. There is hardly a soul on earth who has not at one time or another been soothed by the sounds of music.

Nature helps to make you more aware of yourself and more conscious of your own validity. A walk through the woods or a stroll alongside a stream would remove your focus from the things that trouble you. Simply leaning against a tree and breathing slowly will assist in the centering and balancing of your body, mind and spirit.

There are books. Everything that you ever need to hear or learn is written somewhere in a book. Instead of listening to the late night news, spend fifteen minutes reading some positive or inspirational material. One good book could raise your awareness to such a level that you are motivated to take the few additional steps you may not have taken and thus solve the very problem that seemed unsolvable.

Become more and more aware of the great possibilities that lie within you. Learn to trust your feelings. Tune in to yourself and follow the gentle urgings you find there. Like anything else, it takes practice and a small measure of self-discipline. Your intuition becomes stronger as you exercise it, so keep practicing.

At first, it may seem very ordinary and even boring. But as you keep monitoring your "feelings" and trusting them, you will begin to notice that you are being led in directions that are rewarding for you. It does not matter how complex your life may appear to be, the spirit within you is capable of assisting you to solve all your problems. The information will be given to you, but you will have to make the decision as to what to do with it.

Paul Twitchell became the first Living Master of the ancient science of Eckankar to reveal himself in contemporary times.

CHAPTER THIRTY-ONE

Moving Through Time and Space to Visit Atlantis

"Anyone can predict the future who has mastered the art of soul travel," taught Paul Twitchell, leading authority on the spiritual philosophy of Eckankar.

Twitchell, hailed by many as "this generation's Edgar Cayce," before his death in 1971, divided his time between lecturing, writing, and manifesting almost every phase of extrasensory perception. The seer claimed the remarkable ability to be in more than one place at the same time, and the enthusiastic letters of his followers attested to his skills as healer, prognosticator, and spiritual adept.

The elusive prophet claimed to have accomplished these remarkable feats through the practice of *soul travel*.

"Eckankar teaches the chela [student] to transcend his physical form and explore the spiritual worlds in his soul body," Twitchell explained. "It is a path to God-Realization."

It is by this method that the ancient masters were able to heal the sick, according to Paul, and it is by this same method that he filled his files with testimonials to his similar abilities.

Twitchell's record in the arena of prophecy was steady and impressive. He correctly foresaw the breakup of the Beatles, the defeat of the labor party in England, the arrival of the maxi-skirt, the increase in the popularity of witchcraft, and the rise of the neo-Nazi party.

The seer arrived at these predictions via the ECK method of prophecy, or what he called the ECK-Vidya.

"The ECK-Vidya works on the principle that the world is an interlocking unity which can be observed once we lift ourselves above the regions of time-space," stated Paul. "Within this position we are able to see all as a totality, and all that is needed then is a concentrated effort in one direction, to sort out the powerful magnetic fields around those whom we are reading. Once this is done, we start reading their Akashic records."

DIVIDING THE COSMOS

Eckankar divides the cosmos into several spiritual planes. Among these are the physical, astral, causal, etheric, and soul planes. It is upon the causal plane that the Akashic records are kept. Therefore it is to this plane that one using the ECK-Vidya method of prophecy projects himself. There the records of every soul and every nation are spread before one.

It takes the student a long time before he is able to travel to these planes at will, and certainly not everyone can achieve the same level of spiritual consciousness as Paul Twitchell. Yet even this man had to travel the long road from beginner to a master level of proficiency.

OUT-OF-BODY INSTRUCTION

Twitchell had the advantage of an early start, though. Born on a packet-boat on the Mississippi River, he was taken in as an infant to be raised by the Twitchell family. His foster father had studied with the Indian master Sudar Singh, who had taught the man the precepts of Eckankar and out-of-the-body travel. Kay-Dee, Paul's older sister, was similarly instructed by her father.

Paul, being considerably younger, was not a member of these initial sessions. His first encounter with the art came as a matter of dire necessity, for at the age of five young Paul lay close to death, stricken with pleurisy.

His stepmother, Effie, had never been overly fond of the foster child, and her efforts to save the child were grudgingly given. With Paul's father away in Europe, young Kay-Dee knew the responsibility lay on her shoulders.

By all medical prognosis, Paul should have died. On the most critical night, however, Kay-Dee slipped quietly into the youngster's room. Seating herself as her father had taught her, Kay-Dee performed the necessary exercises to leave her physical form. Soon her *atma sarup*, or soul body, was floating above her dying brother. Gently she eased him out of his disease-ridden body, and then both of them were gazing down at the frail little body on the bed.

"Am I dead, Kay-Dee?" asked little Paul, echoing the query of many who experience this phenomenon for the first time.

"No," she answered soothingly, "but we must take steps to see that it doesn't happen. Concentrate on good health, on recovery."

Within minutes both knew that the boy would survive. The next morning the doctor called it a miracle. Kay-Dee and Paul just smiled and exchanged winks.

When Paul was fully recovered from his near-fatal bout with pleurisy, he joined Kay-Dee in her sessions with their father. The two youngsters soon added new delights to the traditional game of hide-and-seek by playing in their etheric forms.

As Paul grew older, however, the serious business of soul travel replaced his childhood games. A year's study in India with his father's teacher, Sudar Singh, lay the groundwork for what would later become his life's work.

A MAN BORN OUT HIS TIME

Yet he was not quite ready to embrace the totality of ECK. Following his naval duty in World War II, Paul found himself in a confused state.

"At that time, nothing in this century made sense to me," Paul revealed in his biography, *In My Soul I Am Free.*

"I seemed to be a man born out of his time, and for that reason I was not interested in the ordinary man's grubbing for money. I could see that this era in our history was honoring mediocrity until it was fast becoming the stabilizing force of society. I could see our machine age developing an educational system which would produce tame rabbits and robots for the politicians to manage [the famed "Silent Generation"]. I wanted to turn away from the claptrap of this supermarket culture...I wanted to seek the same purpose in life that had driven St. Anthony of the Desert, Jacob Bohome, and St. John of the Cross."

Before finding the inner peace that these men had discovered, however, Paul would take his search to many corners of the world. This period of his life saw Twitchell treasure-hunting in New Guinea, investigating voodoo in Haiti, and diving for pearls off La Paz, Mexico. He also spent several hours before the typewriter, developing the writer's discipline that would later benefit him in his propagation of Eckankar.

THE INNER TEACHER

Throughout this time of social rebellion, however, the seeds planted by his childhood experiences in soul travel were slowly and steadily maturing. The arrival of Rebazar Tarz, Paul's inner teacher, brought them into full blossom.

The phenomenon of the inner teacher might sound bizarre to those unfamiliar with the growth pattern of a psychic, but it is an experience common to a great majority of them. In essence, it involves the appearance of a non-physical entity who, at a crucial time in a psychic's development, reveals truths that could not be learned from books or individuals limited by material consciousness.

It was Rebazar Tarz, a centuries-old adept in the mysteries of Eckankar, who instructed Twitchell in the finer principles of ECK, and finally commanded him to bring these truths before the masses. The final transition from Twitchell's former way of life into the role of spiritual advisor was made when a priest from a temple in Chinatown, San Francisco, informed Paul that he would soon be moving to San Diego, where he would begin his life's work in ECK.

Paul Twitchell addressed thousands of people all around the world. He penned many books, including *The Tiger's Fang, Eckankar, Your Key to Secret Worlds*, and *The Spiritual Notebook*.

TWITCHELL'S VISION OF ATLANTIS

"I vividly remember the ancient continent of Atlantis, the sunken land to which so much mystery and legend is attached," Paul Twitchell told me. "It was through the use of the ECK-Vidya, the Akasa science of prophecy, that I learned from Rebazar Tarz, the great Master of soul travel, that I was able to learn of my past incarnation in Atlantis."

Twitchell stated that the ECK-Vidya enabled him to receive a detailed vision of Atlantis. According to Paul Twitchell:

Approximately 20,000 years ago, during the age of antiquity, there was a fair land in the middle of the North Atlantic. It was an island continent, similar to Australia today, as large as France, Spain, and England put together.

There were chains of small islands, also, one running from Atlantis down to Brazil, and the other across to Portugal. It was via these small islands that so many plants and animals common to both the New and Old Worlds were transported across the ocean.

Atlantis was a flourishing civilization about the 12th millennium B.C. Atlantis conquered all the Mediterranean peoples with the exception of the Athenians, who resisted successfully. Atlantis, seat of an ancient culture, had the largest trade and commerce network of its time.

THE ISLES OF THE BLEST

Atlantis was a Utopian commonwealth which gave rise to many of the early legends. The Greeks called the ancient continent the Isles of the Blest, where the dead made their home. The Welsh called Atlantis, Avalon; the Portuguese called it Antilla, or the Isle of Seven Cities.

Atlantis was the original Garden of Eden. It had a fertile soil and a fine semi-tropical climate. Because of its sea barriers on all sides, Atlantis was isolated for thousands of years and was permitted to develop a great civilization in peace and security. This era of peaceful isolation enabled the Atlanteans to perfect the very elements of civilization which have affected all other cultures down through the centuries. The great sea barriers, on the other hand, enabled the Atlantean armies and navies to conquer other lands while its home front was secure.

I had several incarnations on the continent of Atlantis, but the one which gave me the greatest insight on this island kingdom was the one that I lived as a professor of law at the great university of Semira.

Semira was the capital of Atlantis in those days. Six other major cities serve the island continent, which was divided into seven provinces. During its 18,000 years of existence before the disaster, many of the Atlantean provinces tried to break away and establish their own independence. At one time, for a period of about 200 years, there was a separation of the continent, but then the rebellious provinces were brought back under a central government again.

THE SUGA

At the head of the state was a priest-king who was the intermediary between the people and their Supreme Deity, the *Suga*, a shorter version of that which we know today in the spiritual works of ECKANKAR as the *Sugmad*. The priest-kings were called the *Ekas*, the reigning representatives of God on Earth.

Because of my position as a teacher of law at the vast university which was maintained by the state, I was able to observe the whole of life on Atlantis. It is for that particular reason that I shall use this incarnation as the example from which to speak of my memories of the sunken continent of Atlantis.

Many cultures and civilizations owe their beginnings to their having been Atlantean trade colonies. The great similarities of the peoples of Europe, the Mediterranean, and Central America amaze the scholars. These nations had the same hierarchy of gods, the same system of astrology, the same methods of agriculture, and the same type of architecture. For example, the ancient Mexicans built pyramids, as did the Egyptians, but they both copied from the Atlanteans, whose pyramids were often as high as small mountains.

SEMIRA, MIGHTY CITY

During my incarnation as an Atlantean university professor, Semira was a mighty city at the foot of a great mountain range in the northern section of the continent. The city was ringed by three broad canals and three vast defensive zones of gigantic walls strengthened with copper and brass. Semira had been built on artificial islands, laced with networks of canals, in honor of Poseidon, god of the sea, who had been the chief god of the early Atlanteans. The main canal of Semira was 300 feet wide and 100 feet deep. The canal surrounded the whole city and linked up with the sea six miles away. The city proper was situated on a main island with high walls, towers, bridges, and two zones of land which also had high stones walls which protected the inner sections of the city. Within these areas were temples and palaces and docks for ships from foreign countries.

Within the center of the main island stood a vast citadel which enclosed the greatest of all buildings ever seen on earth – the vast Temple of Poseidon. The temple had been ornamented with increasing splendor by subsequent generations until the whole outside was plated with silver, with the exception of the pinnacles, which had a gold covering. The ceiling was made of ivory imbedded with precious jewels. Within the temple were many solid gold statues of gods, the greatest being that of Poseidon, which was of such a size that its head touched the roof. This gigantic statue represented the god standing in a chariot drawn by six winged horses surrounded by sea nymphs riding on dolphins. The enormous statue was made of solid gold and ivory.

The Temple of Poseidon was surrounded by a large garden which had many fountains, rare trees, and flowers. The garden also contained an exercise ground and a sports stadium.

The Atlanteans were miners, planters, and farmers, but by and large, they were navigators and sailors, who took their ships over the waters to faraway lands to trade. Among the Atlanteans there were also learned architects, lawyers, doctors, artists, writers, musicians, and scientists. The Atlanteans had a kind of airplane with which they could scout their enemies.

MISUSE OF NUCLEAR POWER

The Atlanteans knew much about the theories of nuclear power and were able to fashion some atomic weapons. It was the testing of nuclear bombs which eventually cracked their island's surface and opened the gas chambers beneath, thereby releasing the volcanic fires and earthquakes which sunk a whole continent in less than twenty-four hours, killing millions of people.

I was not incarnated at the time the continent was destroyed, but I had spent a lifetime on Atlantis approximately fifty years prior to its sinking. I was with many who are today the chelas of ECK. I walked the countryside preaching against the atomic tests. We who were of the Order of the Vairag knew what those tests would do to the continent, but few paid us any attention. Some chelas were murdered by the regime for speaking out too loudly against its policies.

As I have already predicted, the same fate that brought mighty Atlantis to her foamy grave will also come to pass in the United States during the early part of the next century unless the testing of nuclear weapons ceases at once!

Since I was a professor of law at the university at Semira, I knew well the codes of law. The first code of laws which appeared on this earth was formulated during the early years of civilization on Atlantis. This set of laws was called the Code of Troana, named after an early lawmaker. The Assyrian Code of Urukagine Lagash, set forward approximately 2370 B.C., was copied from this ancient Atlantean code of laws. So, too, were the Code of Ur-Nammro of Ur and the Code of Hammurabi of Babylon derived from the Code of Troana. Many of today's public laws are direct descendants from this original code which gave the common man his basic rights.

Atlantis was a great nation. Someday soon it will be proven that it existed in fact, and not merely as a legend. Atlantis will then become a part of the recorded history of man's progress on Earth, and its discovery will help to fill in the gap between the beginning of the human race and the start of ancient times.

Ambrose and Olga Worrall, two of the most gifted healers of this century.

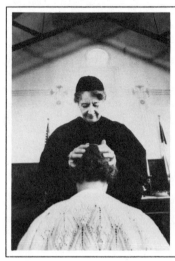

Olga Worrall at a spiritual healing session, practicing the laying on of hands.

CHAPTER THIRTY-TWO

Olga Worrall's
Healing Ministry

Every Thursday morning for many years, hundreds of sick people filled a Baltimore church to receive spiritual healing. And at precisely nine o'clock every night those same people, along with thousands of others who suffered from physical, mental and spiritual ailments, paused for five minutes to give and receive the healing energy which purported to flow into them from God through the hands of a gifted healer.

Ambrose and Olga Worrall established an untarnished record as spiritual healers of astonishing ability which has persisted for 50 years. They worked privately to aid the sick and participated in countless miracles during that time.

The Worralls concentrated much of their healing on sick children. Children with twisted limbs, diseased organs and hopeless prognoses came to the Worralls for assistance and relief. So did adults from all walks of life. A great many of these people improved as a result of the healing sessions, and many were cured.

The Worralls' method of spiritual healing was remarkably compatible with the pragmatic techniques used by most scientists. This was probably because Ambrose Worrall was an engineer and, as such, was a stranger neither to science nor the scientific method.

Olga Worrall was just as scientific. She was not the sort of woman given to vague thinking and incoherent conversation. Indeed, five minutes spent talking with her was enough to convince anyone that she was a far cry from the stereotyped mysterious lady of the occult. Mrs. Worrall was a straight-from-the-shoulder person who believed explicitly in what she and her husband accomplished.

It was this willingness to give straight, unequivocal answers to any and all questions that won for the Worralls the respect of learned people everywhere.

An interesting part of the Worrall's story, apart from the healing ministry, was that they never took a penny in payment for their services.

After Ambrose's death in 1972, Olga carried on as best she could. She participated in a weekly healing service at the Mount Washington Methodist Church and continued to offer both her prayers and her healing energies every evening to those people whose names appeared on her long list.

Until her own passing in January of 1985, Olga Worrall continued an unselfish devotion to her healing ministry. It was in the fall of 1974 that we had the following dialogue:

Brad Steiger: It is a matter of record that you and your husband never accepted payment for your work as spiritual healers. This is rather unique in a society that has become conditioned to paying a high cost for medical treatment. Why did you choose this way of going?

Olga Worrall: In the 1930s when my husband and I gave serious thought to helping people on a large scale, we decided we would never take any money for our ministry. We felt that we did not want to get rich at the expense of sick people. Ambrose decided he would devote his spare time to helping the sick and would work during the day to earn our bread and butter.

Now, I would like to clarify one thing. I have no objection to people being paid for this endeavor if they give their entire time to spiritual healing. After all they must eat and pay their taxes. But they must be paid for their time and not for their gift, and that applies to mediums as well. I feel that a man is worthy of his hire when he is giving his entire time to his work. I object strenuously, as did my husband, to people who commercialize their gift to the point that they become millionaires at the expense of the sick.

I am dismayed when healers, unable to deal effectively with certain sick individuals, blame the patients. These healers project onto a person a guilt complex that is very hard to remove. For instance, they may imply the patient is a sinner and therefore unworthy of God's healing. Or that he did something terrible and therefore cannot be healed. Or that it is his Karma and he must suffer. Well, our Lord does not think that way. Our Lord does not say to those seeking His healing touch, "I cannot help you; it is your Karma that you must not be healed."

I think this attitude on the part of some of these people who set themselves up as healers is what turned the medical profession, as well as the church, against spiritual healing.

How did the medical profession and the organized church react to what you are doing?

When we started in 1930 we had a rugged row to hoe. We were unconventional, and the church took a dim view of what we were doing. Somehow or other theologians forgot that the very foundation of Christianity was built on the gifts of the spirit, especially healing. Healing was practiced by the early church until a certain group of non-spiritual individuals decided that they were the only ones who knew how to interpret God to the laymen. The church and its people have suffered for this.

So all the odds were against us. The church was unsympathetic and the medical profession was rather suspicious.

Average people unacquainted with the various gifts of the Spirit were opposed to our psychic gifts, as well as to spiritual healing, and the more fundamental were certain this was the work of the devil. When they tell me that, I always say I stand in good company, because that is what they told our Lord when He healed. We plodded along in our own way. We never took a patient unless he was given proper medical attention or was under the care of a doctor.

What were we supplying? That extra ingredient that accelerates the normal healing of the physical body. We don't exactly know what spiritual healing is, but it may be akin to electricity. Of course, we don't know exactly what electricity is either. Perhaps someday science will discover the law governing spiritual healing, and then it will be used as an adjunct to medical practice and will enable people to get well much faster.

Has the attitude of the professional community changed?

Yes. I would say after 40 years of practicing spiritual healing the churches now respect us. It recognizes the fact that we were not out to fleece the public. Healing results have been obtained, but we did not claim we were the ones who did it. Only God is able to heal whether He is working through a medical doctor or a clergyman or a healing channel. Without God's power you are utterly helpless.

Would you agree that the acceptance of your spiritual healing is based on these three factors: (1) you receive no money; (2) you take no personal credit for the success you have achieved; (3) you approach the task of healing with a sense of reverence for the source of your healing energy as part of an as yet unexplained universal law?

Perhaps. I might also add that we are not challenging these people. We are not a threat to them. But we are a help. Now, even doctors are more open to the idea of spiritual healing. I have met many, many doctors and they are as a rule very compassionate people. I find medical people are using spiritual healing; these doctors are praying. The dedicated doctors know they are only channels for this healing energy. The use their skills to mend the body, then that something extra takes over and heals.

Clergymen, too, are now more aware than ever of their responsibility in the field of healing. Ministers are told to teach and preach and heal. They do a lot of preaching, but very little teaching, and absolutely no healing in the average church. I salute the Episcopalians, because they accepted the idea of the need to provide their people with a healing ministry and have healing services in many of their churches. I am in the Methodist church. We have been instrumental in keeping the New Life Clinic healing service going because of the healing successes demonstrated. We have people who have started New Life Centers in their own churches after observing ours.

How did the New Life Clinic get started?

This was a pioneer project. It was originated in 1950 by Dr. Albert E. Day, Ambrose, and myself. Dr. Day was the one who had nerve enough to want a healing service in his church. He was severely criticized by his colleagues, who made very sarcastic remarks, such as: "Who do you think you are, God?"

Has your years of experience with the New Life Clinic made an impact on the church in general? What are your views concerning the attitudes of the church leaders?

I feel the New Life Clinic has brought many ministers into contact with spiritual healing in a very simple way. Our healing services are ecumenical. Christians and non-Christians come together. I have a standing joke: All denominations are parked on the front lawn of the church. You come in as a child of God. When you leave you pick up your denomination, because I don't want the front lawn littered. God is no respecter of persons. We are all His children, and when we can have a coming together, then healing takes place. Sometimes it takes months before anything happens. We had one case where it was three years before something happened. But the healing was dramatic.

We must teach our people how to prepare themselves for healing. We conduct a half hour meditation and contemplation that we can hear the whisperings of God. We must be still and stop broadcasting. But how many take the time to listen to what God may want to tell us?

We have six New Life Clinics now, but there should be a New Life Clinic in every Methodist Church in the nation. Our clinic has been accepted as part of the Mount Washington United Methodist Church's ministry. It has not been accepted by the Methodist Church as such. I am terribly disappointed that the theologians are not more interested in finding out what it is we are doing at the clinic. We are getting publicity from various periodicals, and we are known all over the world. Yet, how many of the Methodist theologians are aware of what is going on right under their noses?

The New Life Clinic is living because healings are taking place and we don't take money. My husband underwrote all the expenses involved in our healing ministry. This is one of the reasons I'm sure why we have been respected in this field. We are not making money on sick people.

Has there been any serious analysis of the case work done by you and your husband?

I have thousands of letters from people who testify to the healings. I am not in any financial position to have them documented or to have an analysis made. I am really, frankly, not very interested in proving documentation, because if a person gets well that is all I need to know. That is the important thing. The miracle healings of Jesus are documented in the Bible. What has the church done with all that documentation? Has it analyzed His healings?

If people want to testify to their healings they can do so in writing. We do not encourage them to do so publicly in our New Life Clinic. Our healing service is conducted in a very dignified, very quiet way. When the people come to the rail for the laying on of hands, we don't ask them if they have been saved. It is none of our business. We don't ask them what their denomination is. That is none of our business. Our business is to do the laying on of hands and permit God to use us as a channel, to bring healing into the life of that person.

Would it be fair to say yours is a universalist point of view in that the qualifications of the sufferer is of no interest to you?

Their spiritual needs are our concern. When some ministers ask, "What if nothing happens?" I always tell them that is none of their business. If you are willing to permit God to use you as a channel, whether anything happens or not, then the result is none of your business. Your only business is to permit God to use you.

What are your feelings about the future of spiritual healing?

I hope and pray it will increase. So much work has been done by people like my husband and myself and others – Harry Edwards, for instance, for whom I have great respect. I do feel that present day spiritual healing has made a terrific impression on the lay person. Perhaps one day the church will wake up to the necessity of a healing service, because if it doesn't the church is going to be empty. If we can fill a church on a Thursday morning (which is an odd day) to overflowing with people who are there crying out for spiritual healing, this should be a sign for the churches to provide this type of ministry for all people. These people attend for soul healing as well as for physical healing.

What do you mean by soul healing?

I feel a person is soul sick when he doesn't have communion with God. His soul is crying out for this communion and very often this soul sickness will reflect itself in the physical body. Doctors call this psychosomatic illness. The two are the same thing. If you can bring peace into a man's mind, assure him that he is God's child, that God is concerned about his well-being, that those who have passed on ahead are very much alive and are eagerly awaiting his coming, that we do live after death, then you can heal and bring peace to the soul. This is thus reflected in the physical body and many illnesses disappear.

Do you believe the mind of man is part of the consciousness of God?

Yes! It is part of God. You have a mind that functions outside of the body. When you go to sleep at night you often have astral experiences. There is something in you, something unexplained. You can call it the mind, the God-spark. It is in command at all times. You can describe the physical body; you cannot describe the mind.

Psychiatrists deal in the treatment of mental illness – diseased minds and unhealthy emotions. You are talking about the treatment of soul sickness. Are they aspects of the same thing?

It is the same thing. Psychiatrists recognize the fact that they have to reach or heal the mind first. They will tell you they have never "healed" a person. They have helped, but they have never really cured a person. My husband was once approached by a group of psychiatrists who asked him to teach them "instant psychiatry."

Instant psychiatry?

That is much of what Jesus did. I feel that if psychiatrists would pay sensitive attention to the soul of man, the spirit of man, they could perceive the real cause of a person's sickness. They would have instant psychiatry. They kid me and call me the old Dutch uncle, but I do direct counseling because when I perceive a person's problem I don't beat around the bush. I have absolutely no patience with the idea of blaming other people for what we do. I don't go for that because I was the tenth child in a family of 17, and we were not given every privilege. We were given responsibility and chores to do.

Today young people want responsibility. When I was a school teacher, I discovered that the children who came from poor, yet disciplined, families were on the whole very responsible. Some of the others who were pampered and had every whim catered to were just like a ship without a rudder, irresponsible and undisciplined.

Do you believe then that one is the architect of one's own life and has the responsibility for that life regardless of what happens? Are you saying the onus is on the individual, not the society, to make the necessary adjustments?

Right! I believe that we should help our children to become responsible citizens. The parents should be held responsible for their children's behavior.

What do you think about the use of alcohol and drugs for achieving an altered state of consciousness?

These methods do not achieve true altered states of consciousness. Children want mystical experiences, they want to know a mystical Christ, but drugs and alcohol are not the answer. I would also like to take to task the clergy who are not providing this spiritual teaching in our churches. Our young people want to know about these things and yet they are being denied this knowledge by the very persons who should be providing them with this guidance and information.

We don't have a home life any more. In the old days families had prayer meetings where the parents and children sat around in a circle. Very frequently the sensitivities of the children would be developed or recognized in these circles. We had excellent mediums in the old days, but do we have them today? The children who would have made very good mediums are the ones who are on drugs. Their spirits are crying out for this sensitive communication with the spirit world, and they are not getting it. So they are trying drugs to get into that state of consciousness and the results are tragic.

How about the possibility of possessing discarnate entities?

I know many alcoholics are possessed by individuals who died in a drunken stupor, who knew nothing about the life hereafter. Their churches did not provide them with that necessary information. Those unaware of this phenomenon have become victims of possessing earthbound spirits, and they become alcoholics. I have seen possessing earthbound entities, and my husband and I have been instrumental in depossessing these unfortunate individuals. We have often heard these alcoholics say that something beyond their control had come over them, like a cloud or veil, and they were compelled to drink and continue drinking when they didn't want to.

What type of individual should enter parapsychology?

If I had my way, I would insist that every person hoping to be active in parapsychology be screened first. I believe that this is very important to prevent immature people from becoming involved with a subject they are not able to handle wisely. I believe that a parapsychologist should have a good understanding of psychic phenomena. I wish we had enough good mediums that parapsychologists could sit with. Every parapsychologist should experience this type of phenomenon so that he will be better qualified to handle the subject. I believe that our qualified psychologists are now realizing that psychology has been found wanting, and that parapsychology will provide the answers.

Could you elaborate on that?

Many of our psychologists have been very materialistic and knew little of the inner part of man. Therefore they had not been very successful in healing the whole man. But there are psychologists and psychiatrists now who are becoming more and more aware of the fact that man can have psychic experiences. This knowledge will enable psychologists and psychiatrists to distinguish genuine phenomena from hallucinations.

Psychologists used to dump every unusual experience into the pot of hallucination and condemn people as being mentally insane when they were not. This is pointed out very accurately in Dr. Carl Wickland's book *Thirty Years Among the Dead*. He was a medical doctor and a famous parapsychologist as well. He and his mediumistic wife were able to free many people who were incarcerated for being mentally deranged when they were really mediums having psychic experiences and sometimes experiencing possession. They depossessed these people and brought them back into society. I believe that parapsychology is going to have a great deal to do with stabilizing spiritual healing.

How should the gift of spiritual healing be developed?

I would suggest that every minister, doctor and psychiatrist be taught to be aware of their gifts of the spirit, and utilize these gifts fully and effectively.

Are you saying that everyone can become a spiritual healer?

I am not saying that at all. I am saying that anyone who has a desire to go into medicine or nursing is often a natural-born spiritual healer. These people heal without realizing it. If our doctors were given a course in parapsychology they would be better able to understand spiritual healing.

I have found very few doctors who are not healers, but many of them can't talk about it because the medical profession is so opposed to unorthodox healing. These dedicated doctors do use their gifts *sub rosa*, and many of them have told us they pray before they operate. There are those, too, who are natural-born diagnosticians who receive this knowledge intuitively. They don't "study" intuition in medical school. I know many doctors who are truly holy men.

Do many doctors tell you they possess the gift of spiritual healing power?

They look at me and smile. God love them! My heart goes out to these dedicated men and women who know the source of their power. As one recently said to me, "I know I only repair the body. God does the healing."

Is it possible to train spiritual healers?

No, not unless the person has the potential gift lying dormant. You have it or you don't have it. But you can refine your gift, and you do learn methods that make it possible to use your gift more effectively.

When you perform the laying on of hands, do you intuitively know what to do?

Yes. You know where to put the hands. Certain states do not permit healers to put their hands below the shoulders as protection for unsuspecting people against unscrupulous, so-called healers, and I approve. However, if the healing is going to be performed in a doctor's office or under supervision, the healer can put his hands on any area of the body. I have found though that this really isn't always necessary; very often a hand clasp will heal the person.

Is this a transfer of energy and does it flow from a healer who is prepared to a patient who may or may not be prepared?

I feel that it helps if the patient is prepared. When a person comes to me and says, "Help me," I find this need triggers off that force in me. I cannot turn my healing on at will. The person may ask me for healing, but if there isn't that immediate attunement the energy might be released, but would miss its mark. Therefore, we would continue trying until such time when proper attunement would be achieved.

There must be compatibility then?

Compatibility is one of the several ingredients in spiritual healing.

How does the healer adjust?

The healer and the patient both adjust. My husband always hoped science would come up with a machine that would test the healer and the patient to find out which healer was most compatible with what patient, and then put them together.

Do you think such a machine can be developed by science?

I hope so, because this something Ambrose had hoped for the last 50 years. This would give the subject of healing the scientific approach. However, with common, garden-variety people like me, you can *feel* an attunement. If we had to wait for instrumentation nobody would get healed. A machine will never take the place of a sensitive, however.

You don't know what it is that works through you. You only know that it does work. Instrumentation may be able to guide you.

Perhaps to register wave length. What is it? Is it a component part of electricity? I don't know.

Is that similar to the problem of explaining how acupuncture works?

Right! What is this energy? How can it be captured. We don't know what electricity is, but we have captured it and can turn on a light and see in the dark. If science had to wait until it *knew* what electricity was, we would never have anything. So we use it, and in the meantime try to find out what it is.

Spiritual healing is a phenomenon that has great meaning for you and had for your husband, not to mention the thousands of people you have helped over the years. You and your husband demonstrated conclusively that these gifts do, indeed, work effectively. However, is it possible your gifts may be lost because of a lack of acceptance for spiritual healing?

Not at all! In spite of all past opposition our gifts have flourished and our gifted young people should be developed. I made the statement to a group of ministers that if I had my way every church would have a developing circle that would meet once a week under proper supervision to permit our young people to be able to experience psychic phenomena. You make such a suggestion, and some unenlightened soul thinks it is the work of the devil. Yet God's work will continue regardless of such thinking or opposition.

Through a strict program of spiritual discipline, which includes prayer, fasting and meditation, the author's wife, Sherry Hansen Steiger, who is also an ordained and licensed Protestant minister, has been able to overcome such onslaughts against her physical body as rheumatic fever, a heart attack, the mashing of her spinal column, the tearing of the ligaments in her back, and a shark attack. By maintaining a balanced regimen that recognizes mind, body, and spirit, Sherry, who is in her forties, presents a youthful appearance that continually causes her to be mistaken for a woman in her early twenties.

CHAPTER THIRTY-THREE

Fasting to Cleanse Mind, Body, Spirit

In *The Healing Power of Love* (Whitford Press), my wife Sherry Hansen Steiger relates dramatic instances in which her ability to focus the power of prayer resulted in blessed healing for afflicted individuals. In other more frightening circumstances, Sherry, an ordained and licensed Protestant minister, has found herself the instrument of exorcism, driving out evil or negative entities from men and women who had become horribly possessed.

I made it very clear in *The Healing Power of Love* that Sherry is an extraordinarily disciplined individual. I have never personally known anyone who is able to enter such a deep state of meditation as she is able to achieve. In *Mysteries of Time and Space* (Whitford Press), there are photographs of Sherry bringing down the Light and becoming one with it as she meditated at a Sedona, Arizona, vortex. Incredibly, the sequence of photographs actually captures Sherry transcending the ordinary, material world and manifesting as Light Energy.

Sherry's belief that mind, body, and spirit are one led her first to study nursing. She then moved on to theology at the Lutheran School of Theology in Chicago, where she was later put on staff. A licensed massage-therapist as well as a minister, she has been active in community work and she has served as a youth and family counselor in cities throughout the United States.

She has conducted stress management programs for state boards of education, large business groups, the federal government, the U.S. Navy, and many religious gatherings. Co-creator of the highly-acclaimed multi-media Celebrate Life Program of the 1960s, she also founded the Butterfly Center for Holistic Education in 1972.

Sherry has served on the advisory boards of many educational and health-oriented organizations, and she was one of the founding members of the Wholistic Healing Board through the Institutes of Health and Education, Washington, D.C. in 1978.

I have married a truly Renaissance woman. In addition to all of the above – and so much more that is not recounted – Sherry has appeared in dozens of national television commercials as an actress, and she has written and directed even more! As a model, she has appeared in such publications as *Family Circle, Redbook, Women's Day, Good Housekeeping,* and *Modern Photography.* In 1979, she had a part in *Amusement Park,* a highly-rated television movie of the week.

A minister, a model, a massage-therapist, a meditator, and an exorcist – all rolled into one perpetual motion woman. But above all, Sherry is a Lightbearer, concerned that people truly understand that they can be so much more than desperate individuals trapped in the debilitating ruts of the ordinary. She wants us all to know that we can soar free of the societally prescribed limitations of time and space, and emerge from our cocoons of conformity into beautiful butterflies with borderless horizons to explore.

"The material for our creative transformation from disease to harmony, from illness to wellness is inside of us and exists in us," she says. "Science has proven that an element cannot be changed unless its nucleus is changed. I believe that it is the same with human personality. The inner-most self must change before healing or transformation can be accomplished."

As an important part of her personal program of self-discipline and growth, Sherry very often includes fasting as a vital means of cleansing mind, body, and spirit.

"There is an old German saying," she reminds us, "'If the disease cannot be cured by fasting, it cannot be cured.'"

It is well known that the practice of fasting is an ancient one, which seems to have been employed by nearly every civilization. "The Egyptians believed that one could preserve youthfulness if one fasted only three days each month," Sherry observes. "Hippocrates, considered to be the father of Western medicine, often prescribed fasting to treat critical diseases. Both Socrates and Plato are said to have fasted for ten-day periods to 'attain mental and physical efficiency. According to the famous sixth century Swiss physician, Paracelsus, 'Fasting is the greatest remedy.'"

In Sherry's view, fasting truly is a wholistic approach to wellness and to personal transformation, as it constitutes not only a spiritual discipline and cleansing, but a mental and spiritual cleansing as well. Here, especially prepared for this book, are her comments and recommendations on the rewards of fasting:

The practice of fasting as a spiritual discipline can be found in virtually all religious traditions. From the Islamic point of view, Al Ghassali, a 14th Century poet and mystic, states: "Fasting stands alone as the only act of worship which is not seen by anyone except God. It is an inward act of worship performed through sheer endurance and fortitude...it is a means of vanquishing the enemy of God...Satan, who works *through* the appetites and carnal lusts."

How interesting it is that Christianity says the same thing. Jesus said, "For I tell you truly, except you fast, you shall never be freed from the power of Satan."

The Essene Gospel of Peace, a translation of a Third Century Aramaic manuscript preserved in the Vatican archives, gives a whole treatise by Jesus about health. He gives explicit directions as to how to make an "enema" device out of gourds, as well as detailed instructions about fasting. He says: "All manner of evil and all manner of abominations have their dwelling in your body and your spirit."

In The Gospel of Matthew, Jesus heals a child when the disciples of Jesus had been unsuccessful in their attempts. Later, they ask Jesus why they could not cast out this demon (casting out of demons was a large part of Jesus' ministry of healing). Jesus responded by stating "that kind of demon could only be cast out by prayer and fasting.

Paramahansa Yogananda, the great master teacher and healer from India, pointed out that when animals or primitive people are ill, they naturally (instinctively) fast. He believed most diseases could be cured by fasting, and said that the Yogis recommended regular short fasts (unless one has a weak heart).

Fasting is mentioned 74 times in the Bible. Moses fasted for 40 days as he prayed and lamented over Israel's sin. Right after his fast, he was in direct communication with the Lord and was given the Ten Commandments. Elijah fasted for 40 days, as did most of the prophets. Jesus fasted in the wilderness before his temptation.

Jesus admonishes us to know that the body is the temple of the Spirit, that we should purify that temple. And because the Spirit is the temple of God, it needs to be pure, to be worthy of Him! In the Essene Gospel, Jesus says: "Renew your baptizing with water on every day of your fast, till the day when you see that the water which flows out of you is as pure as the river's foam." (I might add the obvious: We are talking about 2000-year-old river foam.)

THE TRUE POWER OF FASTING

It strikes me that we must be talking about a very important underlying truth about the power of fasting in healing, since it seems to cross over all religions and cultures dating back apparently as far as the earliest records.

Just what is fasting? As a simple definition, fasting means to voluntarily abstain from food, except pure water, thereby giving rest to the entire body. When digestion and assimilation of food are suspended, the elimination of toxins is increased. Blood pressure decreases, and the process of healing is facilitated. Aging and sick cells are removed and regenerated, (provided disease has not reached an irreversible stage). Excess fat and abnormal deposits are consumed as food during the fast, while the cells and tissues of vital organs are preserved. The *elimination of toxins* or poisons from our systems seems to be *the* elemental process of the body, mind, and spirit.

In the body, toxins are harmful substances either produced as by-products of bodily cell function, or from drugs and chemicals. They are eliminated from the body by the liver (in bile juice), by the kidney (in the urine), by the lungs (through exhalation of air), and the bowels (through elimination). I don't think anyone of us needs to be reminded of the facts of toxic substances in the food we eat (sprays and tenderizers, etc.) or of the pollution in the air we breathe. If 4000 or more years ago there was the known wisdom of fasting, how much more do we need it today!

WHY FAST?

There is sufficient research which shows that meat, dairy products, and starchy foods tend to produce large quantities of mucous, which serves as an ideal medium for germs. The modules (pockets) in the intestinal walls lodge chemicals. There are all kinds of little storehouses and buildups of harmful substances within us. Greg Brodsky, in his book *From Eden to Aquarius* says the average American eats *three* times more than needed. Because our food today is so devitalized and devaluated, Brodsky says, the inassimilable part is stored as fat, robbing us of our energy, and collecting poisons – and I might add, making us sick.

Brodsky emphatically states, "There is *no* more efficacious form of medicine available to man than fasting. It represents one of the essential truths of all healing...total elimination...which cannot take place while there is obstruction. Once the body stops digesting, it can begin total elimination of the built-up poisons blocked in the system...to be cleansed on every level – physical, mental and spiritual."

Research from the 70s and much additional recent research, seems to substantiate that those who eat twice as much live one half as long! In experiments with mice (as a testing ground for treatment of man's disorders), it was demonstrated that the life-span could be increased by 50%. How? By fasting! Other research indicates that a pregnant woman who "has a clean body" will not suffer from morning sickness and other distresses which often accompany pregnancy.

According to Jethro Kloss in *Back to Eden*, a diet of acid forming foods and bad food combinations causes waste matter in the system that apparently the body cannot get rid of while we continue eating. This in turn, he states, makes us old and wrinkled. He cites cases of people with old-wrinkled skin who were put on fasts and given sweat baths and herbs to cleanse the blood stream, the intestinal tract and colon. The changes were so dramatic that their own friends didn't even recognize them...they looked 20 years younger! Jethro Kloss says he was himself a case in point, and revealing pictures seem to verify that was true. Many M.D.'s document a wide array of diseases and complaints that have been completely cured by fasting. These include: hardening of the arteries, digestive and elimination problems, glandular malfunctions, circulatory troubles, respiratory difficulties, female problems, frayed nerves, eyes, teeth, weight, children's ailments, asthma, hay fever, arthritis, high blood pressure, psoriasis, multiple sclerosis, ulcerative colitis, acne, migraine headaches, diabetes, cancer, tumors, among others!

FASTING HELPS THOUSANDS OF "HOPELESS" MENTAL PATIENTS

"Controlled fasting has proven to be a safe and effective treatment for schizophrenia, especially in cases where all else failed," claims a noted Canadian psychiatrist, Dr. Abram Hoffer. "Besides curing such psychiatric conditions as depression, paranoia, and anxiety, we're also curing headaches, rashes, stomach ailments, and digestive disorders by fasting.

In a Chicago Hospital, Dr. Theron Randolph said he used a four-day fasting program on more than 7,000 mental patients who were sent to him by doctors who couldn't help the patients any further.

"Through the fasting program we found that 90% of the patients were allergic," said Dr. Randolph, a specialist in internal medicine. "By eliminating allergy-causing foods, after they resumed normal diets, better than one-half of the seriously disturbed patients are now functioning normally."

For at least 35 years Russian doctors have had incredible success with fasting, curing schizophrenics who did not respond to any other treatment. Yuri Nikolayev, a Soviet psychiatrist, was one of the pioneers of this work.

Many doctors consider juice fasting to be *the* #1 healer and rejuvenator. Two of the better known advocates are Dr. Airola and Dr. Ann Wigmore, of the Hippocrates Health Institute in Boston. She believes that almost any disease or body impurity, including cancer, can be eliminated from the system.

To expand upon our "simple" definition, some programs of fasting are more than not eating, although this is a large part of it. Often juices are used to intensify the body's natural eliminative ability and to supply some nutrients. Actually one can find many different types of fasts. There are fruit fasts, salad fasts, grape fasts, grapefruit fasts, apple fasts, millet fasts, etc., lasting anywhere from 24 hours to 60 days.

HOW TO PREPARE FOR A FAST

In *From Eden to Aquarius*, Greg Brodsky outlines some guidelines that I feel are very logical. Some of these are:

Persons over 40 or with chronic or acute disease or anemia should not fast for lengthy periods of time without supervision.

Keep the mind and emotions quiet while fasting.

Don't fast while doing heavy manual labor.

Bathe regularly.

Sauna, steam baths or sweats should be used in moderation.

A fast of less than 7 days or anything less than a series of short fasts in succession, while beneficial, will not usually have a deep, lasting effect.

Drink *lots* of water...to wash out the system.

Limit first fasts to a maximum of ten days...(I would advise a beginner to limit it to three days to start.)

No fast should last 21 days without medical supervision.

The main danger may occur when the fast is over by breaking the fast with foods that are too heavy or by eating too much food. It is suggested to break the fast with juices, then add fruit, vegetables; then once again fresh fruit, then fresh vegetables, slowly returning to solids. There should be no grains, bread, eggs or meat for a time equal to one half the length of the fast.

In the 70s, I was involved with a group of very prestigious doctors, many from the Institute of Health, in Washington, D.C. We formed a "Wholistic" Board for a Wellness Center. After untold hours of discussing just what 'wholistic' medicine was to each of us, and focusing on exactly what the most important diagnostic and treatment modalities should be in this Wellness Center – it was unanimous that the process of "detoxification" was crucial. Fasting, sweats, enemas, colonics and massage were all considered extremely important.

Personally, I think it is very important to assist the body in the removing of toxins, not only during a fast, but as often as possible with sweats. During a fast, sweats are very important, because when the system is finally freed temporarily from the duty of digestion, the stored toxins and poisons literally pour into the blood stream. It is essential to get rid of them!

Supporting the idea and importance of sweats (which can be baths, sauna, steam or other) is some fascinating research from Russia. According to Dr. Boris Wydoff, former physician to the Russian Olympic team, a 30-year research project in Russia led to the conclusion that five out of every eight pounds of substances taken into the human system, passed out again through the *skin*, leaving only three pounds to be passed by the bowels, lungs, and kidneys. Consequently, Dr. Wydoff states most physiologists agree that the "skin exhalation" of toxic substances is very abundant and effective. Most physicians also agree that many toxic substances are absorbed through the skin to begin with, as well as by breathing in or ingesting. The skin is actually the largest organ of the body.

Water permeates *everything* in our bodies and is the basic medium of our chemistry. Our bodies are composed mostly of water. It's easy to understand the wisdom of the ancients and the knowledge of modern medicine focusing on the cleansing of the body until it runs clean once again. After all, even to keep our *cars* running well, we are supposed to change the oil every 2,000 miles or so. And we live in our bodies.

Fasting For The Health Of It by Jean Oswald and Herbert Shelton is full of testimonials and actual case studies of cures, from cancer to depression, achieved by fasting.

Dr. Robert Mendelsohn, former Professor at Northwestern University Medical College and Past President of The National Health Federation, indicates that if you tell your physician ahead of time you're going to fast, you'll probably get a very negative reaction. Dr. Mendelsohn advises, "If you are ready to try a way – that may be new to you – of getting well or, of staying well, I prescribe heavy doses of fasting!"

Uri Geller, the Israeli psychic, set kids to "spoon bending" all around the world.

CHAPTER THIRTY-FOUR

The Controversial Uri Geller and the "Space Kids"

In the times that I have been with Uri Geller, I have seen him exercise abilities that I am convinced must be presently categorized as paranormal. Although there are professional magicians who claim to have caught Uri "cheating," I maintain that he does have genuine "psi" talents.

At least a portion of the controversy that rages about Uri Geller, the remarkable Israeli psychic, has to do with certain assertions that he combines a "blood-of-the-gods" genetic inheritance with the UFO contactee pattern of having received his superhuman abilities directly from a UFO when he was a boy.

An interesting kind of phenomenon has occurred as Uri Geller has toured throughout the world to demonstrate his unique psychokinetic abilities. Wherever he performs, wherever he appears on television or radio, thousands of individuals, especially boys and girls under the age of 17, begin to go and do likewise – they bend spoons and repair broken watches with psychokinetic ability alone.

When Uri Geller appeared on NBC's *Today* show, he suggested that people watching at home should do as he does – get out their broken watches and use their psychic powers to will them to start working again.

After Uri's remark, representatives of NBC said that the network switchboard "lit up like a Christmas tree." Arthur Oppenheimer, public relations director of the *Today* show, said, "We were swamped with hundreds of phone calls from viewers who said their watches had started working again during the show."

A check with NBC affiliates in cities such as Atlanta and Chicago indicated the same kind of response. Letters poured into the various stations. Since the *Today* show has approximately ten million viewers nationwide, Arthur Oppenheimer has suggested that, gauging from the New York response alone, "It's clear the experiment must have worked with thousands – it could have been as many as forty thousand people."

In Denmark, seventeen-year old college freshman Lena Duuse emerged to be declared, "The most powerful psychic I have ever come across – and that includes Uri Geller!" by Dr. Richard Mattuck, Senior Physicist at Denmark's prestigious Orsted Physics Institute at Copenhagen University. Under strictly controlled experiments at the Institute, the teenager used the power of her mind to bend thick iron nails (even while one was encased in a sealed, glass container), to divert a compass needle, to speed up time on a watch, and to boost the temperature on a thermometer.

Lena does not intend to offer competition to Uri Geller, however. She is a shy young lady who prizes her privacy far above international fame and controversy. Although she did appear at a press conference with Uri Geller on one of his visits to Denmark, she has since adamantly refused to talk with any member of the press. She just wants to be a normal girl.

In explanations of human character, the word "normal" can offer a stumbling block in many situations. It may be that it is quite normal to have abilities such as those of Uri Geller, and that most children have these abilities carefully tutored out of them as they progress through the average educational institution in the Western world.

Or it may be, as some people have suggested, that a root race is now emerging in which abilities such as bending metal, influencing one's environment, and developing and expressing all sorts of psi abilities would be considered extremely normal.

For many years now, those who study various esoteric teachings have been predicting the dawn of a new root race, with births occurring on a planetary scale. The children will represent a quantum leap in terms of their advancement on the evolutionary scale.

In my own travels around the United States, I have met many of these superkids after my lectures and public appearances. I have been especially pleased to note that most of them are developing spiritually as well as psychically, and that the majority of them seem to tire quite rapidly of "show-off" psychic manifestations. None of them have been interested in public demonstrations of their abilities, although a good number of them, quite understandably, have become minor heroes to their playmates and friends, and some have caused a certain amount of consternation and confusion in the classroom.

In one instance I was told of a young boy who was a veritable demon according to the testimony of his mother and mother's best friend. He was the bully on the recess playground, and he was abusive to his parents and to his siblings. All in all, he was a quite disagreeable boy.

After watching Uri Geller on television and grunting something to the effect that he could do those same things, he began to bend spoons and to develop the wide range of psi abilities that the personable Israeli psychic possesses. And after having developed these abilities, he underwent a metamorphosis of personality and was transformed from demon to saint. He now spends his time diplomatically breaking up the fights of his friends on the playground and soothing the egos and injured feelings of his classmates who may have suffered physical or mental injury at the hands of others. He has now abandoned his psychokinetic abilities, and he seems no longer interested in his clairvoyant talents. But his mother thankfully acknowledges that he has maintained an interest in growing spiritually and becoming a tranquilizing influence at home and in school.

In November, 1975, during a telephone conversation with Melanie Toyofuku, an associate of Dr. Andrija Puharich, I learned that she had just returned from England and an examination of a number of the superkids there. Melanie was engaged in a worldwide project of investigating young people with extraordinary mental abilities. She was conducting her studies without fanfare and without a desire to spotlight the young people she was investigating. She was seeking only to learn more about them so that she might help them and help prepare society for their super talents.

When I arrived at Andrija's estate in Ossining, New York, I found it marvelously advantageous that, in addition to Melanie and Andrija, I would be speaking to Gene Roddenberry, the producer-creator of *Star Trek*. Since Andrija and Melanie had worked so closely with Uri Geller, and since Gene Roddenberry's televised series had influenced literally millions of young people all over the world and acquainted them with areas of the mind in which they could "boldly go where no man had gone before," they seemed an ideal trio with whom to discuss the worldwide production of little Uri Gellers.

ANDRIJA PUHARICH: In reviewing what's going on right now, the unusual psychic phenomena which are popping up all over the planet, nothing is unique; it's all happened before. It's an old story. But what seems to me unique is the fact that the onset of the phenomena has been orchestrated. Melanie and I are really prime witnesses to that.

On November 9, 1973, during tape-recording sessions with SPECTRA [an alien intelligence said to have monitored Earth for thousands of years] it was hinted – though it wasn't said specifically – that Uri would do something unusual with electromagnetic communication. (By the way, November 9 was also the day that Uri was teletransported from New York

City to my porch here in Ossining.) I didn't know what SPECTRA might be referring to; I couldn't interpret the statement. But a few weeks later, November 23, Uri appeared on BBC television, and it was like he was an orchestra conductor with a baton. When his baton came down, thousands of people – nobody knows how many people – reported strange events happening at home. Clocks that hadn't worked for years started running; chandeliers began to swing. The British press was saturated for three months, and it's still happening.

Wherever Uri has been – South Africa, Japan, Australia – whenever he goes on television, the phenomenon occurs. I don't even try to guess how it works. Not to give McCluhan a pat, but somehow the medium is the message. The medium does carry the message immediately, and we don't even know what the message is!

The super kids that I've run into are not at all like Uri. They're like the ones you've mentioned, Brad, who don't even want to be known. This little kid from England told me he was up in a spaceship last night. He said he told them, "Don't bug me! I've got to study for exams!" But they said, "You've got to come up here." He said, "Well, then you've got to help me with my exams." So he goes up to his classroom in the spaceship, and they give him a whole bunch of equations and he's told immediately to send them to me.

We talked for sixteen minutes on the transatlantic call, with him telling me all these equations. I haven't had time to study them. I don't know whether they're valid or not, but he's really a brilliant mathematician. That's his *forte*. So I can't even begin to understand these kids or define them myself. To me it's like some kind of biological time bomb, and both our leaders in society and science are totally ignoring it.

Nobody really wants to look at the problem, at the phenomenon. They're afraid of what they might see, and that includes some very beautiful people who are turning their backs on the whole phenomenon of the super kids. They just don't want to look at what's underneath the surface.

MELANIE TOYOFUKU: Responding to Andrija, these children really do seem to be quite different. I think we have a tremendous responsibility – since they are on Earth, and they are Earth children – we have a tremendous responsibility in grounding them so that they can be effective on Earth, so that they can function here, and so that they can bring down that knowledge to Earth level and share it with the rest of us. It's probably easy for them to be "out there," and their problems are created when they try to interact with social systems and Earth education and Earth families and Earth life. For us to emphasize their "up-thereness," I think, is a tremendous disservice to them. What they need is integration on Earth so that they can then allow their cosmic knowledge to be effective. We all have to learn from them, for, in a sense, they bring clues to our survival.

BRAD STEIGER: *I think we should point out that some of these children are emerging in locales where Uri Geller is totally unknown.*

PUHARICH: Yes. I was in Mexico in May, and Uri's never been to Mexico. I was absolutely amazed when a flood of people got in touch with me after I did a television talk-show. And out of this came a bunch of what I call space kids – kids with these unusual psychokinetic powers, etc. None of them had seen Uri. None of them had heard of Uri. So that's one clearly documented experience that I have. I have two space kids who are living with me now who are from Colombia, and their abilities had manifested long before they had heard of Uri. So there are kids all over the world who are developing the same kind of abilities who have not been subject to Uri's baton influence.

One aspect of American culture that certainly could have been a preconditioning factor for Uri Geller and the super kids would be "Star Trek." On that marvelous program, which has become a cult, even for kids who weren't even born when it was originally shown on television, there are a number of individuals whom the stalwart crew of the Starship Enterprise encountered who had all sorts of remarkable abilities, who could materialize bouquets of flowers, who could dematerialize phasers out of the hands of Captain Kirk.

GENE RODDENBERRY: We wrote a couple of episodes about individuals who had such unique talents. As a matter of fact, our second pilot – and the one that sold the series – was on that subject when [actor] Gary Lockwood began to find out that he could, after having undergone a strange experience in space, accomplish things like moving a glass of water without touching it. And then he developed more and more power.

We did the same thing in *Charley X*, which is about a boy who had been raised on a strange planet. But in both cases we did draw a moral. We did echo sort of a warning that may have something to do with why such things appear slowly.

In both cases we had the people destroy themselves because they got too much power too fast. I think it would certainly be a danger situation if a child or an adult had this kind of power without having the kind of philosophical background and morality to balance the power as it becomes greater and greater. I think power does corrupt, and I think that even the innocence of a child is no protection against that.

PUHARICH: In my view, the evidence is accumulating, very rapidly in the last few years, that more and more people are being turned on by powers they don't understand. Rather than being some evolutionary breakthrough, some freak genetic thing by cosmic ray induction or something, there does seem to be this thing where the people who receive these powers are able to communicate with some other source outside themselves, perhaps some extraterrestrial source. So you have to make the assumption, or at least I do, based on the UFOs I've seen, the UFO photographs I've taken, the UFO landings I've seen, and a lot of concrete experience, that there is some kind of intelligent system that is aware of us and can override anything we do.

I make this basic assumption: They are not our equals. We're pretty low creatures compared to the kind of stuff they're dazzling us with. So we ask questions like, "Are they going to take us over? What the hell are they interested in us for? Who are they? There are billions of other planets, why don't they fool around with them? Is this for the good of humankind, or is it not for the good of humankind?

Unfortunately, these kinds of questions too quickly deteriorate into the theological arguments about Satan and who's running the world, which I think, in most cases, are rather sterile, because people don't really know what they're all about when they talk of these things. I would prefer to go to my own direct experience in looking at each of these space kids, these super kids, as individuals and in spending time with them and living with them and eating with them and exploring the farthest reaches of their consciousness.

I have found in my sampling of the kids, which admittedly is not very large compared to the thousands who are around, that not one is given to what we would call evil or negativity. We also know that Uri Geller has never been able to use his powers for petty larceny. He can't control, he can't dominate, he can't override his abilities. So what we would call negativity or evil does not seem to reside in these kids, but it does reside in our generation, in the older generation.

MS. TOYOFUKU: And they are very easily bored with spoonbending, etc. They're not too much into passing their abilities along or in teaching them, but in asking, "If I can bend metal, maybe there are other things that are possible, that are more interesting than bending metal."

There is an interest in further development, and I think that's really important.

Just a generation or so ago instead of going off into spaceships and receiving teachings, such individuals were astral traveling to Tibet and receiving teachings from ascended masters. Don't you think we're seeing an update of the same kind of phenomenon?

PUHARICH: I think so. These space kids seem to fit into different categories. I'll outline them for you.

There's a whole group who claim to go undersea. They have undersea cities that they all recognize. These are meeting places. It's like going down to the local pub.

There's another group that know of places on Earth that are buried, like under the polar cap somewhere – cities that are there ready to be opened up.

Then there's another group who go to places that are traditional – as you've said, the Tibetan mountains, the Andes, Mt. Shasta, etc. All these traditional places which are associated with mountains and cold and the White Brotherhood sort of business.

But the bulk of them go to places that are not clearly recognizable. The funny thing is, when two of them meet in a spaceship, they start swapping notes. It's really funny, and they're very cool about it.

One of the principles of the Starship Enterprise was noninterference with the process of any culture which they might encounter. How do we interpret what is happening on Earth with these super kids? Is this noninterference?

PUHARICH: Well, let's just take a quick skip through history. I think there's evidence textually in Egyptian, Hebrew, early Greek literature, Hindu literature, and many other ancient texts, that there have been people from some other place arriving here on Earth in things that we now call spacecraft. Whoever these people were, they lay down instructions for humanity, but not with a very heavy hand, because teaching should be a gentle thing. The heaviest hand that we seem to have seen laid on man from some other place is in the Old Testament when Jehovah lays down the law and says "Do it my way or else!"

But if you look over five thousand years of history that we've got on the books, it seems to me that the presence of the UFO intelligence has been seen, but scarcely felt. It's not obvious. It's not accepted by religion, not accepted by scientists. So I'd say the influence from a historical point of view has been very gentle, like a father who's seldom around, but his presence is still there.

RODDENBERRY: I think all religions come together, because if the Gods are indeed all-powerful, they could have gone "Zap!" and all men would have been good.

PUHARICH: Sure, but that's the whole thing of free will. The Gods want you to learn by mistakes and go through trial and error. Hopefully, over eons and eons of evolution, man will bootstrap himself to some equal place in the councils of the universe.

Andrija, you talk of space and planets, spaceships. Is there anything in your research which would prohibit you from also talking about these entities having come from other dimensions, rather than from outer space?

PUHARICH: Oh, no, I'm glad you brought that up. People immediately get the idea when you talk about spacecraft that they are from our three-or-four dimensional frame of reference. Forget it! Absolutely not! The one conclusion I have about the nature of spacecraft, having watched them all over the world, photographed them, having actually seen them on the ground, is that the one thing they can do is to transform from this dimension to somewhere else. My basic assumption is that what is called the spacecraft is indeed a time machine that can transform from one dimension to another.

Why has Uri Geller recently denied the whole UFO aspect of his work?

PUHARICH: When Uri found out that people did not like the idea of

SPECTRA and HOOVA, he chose to deny them at a point which is well marked in time, in January of 1974, when he realized that his speaking of them might hurt his show-business career. From that moment he began to back-pedal.

But, believe me, he was a witness to every event. We've seen the spacecraft. He's photographed them. I've photographed them. I've seen him go aboard them, and we've all been in the same place.

RODDENBERRY: Yet when Uri gave me a copy of his own book three weeks ago, it included all these things in it. He very specifically talks about going to the spaceship and finding the pen cartridge inside, and he also has a photograph of the UFO that he took out of an airplane window.

Uri's acceptance or denial notwithstanding, where is the UFO mystery leading us in terms of our social transcendence? What do you see as the big picture?

PUHARICH: I know that the phenomenon essentially is not what we could call an emergent phenomenon. By that I mean, there's not a little chain here called material world, material science, and if this chain grows outward the last flower that appears is the flower of these space children. I think something has come from the outside. The reason I say that is, as I said earlier, you can't deal with this thing either on a three-dimensional scale or a four-dimensional scale. You have to get into higher dimensional phenomena. This is what bugs all of us. We'd like to be able to package it in cellophane in 3-D and say we've got it all wrapped up, but the phenomenon is not like that.

The "big picture," as you phrase it, extends outside of our dimension, beyond our scope of vision, of hearing, of communication. We're very much like a prisoner who's in a cell who doesn't know what's going on outside. He has no doors, no windows. Every once in a while somebody shoves food under the door, and he tries to imagine who's on the other side, but he doesn't really know who or what. He can only decode the message in terms of his own little black box, and this is the kind of black box all of us live in. I think it's very much a bigger picture than any of our speculations from theological to science fiction to philosophical to physical science have considered.

I do think it's a phenomenon that will eventually become clear, but it's not going to become clear with the ordinary 3-D vision that we exercise in contemporary science. I think we're going to have to develop what I call a whole race of "psychonauts" – talented people who are able to cross dimensional barriers. And there are such people. I've worked with them. They can see into the future. They can see into the next dimension. They can bring back reliable, hard information that can be verified in the 3-D world.

I think it's going to take an enormous amount of data collection with these psychonauts, who can escape from the fourth dimension and the fifth dimension and the sixth dimension and tap other civilizations, get aboard spacecraft physically, be teletransported from here to some other civilization. I think we're just at the beginning of a whole new age of exploration; and, to me, it probably is much more exciting than the time when the first little old Neanderthal man dug out a canoe and sailed forth. That little Neanderthal and his canoe led to the great age of exploration, but the exploration on which we are now embarking will be much greater than landing on the moon or going to Jupiter.

I think that everybody should be aware that we are dealing with exciting new phenomenon which will make the present way of life seem archaic and primitive – as we look at man in the Paleolithic Age. I think we are on the threshold, and we have all the tools, all the opportunities. All we have to do is remain cool about it and not try to preserve old ideas, old systems, old philosophies of science, old religions, old political forms.

I think we should imagine that the world never existed before and we're starting from scratch. We've got the opportunity to create a whole new world. My son will probably see all of these things happen. I may never see it. But I'm encouraging him to follow this path, and he follows it happily – because it's fun!

RODDENBERRY: I don't know whether the children who see themselves in a spaceship or in Tibet actually go to a Tibet or a spaceship as we know it. But I think it is possible that the power of thought allows them to create a place, not an imaginary place, but a place that is as real to them as reality.

I know that when I am writing very well, and I create (I don't know where that comes from either) a different planet, a different society, during the time I'm writing, it's as real to me and as solid as this table top. I have smelled the smell of a campfire with an odor from no wood you'd ever have on Earth. There has been quite a reality there. I sometimes wonder how much farther one would have to go until indeed it became real.

I don't know how many worlds are going on all at once. All of us here may be living in a different one in which we just sort of correspond. We're reaching each other through those dimensions.

I think an exciting explanation, an exciting way to look at things, is that the ultimate power, the ultimate particle, the ultimate meaning, is thought itself.

MS. TOYOFUKU: I completely believe that there is an evolution going on right now. In Queen Victoria's time, for example, some women began menstruating at the age of 21. Today we're menstruating at 10. I think that a kind of biological evolution makes it a lot easier for people to accept a psychological and a spiritual evolution, and the children are in that kind of evolution.

The children have evolved to the point where they're transcending. All that's happening is transcendence. I think that transcendence is the important thing. Some people transcend on a religious level. They commune with God, and that's enough for them. You mention space civilizations to them, and they get very upset. With the space children, religion upsets them. They're in another kind of space with another civilization. All of that to me is comfortable.

I think that arguments we create, whether it's a UFO, whether it's a Jungian thought-form, whether it's collective unconscious, all that is less important to me in terms of an argument. All of it is totally acceptable to me, and I think it depends upon your personal belief system as to whichever cosmology you wish to believe.

The important thing is that if we are indeed here as part of the evolutionary process, which I believe we are, then our commitment is to be effective in creating a transcended planet, so that we survive in light and be the best that man can be. And if it requires some discretion to do that, some altruism, some help, then we should do it.

CHAPTER THIRTY-FIVE

The Master of Mind Over Pain

He lies on a bed of sharpened nails while a husky member of the audience crushes a chunk of cement on his body with a sledgehammer.

He stretches serenely on his nailbed while heavy men from the audience stand on a board placed across his chest.

He leaps from a raised platform onto a bed of nails with his bare feet.

He pushes a nail through a one-inch board, his hand protected only by a handkerchief.

He bends bars with his bare hands. He is Komar.

Komar is listed in the famous *Guinness Book of World Records* as holding the record for the hottest firewalk. According to the book's editors: "The highest temperature endured in a firewalk is 1,220°F. for 25 feet by 'Komar' of Wooster, Ohio, at the Phoenix Psychic Seminar, Arizona, on March 7, 1975. The temperature was measured by a pyrometer."

The *Guinness Book of World Records* credits Komar with two additional international record feats: "The duration record for non-stop lying on a bed of nails [needle-sharp 6-inch nails, 2 inches apart] is 25 hours 20 minutes by [Komar] at Wooster, Ohio, July 22-23, 1971. The greatest live weight borne on a bed of nails is also held by Komar with four persons aggregating 1,142 lbs., standing on him on the *Mike Douglas Show* on TV in Philadelphia on March 26, 1974." Komar also performed this feat in Chicago while sandwiched between two beds of nails and supporting an aggregate 1,642 lbs.

PAIN TESTS

On July 17, 1973, my research organization, Other Dimensions, arranged for medical tests to be conducted at the Pain Rehabilitation Center, a unit of St. Francis' Hospital in LaCrosse, Wisconsin, by Dr. C. Norman Shealy, recognized as one of the most knowledgeable authorities on pain in the United States. The subject of the tests was Vernon E. Craig – better known as Komar, the Hindu Fakir. The objective of the tests at the Pain Rehabilitation Center was to find out how Komar is able to control pain, to seemingly fly away from intense physical discomfort.

Dr. Shealy was willing to undertake the tests because he is interested in any technique that may offer aid in the alleviation of pain. As a neurosurgeon, Dr. Shealy has a thorough knowledge of the relationships of pain to the nervous system and the brain. At that time, Dr. Shealy was the Chief of Neurosurgery at the Gunderson Clinic in LaCrosse, associated with the neurology sections of both the University of Wisconsin and the University of Minnesota, and was widely published in leading medical journals.

The remarkable Komar appears many times in the authoritative Guinness Book of Records as the holder of world records for incredible feats of pain control.

The plan was to put Komar through a battery of preliminary tests and evaluations in the morning, then run him through some of the same tests after lunch – this time while hooked up to various electronic instruments. Dr. Shealy wanted to measure Komar's responses to pain on the EEG and EKG machines, which would track his heart and brain reactions to the pain stimulation. He also wanted to use a galvanometer to measure skin and muscle response, and a special instrument for measuring changes in body temperature.

Dr. Shealy began his investigation by assuming that if Komar did not have congenital analgesia (no physical awareness of pain – a rare condition with which certain persons are born), then he probably had considerable ability to control his mind.

A complete neurological work-up was given to Komar. The test results determined that he is a relatively normal subject, both physically and neurologically. He apparently does not have congenital analgesia, and is as sensitive to pain as anybody else. Dr. Shealy observed that Komar had no apparent damage to his back from lying on his bed of nails three times a day during the preceding week. There were marks on his back, but these did not appear to have created punctures.

RESPONSE EVALUATIONS

Following the neurological and physical examinations, Dr. Shealy began the pain response evaluations.

He applied a tourniquet to Komar's right arm.

Shutting off the blood can have some persons writhing on the floor in agony after just two minutes. Komar, who said he was disassociating himself from any pain that might occur in his right arm, advised the doctor he felt no discomfort.

Dr. Shealy removed the tourniquet after five minutes and seemed surprised that Komar reported absolutely no pain.

Next, Komar was asked to plunge his arm into a bucket of ice cold water and see how long he could stand the freezing sensation. Komar withdrew his arm from the water after thirty seconds and said he could not stand it any longer. He was then asked to try the same test again – but this time he was to try to control the pain.

Komar placed his arm back in the freezing water. Two-and-ahalf minutes later, Dr. Shealy withdrew Komar's arm from the ice-water. Komar reported no pain during the second immersion.

The test was followed by the running of a nineteen-gauge needle through Komar's biceps.

Komar willed himself into a trance and reported feeling no pain; as a matter of fact, he didn't even flinch.

Dr. Shealy brought out a battery-powered electric rod that is used to test pain thresholds. The amount of charge can be intensified by advancing a lever on the rod.

Komar was able to withstand the maximum charge without feeling any pain.

After lunch Dr. Shealy continued the testing. The schedule included a rerun of the ice-water test, the needle through the arm, the bed of nails, and Komar's reaction to hypnotic suggestion. Dr. Shealy also wanted to see if Komar could cause body-temperature changes at will.

Tests were made of Komar's responses while he was in a normal state of consciousness and awareness. The complete battery of monitored tests took the better part of an hour.

The results turned out to be what Dr. Shealy had expected. The electronic instruments showed that Komar was able to launch himself into an altered state of consciousness. In this state of mind, he was able to disassociate himself from the pain whenever he wanted.

In discussing the Komar experiments, Dr. Shealy said that "lying on a bed of nails is thought by most individuals to be extremely painful and to require great will power. We fully expected it would require a theta state of brain activity. The obvious physical principle of dispersing a large surface area over a number of nail points prevents serious pain or injury. The minimal discomfort brought about in my bed-of-nails test (with no previous experience) is evidence that the procedure is not a major physical threat. Nevertheless, the ability to stay on such a bed for twenty-five hours or to have 1,142 pounds pressed on the abdomen and chest, demands considerable mind control.

Brad Steiger (third from left) checks Komar out for himself, with the help of his young sons and a next-door neighbor. Photo circa 1973.

"THE INNATE ABILITY TO DISTRACT PAIN"

"It is obvious from the ice-water test that Komar has an innate ability to distract his mind by going into at least an alpha state, and in it having control over his autonomic nervous system. Presumably, in his more stress-filled public demonstrations, he uses that state of mind to prevent pain and body damage. There was no sustained theta state in the current experiments."

Dr. Shealy concluded his comments of the test by saying that Komar, who has had no formal Yoga training and no neurological deficit, *can mentally distract pain from himself.*

AN ORDINARY LAD FROM OHIO

Vernon Craig was born in 1932 in Hamilton, Ohio. As a child, he had an interest in rare plants. At one time he had in the family home a collection of rare tropical plants which included 150 orchids and more than 1,000 cacti.

When he was a teenager, Craig found employment with an amusement park near Hamilton. He doubled as a waiter and a magician's assistant, and became an understudy in an aerialist act. He left carnival life to learn cheesemaking, and he was soon promoted to chief cheesemaker.

In spite of success in the cheesemaking business, the future fakir felt the need to work with plants. When he learned that the College of Wooster was looking for a head gardener, he submitted a letter of application and was hired. While he was head gardener, he joined the Wooster, Ohio, Jaycees, serving as chairman of the Mental Health and Retardation Committee.

It was as a member of the Jaycees that Craig was asked to entertain at the barbecue, where his first firewalking exploit took place. It was another Jaycee project that prompted Komar's attempt to break the existing world's record for lying on a bed of nails. The champion, an Australian, had done it for twentyfive hours, nine minutes; and Komar would be aiming for the astounding time of fifty-six hours!

A COMFORTABLE BED OF NAILS

Komar arrived at the Chamber of Commerce office in Wooster's public square at 7:30 on Thursday morning. Reporters scurried around, jostling for positions that would afford them the best views. At 9:00 a.m. EST, Vernon Craig lay down on his bed of nails.

A crowd gathered. For hours Komar answered their questions via a public-address system. Most of their questions related to the pain, the sharpness of the nails, and "Are you bleeding?"

These questions almost cost the Hindu fakir his record. Needless to say, it is difficult to shut thoughts of pain out of the mind when one is being constantly questioned about that very subject. There is every reason to believe that Komar would have achieved his goal of fifty-six hours if he had been allowed privacy.

Komar rose from his bed of nails at 10:20 plus fifteen seconds on Friday morning, July 13. Although he had not reached his goal of fifty-six hours, he had established a new world record, exceeding the existing time by eleven minutes.

And Komar reported no pain, only a "tingling sensation."

On August 23, 1971, Vernon Craig received a letter from Norris McWhirter, managing editor of the *Guinness Book of World Records* confirming the new world's record. At the time, Komar was listed in *Guinness* as holding the world's record for having the most weight (825 pounds) on him lying on nails. Since then, the Hindu fakir bettered his own record with a figure of 992 pounds, established at the International Aquarian Age Conference held at Honolulu, Hawaii, in February 1972; and with the total of 1,142 pounds set on the *Mike Douglas Show* in March, 1974.

Although Komar's record-breaking session of nail-lying has brought him international fame, he remains modest about his achievement. He describes himself as "an ordinary man who suddenly developed certain abilities."

But how many "ordinary" men are able to lie for hours on a bed of sharpened nails?

Or leap barefooted onto the same kind of "cushion"?

Or walk up a ladder with swords for steps?

Either "ordinary" is badly in need of redefinition, or the vast majority of people are living at a level of self-awareness that is far below ordinary standards. Komar believes the latter to be the case.

WE MUST BOOST OUR LEVELS OF AWARENESS

"Scientists are saying that most of us use only about ten percent of our mental capacities," declares Craig. "I try to get across to the people who come to see me that it is possible, with proper discipline and training, to utilize much more than ten percent of their minds.

"Through concentration, I must place my body into a state of relaxation in which body tissue becomes more resilient. Once that state is reached, the tissues give, with the result that the nails do not penetrate as deeply as when the body is tense. Many think that the thing to do is to tighten up the muscles, but nothing could be farther from the truth."

Komar also states that he uses no substances to toughen his skin. "That is, unless ordinary soap and water can be called hardening agents."

Some might think of local anesthesia, such as the dentist's Novocaine, as one explanation for Komar's ability to defy pain. Komar denies this, saying that he is able to feel pressure from the hundreds of nails next to his skin, but no pain.

"If, while I am on the nails, someone were to insert their finger between the nails and touch my back, I would know it," Komar explains.

"I maintain this state while I am actually on the nails. But immediately after I get up, if someone were to stick me with a hat pin, I'd probably go straight up.

"In a sense," says Komar, "I out-think the pain. The mind can be disciplined to accept only one sensation at a time. *By filling the mind with another sensation, pain is displaced and the body ceases to react to the painful stimulus.*

"In a more profound sense, what happens during my demonstrations is more like disassociation of mind and body. Just before I jump onto the nails, for example, I pause momentarily, pick out an object a short distance away, then focus my mind on it. At other times I visualize a little ball – sort of a third eye – as I begin. I picture that little ball going out of my head with my mind following."

Komar repeatedly emphasizes that he does not consider himself a mystic or psychic. Referring to his sensation of being out of the body, he hastens to point out that it is only a sensation, not an actual out-of-body experience.

"I do not picture myself as standing apart watching the action in an astral body or anything like that. The demonstrations can be frightening. I don't even like to watch the filmed performances on television, although I have done so several times. When I am on the nails, I picture something pleasant or funny.

"Sometimes I feel as if I am lying in a field of flowers, usually daisies or clover. It's a sensational feeling, as if I am free of the body."

Perhaps one reason why Komar does not like to watch his demonstrations on television is because by his own admission, he has an unusually low tolerance for pain!

"I can hardly walk around without my shoes and socks," says the man who has walked twenty-five feet across a bed of coals hot enough to melt away the legs of his rayon pantaloons. "Even with shoes on, it hurts my feet to walk on a gravel path!"

I asked Komar if he could recreate exactly his mental process as he lay on a bed of nails.

"Through the years, I have programmed my mind," he answered. "Somehow I have a good working system between the subconscious and the conscious; and whenever it's needed, my subconscious takes over.

"Anyone who has attained self-mastery will know exactly what to do in any instance of pain. Usually, and in my case particularly, I stop pain before it even occurs. Most of the pains we're talking about are totally alien to my body, because I've never had them."

"Right now if I would bring out a bed of nails," I asked, "what's the first thing you would think of?"

"The humor of knowing I have to lie on it would put me in a relaxed state of mind," Komar laughed.

"A happy person doesn't have pain! A happy person is a healthy person. I'm in a very positive frame of mind when I lie on the nails. There is an initial sensation. I can't call it pain, but I know the body is being damaged at that point.

"But then the subconscious seems to take over. When 1,100 pounds are on me, I know that they will not puncture my body. I think the subconscious is letting me know.

"There are times when I am about to firewalk when I know I am not ready to go across those coals. If I did at that point, I would be burned. I just know when I am ready.

"I start to walk toward the bed of coals, and if I'm not going to go across them – if I'm not in the right frame of mind – I stop within a couple of steps of the coals. It's happened on only a couple of occasions. I'm aware of people and everything around me, but they can see I'm in a trance-like state to a degree.

"One doctor seems to think I might be down as low as the delta brainwave state at the time I go across the coals. This, he feels, might prevent me from feeling the sensation of pain, but he does not know what could cause me *not* to be burned. This is what is amazing to the medical field. My clothing isn't even affected!

"It might be it's possible to build up a mental field so strong that I can put a layer of 'something' between my feet and the coals.

"I feel heat, but yet don't feel it – it's a weird sensation that I cannot adequately describe.

"I cannot talk after I get into that state of mind. I walk around and around the coals, blocking them out to the point where they don't exist anymore. Although they're there, in my mind they don't exist.

"When I get so convinced, I walk a few steps away from the coals, raise my hands to let everybody know I'm coming through, pull up my pantaloons, and start to walk across."

Medical men are interested in the condition of the skin on the fakir's feet after they have watched his demonstrations. One physician, after a particularly critical examination of Komar's feet, was moved to proclaim that, "There are many who would be happy to have skin like this. His skin is as soft as a baby's."

MODERATION

Komar's approach to eating and the use of alcohol can be summarized in one word: Moderation.

He follows no specific diet, but says he is not "heavy on meat." Komar also says he enjoys an occasional social beer.

With reference to sex, Komar follows the same principle: "Moderation must be the rule."

He believes that excessive sexual desire results from "thinking about sex," and in extreme cases becomes an obsession. He believes that excessive desire can be controlled by the same method he uses to block pain.

"If it's possible to out-think pain," Komar explains, "it should also be possible to out-think frustration resulting from unsatisfied sexual desire."

He is not, however, so moderate in his attitude toward drugs. Komar says that he uses no drugs whatsoever, shunning even aspirin. He seldom drinks coffee because he feels that it is too much of a stimulant.

Even though Komar makes no claims of psychic power, he has been encouraged to try healing. Komar says that many psychic sensitives have told him that they feel he has this power, but that he is waiting until he learns more about the subject.

It would appear that he knows more than he admits, because he claims to have kept himself free of sickness for the past twenty years, except for an occasional case of minor "sniffles."

REINCARNATION

Komar and Brad Steiger were among the lecturers at the First Aquarian Age Conference, Honolulu, February, 1972

It is difficult to talk to Vernon Craig about his life and career as Komar without returning again and again to the subject of reincarnation.

Although Craig lays no claim to being the present incarnation of a Hindu fakir, yogi, or swami, and he remains skeptical toward the doctrine of reincarnation itself, his statements reveal not only a knowledge of the subject, but a conscious pattern that to some extent contradicts his expressions of doubt.

Craig speaks constantly of his fascination with things of an Oriental nature, yet gives no indication of how this fascination originated. Certainly there was not much in the "hellfire and damnation" brand of religion that was promulgated in his childhood home and community to encourage interest in peoples and customs that were most surely dismissed as "heathen."

In addition to an interest in the Orient, the young Vernon Craig was drawn strongly to stories with a jungle setting.

Was it memories of a land of trees, vines, and flowers that led Craig to become interested in horticulture, an interest that predated even his discovery of Yoga?

And was it a sense of the familiar that led him to the woods to meditate and to receive some of the earliest indications of the extraordinary powers of mind he was destined to develop?

In the case of Komar, reincarnation is a more plausible explanation than possession. When an alien entity takes control of a living person, it does not claim to be a former incarnation of the subject. In cases of apparent reincarnation, on the other hand, the entity speaks of a former life, not a period of temporary control.

When Craig is performing as Komar, he retains his own appearance, mannerisms, and tone of voice, as opposed to cases of possession in which the subject often undergoes changes of features, behavior, and speaks with the voice of the possessing entity. The fact that the Hindu fakir has no memories or intimations of a previous existence can be explained by the Hindu belief that one should not try, or be encouraged to try, to remember former incarnations. The Hindus believe to do so is to bring about an early death and incurrence of bad karma.

The same dogma may be responsible for Vernon Craig's attitude toward the paranormal aspects of his abilities. Is his skepticism a mask for his reluctance to pursue the subject, lest he remember the reasons for things for which he now says he has no explanation, or for which he offers logical ones?

THE SIX STEPS TO SELF-MASTERY

By Komar

When I am not performing dramatic demonstrations of pain mastery, I am working in an Ohio cheese factory, not secluding myself away in a Himalayan monastery.

I am an average man with average physical abilities. *If I could learn to control pain, then so can you!*

When man thinks of himself as human, he places limitations upon himself.

But when man thinks of himself as a god, he gains unlimited abilities and control over both his mental and physical health, and over any pain which might threaten his general well-being.

Man is a god – or at least has the potential to become a god.

Remember Your Inherent Powers

But humankind has forgotten how to use so many inherent powers. Through the development of mind and body, today's men and women are able to regain these abilities.

Through my lifetime involvement with humankind, I have learned how to apply many of the universal truths as taught by all the great masters of the past. I have used many of these truths in my work with mental retardation, mental illness, and with men confined to penal institutions.

As I worked with so-called "normal people," I discovered that they, too, were only using from two to ten percent of the brain power available to them. That is when I set out to prove through my demonstrations that all men and women are somewhat mentally retarded, due to the fact that they are not using the full potential of their brain power. There are universal steps toward the development of god-like stature in which people may develop themselves to the point where they feel no unnecessary pain, no stress, no torment due to emotional factors.

Learn To Make The Most Of "Now"

People bog themselves down with worry about trivia. The average man and woman worries about yesterday and tomorrow – the past and the future – and cannot see what is happening to them today.

Everyone must learn to make the most of now.

Yesterday is past and can never be regained.

Tomorrow will take care of itself.

If you seek to control the pain and afflictions which offend your body, then you must start living in the present.

Relax Mind and Body Together

The first step toward pain control is a recognition that you must learn to relax mind and body together.

When you are able to do this, you will find peace of mind. You will become a healthier individual, and you will find your true position in the ever-moving stream of life.

Once you find that wonderful peace of mind within yourself, you will realize that both personal and external problems may be neutralized through the peace which abounds within.

Create the World the Way You Want It

Before a person was born into the world, his world did not exist. He created his own world.

If, therefore, you live in what you consider an ugly, cruel world, then you have, in essence, created that world for yourself. Your world is ugly and cruel because that's the way you want it.

If you hate yourself, then you also hate everyone else.

The essence of love – and the first step toward pain control – must begin within each person.

Just as I learned to master pain so that I can walk unharmed through red-hot coals, or lie unmarked on beds of nails, so can you learn to control the pain of backache, arthritis, headache, or any other affliction that might decrease your full enjoyment of life.

Everything about your pain is not bad. Pain is a danger signal – an alert. It can be like an internal alarm going off to warn you that a fire may be raging someplace where you may not have checked recently.

It is not that we want to eliminate your body's ability to transmit pain signals. But there is no use in suffering needlessly, especially when the cause of the pain may present little actual danger to the overall health of the body.

Rising Above Stress

Sometimes the stresses of daily living, the many tensions one experiences on the job, or the fear of there being something seriously wrong with the body can magnify the pain signals out of all proportion to the actual reason for the transmissions.

And as I have repeatedly pointed out, there are all too many instances where certain stresses and tensions can so work upon the imagination, and upon certain psychic needs of an individual, that pain can be created when there is no need for a danger signal of any kind.

Perhaps the crux of what I am saying is this: We must first understand that pain is the body's natural danger signal. When we have sought medical aid to alleviate as many of the true danger signals as possible, then there is no purpose in suffering needlessly from pain. Instead, we can learn to control pain – and, in many instances, eliminate completely those signals which originate from stressful situations in our lives.

Today's medical science has established the fact that anywhere from 60 to 90 percent of the pain that men and women suffer lies in their minds; and it's caused by frustration, depression, worries, emotional stresses. Subconsciously, too many men and women simply do not have the desire to rise above their sicknesses.

If a man or woman believes he has nothing to live for, if he simply goes about a day-to-day routine complaining about everything imaginable, then pain and illness will soon become a part of his life. Mastery of self, once attained, will control pain. Through self- mastery, a person will become better in every aspect of life.

If we learn how to control physical pain, we can also learn how to control emotional pain and face the problems and disappointments of life with a more positive attitude.

So many men and women apparently wish to achieve a full exercise of psychic abilities, healing abilities, and self-control of pain; but people fail to realize that once they have achieved mastery of themselves, they will have all these abilities at their command.

These are universal truths. They will yield the self-mastery necessary to control all pains and afflictions of the physical body.

1. EGO – the magic of believing in oneself.

2. POSITIVE ATTITUDE – which is so much more than merely positive thinking.

3. RELAXATION – which goes hand in hand with physical exercise: without first tuning the body, it is difficult to tune the mind.

4. PROPER BREATHING – the Yogic breathing techniques of complete breath and rhythmic breathing, which everyone can learn, and which, once accomplished, will put each individual well toward the goal of pain control.

5. CONCENTRATION – the ability to focus the mind and remove it from external tensions.

6. MEDITATION – a passive form of concentration. Most people never achieve this state. It is the sheer ecstasy of being in tune with the subconscious, the superconscious, the universe, or the god-self, whichever has the better meaning to the individual.

Acquiring Strength and Self-Esteem

Nature's plan is to produce strong individual expressions of herself. She will be glad to give you her aid in becoming strong. The man who wishes to strengthen himself will always find great forces within him to aid in the work, for is he not carrying out one of nature's pet plans and one for which he has been striving throughout the ages? Anything that tends to make you realize and express your mastery tends to strengthen you and places at your disposal nature's aid. You may witness this in everyday life. Nature seems to like strong individuals and delights in pushing them ahead. By mastery we mean mastery over your own lower nature, as well as over outside nature, of course. The 'I' is master, forget it not, O, student, and assert constantly."

You must learn to accept and to strive for that "I" that is within you. And, once again, you will gain the proper kind of self-love within. It will swell out and show and reveal itself to the world. You will not have to run around and tell everybody, "I love you; I love you," because when you love yourself, it shows that you love the rest of the world as well.

Believe In Yourself

You must learn to believe in yourself because, if you do not, you cannot convince anyone in the world to believe in you. When you start to believe that you can accomplish things – that you can be whatever you want to be – then you have begun to believe in yourself.

As you believe in yourself, you will gain a beautiful outlook on life and become more a part of the world. Instead of being in the world, you will become *part* of it. This is highly essential. The mind is the working tool of the ego. Work and strive toward this development.

As children we are programmed to believe in various things in regard to our world. This often leads to what I call "environmental retardation." We must make the first move and begin to change our world. If our world is not a happy one, we must change it. This is all a part of ego, because each of us has the ability to create a wonderful world and to live in a wonderful world.

But you, and you alone, are the only one who can do that, because you are the only one who lives in your own individual world.

I do not live in your world. No one else lives in your world – unless you want them to live there with you. If those persons you admit into your world are very negative individuals, then they will have an influence on your world and make it an unhappy world once again.

Ask yourself, "What do I really think of myself?"

If your answer is, "Not much," then it's high time you set as your goal the systematic and continued development of selfesteem and the strengthening of your ego. You must have a positive attitude. You must learn to be positive within every molecule of your body.

Negative thoughts can cause almost any kind of illness – ulcers, blindness, paralysis. On some occasions, negative thinking has even produced death.

If you will yourself into a negative situation, you can become very ill. Start now building your ego to produce positive thoughts – even if you have to go to the point of getting away from family and friends who are very negative. You must learn to have a positive attitude around you at all times.

A little bit of negativity is not bad; it does make the world interesting. But you must have little goals that you set and reach in order to keep building yourself all the time.

You must not be afraid to strive for goals for yourself that might seem impossible to you right now.

Positive attitude will lead you to expect the most of yourself as an individual and as a human being: This is short and simple, but true.

CHAPTER THIRTY-SIX

The Magic of Music

When Bill Reddie was music director of the Sands Hotel in Las Vegas, he may have discovered his soul by accident – inside an electronic sound synthesizer – and, in the process, opened the door to a more complete understanding of what music and the primal sound may really be.

Reddie, the president of Electronic Music Research, Inc., has for some time been seriously searching for the common denominator he believes exists in music that will explain the universal language of this ancient medium.

His electronic music lab consists of a series of tape recorders hooked into an ARP electronic synthesizer, complete with keyboard, speakers and other electronic components specially designed by Reddie and his associates to produce entirely new concepts of music. At the time of Reddie's experience with what may be the highest realms of consciousness, he was experimenting with a technique of composing that was entirely intuitive. He describes this process as extemporaneous composition.

As he explains, "My over-all approach had become more and more intuitive. I was not intellectually planning the outcome of a given musical sequence. It was all coming off the top of the head and simultaneously recorded on tape.

Nothing was planned out. Whatever I felt like playing on the keyboard was recorded on several individual tracks. As the tracks were all used up,

I would conclude the composition, not really knowing exactly what I had until I played back everything simultaneously.

"It was during one of these playback periods that I had this incredible contact with whatever was in my music. It began with a feeling of tremendous heat which completely enveloped my body. Next, I broke into convulsive sobbing, the kind that comes from somewhere deep inside. I couldn't stop it. I remember thinking at the time that I must be going mad.

"Nothing seemed to stem the sobbing. I was finally compelled to shut down the equipment and leave the studio."

SECOND STAGE

Reddie was unable to muster the courage to return to his research studio for three days after this traumatic experience. During those three days he frequently broke into the sobbing again. Upon his return to the studio, the second and most rewarding part of the phenomenon occurred.

Once he was able to resume his work he became, at once, unbelievably prolific. He composed a total of 40 new original musical creations – each eight to ten minutes long – in the space of four weeks. By any measurement of creative production this achievement is phenomenal. All the new compositions were realized as the result of a nearly pure intuitive approach and were constructed in a free-flowing style, unhampered by the rules of accepted musical form or harmony.

The effect of this new music was enhanced by the electronic quality made possible through the synthesizer, which gives each piece a character and individuality that could not be achieved with traditional instruments.

What happened to Bill Reddie to cause all this? "In retrospect I have come to the conclusion that some unknown factor was present in that particular sequence of musical frequencies, and it caused me to release some very deep feelings. I can assure you, I have not been the same since. I hate to use the expression, because it is so overworked, but I felt I was actually reborn.

"At first it was a little frightening. Then it became extremely exhilarating as I realized that I am, and always have been, the master of my own fate and evolvement as a human being. Incidentally, after this transformation experience other paranormal experiences have become part of my daily life."

Since he discovered his essential self, or as he puts it the core of his being, somewhere in the random groupings of musical frequencies he composed by intuitive creativity, Reddie and his associates have been able to repeat the experiment with others. The same dramatic release of emotion doesn't always occur, but there is frequently a deep, inner awareness at another level of comprehension.

As a result, Bill has produced a recording of some of his spontaneous compositions and invited a number of psychologists and therapists to use this music for therapy and evaluation. Test subjects have responded to the music in a variety of ways and the cumulative evidence attained so far would seem to indicate that he has successfully isolated some of the x-factors of music and rearranged them in a new order.

The thrust of the research now being conducted is the isolation of more and more of these x-factors and their rearrangement into structures of musical frequencies that will evoke a common emotion in all listeners.

Reddie freely admits his search for this common denominator has not yet been successful. He has not found one single note or frequency which could be described as the elusive primal sound, but he has found traces of new musical configurations that affect people. He believes these discoveries to be important and should be catalogued and filed for more comprehensive study.

The first collection of Reddie's electronic music, *Atlantis Revisited*, was released to the public by his own recording company, Channel One Records. The stereo album was given this title after numerous test subjects strangely had a common memory pattern emerge as they listened. They felt they were remembering a past life in legendary Atlantis. This past-life recall is one of the psychic or paranormal phenomena which frequently occurs when people are exposed to Reddie's electronic music.

The brilliant Bill Reddie is one of the early pioneers of New Age Music.

SECOND LANGUAGE

Music is a second language for most of us. We know certain types of music speak to us in a special way and that music evokes emotional responses in people, even if the reasons for these responses are not understood. Because music as we understand it is a function of at least one of the five senses, it becomes a familiar medium.

Music stimulates memory patterns and encourages sentimentality and nostalgia. Music has the potential for good or ill.

Bill Reddie says music and sound vibrations are neutral and, like all forces of nature, can be exploited for the benefit or detriment of society. His driving motivation is to produce music that will permit people to journey inward and discover new dimensions of their being.

"I use the term common denominator for lack of a more suitable description of what we are looking for. We know music is a language which speaks to people at a nonverbal level. We know there is a very definite pattern to musical language, but we know only a few of its characteristics as they have been preserved in the diatonic system and the well-tempered scale. Every good composer knows there is far more to music than we can, express effectively at this point.

"We are trying to isolate this common denominator. When we do, we will attempt to reorganize its harmonic and rhythmic structures in a more orderly manner. In other words, we would compose music that would predictably cause the specific reaction we want. We could then be able to generate whatever emotion is called for. To date, composers are at best touching upon the common denominator factor merely by accident. We really do not understand why a certain passage or sequence of bars or a musical phrase will consistently cause a certain effect. We are equally hard put to explain why other passages and formations cause no effect whatsoever.

"It is my conviction that the human organism knows and responds to these common denominators automatically, without any assistance from the conscious mind. This deep response has nothing to do with the conditioned reaction of the ear to music – or the way we think we hear music."

The existence of entire new dimensions of music has been known to creative composers for years. In a sense, composers have been locked into the diatonic system and the well-tempered scale. All the sounds we understand as music conform to this system. Innovators, like Reddie, believe they can at last progress to a much larger range of sound frequencies and combinations. He explains it this way: "In electronically produced sound we are in command of literally every frequency in the audible spectrum. We can add or subtract harmonic content of a given frequency at will. For hundreds of years composers have been able to hear these sounds, to sense them with their inner ear.

"Up to now these areas of invisible sound have been inaccessible. We have tried to tap them by using quarter-tone music. But the musical instruments are too rigid in construction to capture these sounds properly every time. It is a terrific responsibility for the musician to faithfully reproduce exactly what the composer heard (or thought he heard) at each performance.

MAJOR BREAKTHROUGH

"The only way this can be achieved is by pure accident or by some mathematical means. Since the mathematical approach cannot be applied to the well-tempered scale, the next step forward called for a major breakthrough in music technology. We have that breakthrough in electronic music.

"With traditional musical instruments we are bound by the limitations of the physical range of the instrument. Take the clarinet for instance. A clarinet sounds like a clarinet because of the harmonic envelope created by its construction and the material from which it is made. It is true that certain alterations can be made to the harmonic envelope of the clarinet to give it an expanded versatility, but the sound can still be recognized as being that of a clarinet. This is basically true of all musical instruments. They are designed to conform to the musical scale as we know it – seven primary notes and variations of these notes.

"Every composer has heard sounds in his inner ear which existed somewhere between the black and white keys of the piano, but have been beyond his ability to   translate into music because there were no instruments capable of reproducing these sounds. Electronics is changing this. We know that all sounds are vibrations of varying frequencies and wave lengths. Now, I can not only translate what my composer's ear hears, regardless of the frequency, and record it as I hear it onto recording tape, but I can be assured of a faultless repeat performance without coping with the shortcomings of inadequate acoustics.

Reddie is one of the pioneers in what is still a relatively new medium of expression. The theory of his work is not too difficult to understand once one accepts the fact that music is sound vibration, and that these vibrations have an effect on the human organism at two levels at least: the physical/mental level, where emotions are responsive to musical stimulation, and at a subliminal and as yet uncharted area deep within the human organism.

ENERGY AND PERCEPTION

This latter area is where Reddie encountered his personal transforming experience and where others are obtaining similar effects. Little is known about this domain of unseen energies and perception. It has been established that there is clearly more to the human condition than the physical matter which constitutes our bodies. Yet, we can only speculate what these energies and supersensory perception qualities are all about and what they mean. For many, this exploration of electronic music is more attractive than some other areas of psychical research because the research is based on a physical manifestation rather than mental or spiritual phenomenon.

THE "PHILOSOPHER'S STONE" OF CREATION

Reddie believes sound is the philosopher's stone of Creation. He says that "All nature has a vibratory rate. Therefore, all matter has a vibratory rate consistent with its content. If we cannot see matter which has been altered to the degree that it disappears from sight, that does not mean it has ceased to vibrate. That particular manifestation which once existed as solid-appearing matter has merely risen in vibratory rate to the extent that our eyes can no longer perceive it.

"I believe many of these invisible vibrations can be sensed or felt. As far as other forms of life are concerned, plants and animals do a better job of coping with these unseen and unheard vibrations because of their place in nature.

"These 'lower' creatures simply perform the function given to them by nature and don't have to worry about the incoming data they receive from their environment. They just do their thing without having to weigh everything and pigeon-hole what they perceive for careful, and often postponed, evaluation. Man on the other hand, instead of being able to process this incoming data automatically, must – by his nature – attack what he perceives with his reasoning faculty. Perhaps electronic music will help humans to realign the vibrations of nature into patterns which we can understand and attune to."

Reddie theorizes that the music of the future will not resemble the music of today. The concept of musical composition that has served us so well for hundreds of years will, of necessity, fall by the wayside. He believes this change will not take place in our lifetimes, and may not happen until the era of 2500 A.D. By then technology will have advanced to the point that present day musical construction will be relegated to history. From a musical viewpoint we are living in an over-stimulated era that will serve to hasten the progress from old to new.

FEELING SOUND

Reddie feels: "Movies and television will have musical scores that truly identify with the emotional content of the script. These scores will most probably not sound at all like present day background music. You may not hear the sounds, but you will certainly feel them.

"It will also be possible to control personal environmental conditions through the inaudible frequency structures. You may be able to create any number of effects for health, self-improvement, relaxation, and romance simply by going into a room that has been specially rigged to facilitate the use of electronic stimulation.

Reddie reminds us that the forces of nature are neutral until they are manipulated by man. It becomes extremely important to have men and women of high purpose involved in this research. When we consider the power that will become available with the discovery of the origin of these undiscovered energies, and the frequencies which govern their function, we cannot be too careful.

He also believes the potential of electronics will eventually lead to unheard of methods of producing the sound of music, including laser arrangements of multifaceted configurations. It will become possible to produce the music of a painting into sound. In Reddie's estimation, the potential for entertainment, personal meditation, spiritual development and creativity are unlimited.

BRAINWAVE MACHINE

"I have been able to activate a synthesizer and to control it with a brainwave machine. These experiments may result in more new musical configurations electronically produced. Biofeedback offers great potential in electronic music. However, it costs a small fortune to make a total commitment to this because of the tremendous cost of the equipment required.

"Quite often in research one finds that in order to complete a project you have to invent your own equipment or apparatus. For instance, I have been told by persons who have a high degree of psychism that they can perceive a multicolored energy field emanating from, or created by, musical sound. The problem here is that there is no apparatus presently available which is capable of recording this phenomenon. It will have to be invented. To date we have not advanced far enough with our 'bio-music' experiments to state definite theories."

Bill Reddie answered one of my questions on the futuristic aspects of his music in a very direct manner. I asked him whether he felt that traditional music is sort of a musical kindergarten – and that the areas of electronic music are in a more advanced stage?

"I certainly do *not* consider traditional music a musical kindergarten! To do so would be to deny the greatness of Bach, Wagner, Beethoven, and the rest. The same goes for pop music. All of them contributed something to the whole, some more than others, and for me to hold such an opinion would border on lunacy. I do feel that all the famous or near famous composers would be the first to probe into these new areas if they were alive today. It was a dissatisfaction with the status quo that served to project them to greatness with their own innovative compositions in the first place. The areas we have chosen are definitely futuristic and advanced. But let's not forget that Wagner was advanced for his time, and he bore the scars to prove it.

BUILT-IN RESISTANCE

"Some modern composers have been able to apply the positive manipulative forces of music and have a higher batting average than others. This is due to the fact that these composers are more in tune with the universe. Still, I feel that all of them have been hampered with the built-in resistance caused by the diatonic system and the well-tempered scale we talked about earlier."

He continued: "I believe the basic creative energy is nonverbal by nature. It is imagination and intuition. It is like being in two worlds simultaneously. You learn how to tune out the material world long enough to grasp a concept and bring it back through a sort of transposition which makes it possible to reapply them with the tools of the material world.

"It is a contact made with the true realities, cosmic force, creative energy, God, or whatever name you wish to give it. The quality of the contact made depends on the composer. All that he needs exists, but it is up to him to discover what way works best for him individually. His music will tell you much better than words how well he has succeeded in contacting that all-embracing creative force of the universe.

"To say that inspiration is a causal factor in composition would, in my opinion, be incorrect unless you were to equate the word inspiration with excitement. In other words, a composer receives an original musical concept by personal contact with his true reality. He then becomes excited or inspired by the inherent possibilities of the concept. From there on his excitement will give him the impetus and energy to act upon what he has perceived by taking pencil or pen in hand and committing the idea to paper.

"Of course, I no longer use this method. When I compose electronic music I do just the opposite. The last thing I do is write the notation of my compositions. The method I use is one whereby the creative idea is almost simultaneously recorded on magnetic tape in multi-track form. All the music comes off the top of my head. The last function performed is the commitment of the piece to paper. I feel that this technique allows the composer to remain in contact longer with the creative force, leaving the more intellectual and physical chores for a later time.

"In passing, it should be added that this is precisely the process used by jazz musicians, the only difference being that they usually improvise around basic outlines that serve as springboards for their extemporizing."

PSYCHIC POTENTIAL

An interesting sidelight to the research conducted by Reddie's Electronic Music Research group has been the increased awareness by the test subjects of their own psychic potential. Many have experienced vivid color and nonverbal phenomena while listening to Reddie's electronic music compositions.

Of course, some are frightened by this experience. Once it is explained to them that they are allowing this fear to enter their sphere and that they can control it if they want, they often begin to enjoy a freedom previously unattainable to them.

Reddie remarked that others who have worked with his electronic music have told him of experiencing the phenomenon of past-life recall or genetic memory or whatever is causing this impression of a former life.

Still other test subjects received visions of what they would be like in the years ahead if they continue to live the way they were at the time they listened to the music.

A number of educational institutions have purchased music for their own research and evaluation projects. He and his associates are very hopeful a creative role will be found for Music therapy and other constructive applications in learning institutions. Some headway has been made in this direction and more is anticipated this year.

Perhaps the most significant early results of Reddie's electronic compositions come from two Arizona psychologists. One psychologist has been using the music to delve into the workings of the criminal mind with some good results. In this case, there is insufficient evidence to make firm conclusions, but the reports indicate some useful function is being served by playing electronic music to inmates of prisons, some of whom may be criminally insane. Electronic music may make treatment of these serious disorders a reality.

There may be many physical applications for music which could make it possible for music vibrations to go right to the essential self and assist in a cleansing and transforming operation that may cause positive realignment of the individual's life forces at all levels of existence.

Music, music, music. It is all around us, even when we cannot hear it with our ears. Apparently this unheard music, in combination with or underlying the music we can hear and be aware of, is capable of affecting the human organism in profound ways – to the point that an entire life can be transformed and redirected.

CHAPTER THIRTY-SEVEN

UFOS, Man's Genesis, and Our Coming Help From Other Worlds

On that warm night in August, 1970, the sky looked very much like a gigantic blackboard on which some superior intelligence had industriously laid out a mammoth connect-the-dots mystery in luminous chalk. Olof Jonsson and I sat on the balcony of a Wisconsin lodge. Suddenly, someone in our party noticed a bright object traversing the night sky. "Is that a satellite?" she asked, "Or is it an airplane? Or. .. ?"

The object suddenly stopped dead still, answering the two questions that had been asked. Neither a satellite nor an airplane can instantly suspend motion in mid-flight.

Then came the third question: ". . .or is it a UFO?" By now the object appeared to be flashing different colored lights in a sequence of red, greenish-blue, and white, as if it were attempting to establish contact with intelligent life on Earth's surface.

"I will try to answer them with telepathy," Olof said.

"Just don't ask them to land!" one of our group requested.

"No," another said, echoing the previously expressed sentiments. "No trip to outer space for me right now. I have to be back at work tomorrow."

After a few moments, the object made a rapid movement to the left, then began moving a course drastically altered from the one that it had been traveling. Whatever we were watching steadily accelerated until it was out of sight in a matter of seconds. "Friends of yours, Olof?" I asked jokingly.

Olof smiled, but his manner was strangely serious. "Perhaps they were very old friends."

BEINGS OF COSMIC HARMONY

When Olof was a child of four or five, he used to take great delight in playing by himself near a small stream that ran by his home. As he made leaf-houses among the water grasses and sailed toy boats between the lily pads, the child was aware of other presences near him.

"They may have been the same entities that so often represent them-selves to small children as fairies and wood sprites," Olof told me. "But, somehow, on occasion, I believe that I was able to see them as they really were. They were taller than I, but not nearly as tall as my parents. They were, perhaps, just under – or just over – five feet tall. They had much larger heads and proportionately much smaller bodies than an adult human. Their skin color varied from bluish-green to gold brown to a shade of gray. It was they who began to tell me wonderful things about the universe and Cosmic harmony."

Who were these strange beings?

"I felt that they were friends, that they wanted to teach me and to help me," Olof answered simply. "Now, I feel that they may have been from another solar system or another dimension. Of course I am still convinced that they are friendly and intend to help man as much as they can without interfering in his own development and free will."

Because of his early contact with beings whom he believes to have come from some other world or dimension, Olof Jonsson does not scoff at reports of unidentified flying objects.

"In their traveling to other worlds or dimensions, the flying saucer occupants have learned to eliminate Time," Olof said. "Once a technology has learned to conquer and control Time, everything can happen *Now*."

EARTH IS A GIGANTIC LABORATORY

It is Jonsson's psychic impression that human life did not originate on the planet Earth.

"I believe that man was placed here by some higher intelligence," he has remarked. "In the beginning there were maybe fifty or one hundred men and women. Homo sapiens is a vast experiment being conducted by Cosmic beings. Earth is a gigantic laboratory."

Who are these Cosmic experimenters?

"They have life-spans equal to thousands of our years," Jonsson be-lieves. "In their world, they have solved all the myriad problems of existence that we are still fighting on Earth. They have cured all known diseases. It is impossible to achieve one hundred percent harmony on the material plane until all diseases have been conquered.

"I have already described the appearance of those beings whom I saw as a small boy," Olof said. "In essence, they are similar in appearance to man, but they have achieved complete control of mind and they may shape their fleshly bodies in a manner that is most appealing to those with whom they communicate. Throughout man's history, these entities may have appeared as angels, god-like beings, fairies – even demons and devils if it suited their particular purpose."

THE COSMIC SCIENTISTS RETURN

Olof Jonsson believes that the UFO phenomenon is simply physical evidence that the Cosmic scientists are returning in larger numbers to study the progress of their great experiment.

"Although there have always been a number of "Watchers' on duty," he states, "more of them are now arriving to keep man under careful surveillance as he enters the New Age of Aquarius. A period of cleansing may be necessary here on Earth, because there are too few Homo sapiens with enough responsibility to balance those with too much power.

"Our Cosmic Masters may see that the time is soon upon Earth when another cycle of the rise and fall of a civilization and a culture must be completed, and they stand ready to assist man in the transition from the degenerative, destructive pattern in which he was traveling with his misapplied science to a plane of higher consciousness in which the false and outworn will be destroyed and discarded.

BECOMING A CITIZEN OF HIGHER DIMENSIONS

"Man will still be man and will still function as a human being," Olof assured his listeners, "but his frequency, his vibratory rate, will be raised to a finer, more etherealized level. Man's sense perceptions will be heightened. His sense of Cosmic Harmony will be filled with true understanding of peace, love, and brotherhood. The increase in the vibratory rate of this planet will permit man to transcend the old physical boundaries and to become a citizen of a higher dimension, with a new depth of insight that will enable him to live in brotherhood with his fellowman and with beings from other solar systems and other planes of existence."

Is there any way in which man might prepare himself for the new age?

"Yes," Olof nodded, "there is one excellent way by which each man might attune the frequency of his own individual being. Each night before meditation, call upon Supreme Intelligence by whatever name you know God, and ask for his Harmony to aid you in attuning with the increased vibratory rate that has begun to permeate all living beings who stand at the dawning of the Age of Aquarius. Then meditate, allowing your consciousness to attune itself to peace and harmony. The New Age will require many of advanced attunement to offer assistance to those of denser frequency, who will flounder helplessly at the time of the great transition and change."

Once, as we sat in a moment of quiet reflection in the living room of the psychic's home in Riverdale, Illinois, I asked Olof if he ever felt that he himself might have been "planted" on this world by beings from another planet or dimension.

After a moment's consideration, Olof answered, "No, I have never thought that the physical Olof Jonsson may have been placed here by entities from a flying saucer. But I must admit that I have never really felt that I was of this world. I believe that I may have lived before elsewhere in this universe and that I have reincarnated on Earth for this temporal existence."

Have you ever felt, though, as if you might be receiving instructions from beings or entities from other spheres of existence?

"Sometimes," he admitted. "There are times that I feel that there are things I must do in this world. Many times when I am doing an experiment, I can feel that there is someone outside of myself who wants me to do it, to show this materialistic world that there is a more lasting element to its existence. I suppose I must confess that since earliest childhood I have felt that I must live my life to fulfill a role here on Earth. It has always seemed my specific duty to spend my most vital energies in an attempt to convince my fellow humans of the reality of the spiritual spheres of being."